APPLICATION SHORTCUTS

These keystroke/mouse functions are supported by ma[ny]
applications. Other shortcuts are often listed on the me[nus or com-]
mands themselves.

Open new file	⌘-N
Open existing file	⌘-O
Save current file	⌘-S
Close current window	⌘-W
Cut selection	⌘-X
Copy selection	⌘-C
Paste selection	⌘-V
Undo previous action	⌘-Z
Quit application	⌘-Q
Print file	⌘-P
Cancel printing	⌘-. (period)
Show/Hide Ruler	⌘-R
Find file (System 7 only)	⌘-F
Place grave accent (`) over following character	Option-'
Place acute accent (`) over following character	Option-e
Place circumflex (^) over following character	Option-v
Place umlaut (ü) over following character	Option-,

ALL-OCCASION SHORTCUTS

These shortcuts can be employed whenever the Finder or other application
is active.

Eject floppy disk in internal drive	⌘-Shift-1
Eject floppy disk in external drive	⌘-Shift-2
Take a "snapshot" of current screen	⌘-Shift-3

Books that Work Just Like Your Mac

As a Macintosh user, you enjoy unique advantages. You enjoy a dynamic user environment. You enjoy the successful integration of graphics, sound, and text. Above all, you enjoy a computer that's fun and easy to use.

When your computer gives you all this, why accept less in your computer books?

At SYBEX, we don't believe you should. That's why we've committed ourselves to publishing the highest quality computer books for Macintosh users. Externally, our books emulate the Mac "look and feel," with powerful, appealing illustrations and easy-to-read pages. Internally, our books stress "why" over "how," so you'll learn concepts, not sequences of steps. Philosophically, our books are designed to help you get work done, not to teach you about computers.

In short, our books are fun and easy to use—just like the Mac. We hope you find them just as enjoyable.

For a complete catalog of our publications:

SYBEX Inc.
2021 Challenger Drive, Alameda, CA 94501
Tel: (510) 523-8233/(800) 227-2346 Telex: 336311
Fax: (510) 523-2373

THE MACINTOSH HARD DISK COMPANION

THE
MACINTOSH®
HARD DISK
COMPANION

J. Russell Roberts

SYBEX®

San Francisco • Paris • Düsseldorf • Soest

Acquisitions Editor: Dianne King
Developmental Editor: Kenyon Brown
Editor: Jeff Kapellas
Technical Editors: Nick Dargahi and Lillian Chen
Word Processors: Susan Trybull and Ann Dunn
Book Designer: Helen Bruno
Technical Art: Delia Brown
Screen Graphics: Arno Harris
Desktop Publishing Production: Len Gilbert
Proofreader/Production Assistant: Arno Harris
Indexer: Ted Laux
Cover Designer: Ingalls + Associates
Cover Illustrator: Harumi Kubo

Library of Congress Card Number: 92-80426
ISBN: 0-7821-1058-4

Manufactured in the United States of America
10 9 8 7 6 5 4 3 2 1

TO

Anthony Kalani

Gloria Neil

Moana Dawn

(the other members of Lost Patrol

Expeditionary Forces)

and Base Commander Baca

ACKNOWLEDGMENTS

I'd like to extend my appreciation to the people whose talents, advice, expertise, and support helped make this project possible. It may be my name on the title page, but this book is in fact a collaboration, and I owe a debt of gratitude to all my co-contributors.

At SYBEX, my heartfelt thanks go to editor Jeff Kapellas, who deftly navigated the whitewater of shifting schedules as well as my torrent of text, all with good grace and humor. Also, I'd like to thank acquisitions editor Dianne King, who conceived of the project in the first place; developmental editor Kenyon Brown, who helped shape the book into its present form; Nick Dargahi and Lillian Chen, for their thorough and thoughtful technical editing; typesetter Len Gilbert; book designer/artist Helen Bruno; proofreader, production assistant, and screen graphics artist Arno Harris; technical artist Delia Brown; and indexer Ted Laux. Additional thanks go to David J. Clark and Janna Hecker Clark.

In New York, I'd like to thank Sheldon Cotler and the staff of Sheldon Cotler + Associates, especially Leonard Vigliarolo, Peggy Malone, and Tony Limuaco. Their gracious offer of workspace and computer access helped me meet deadlines without sacrificing my sanity. I also appreciate the support, both technical and emotional, that was provided by Eric Rochow of The Gunnar Group, Joe Freedman of Sarabande Press, and Daniel Gross of FLOW Research, Inc.

CONTENTS AT A GLANCE

CONTENTS

P A R T   T W O
WORKING WITH HARD DISKS

4 Organizing Your Disk   99

5 Protecting Your Data   133

P A R T   T H R E E
WHEN SOMETHING GOES WRONG

P A R T   F O U R
MAXIMIZING HARD DISK PERFORMANCE

xviii

11 | The Well-Connected Macintosh— Networks and Hard Disks   315

A P P E N D I C E S

INTRODUCTION

Y ou get a lot when you purchase and use a Macintosh-compatible hard disk. You get increased productivity, overall convenience, and the ability to do some things that are not possible with floppy disks alone. You get so much that nowadays a Macintosh without a hard disk is hardly considered functional. Just the advantage of having data centralized and easily accessible can make your hard disk an indispensable addition.

However, hard disks also bring an entirely new set of issues, options, and problems. Without effective hard disk organization, data can get lost in a clutter of files and folders. Centralization is a double-edged sword: it's bad enough when a floppy is unreadable, so the prospect of a hard disk malfunction wiping out all of a user's data can strike fear into the heart of even the bravest user. Just getting through the jargon of the hard disk marketplace—*SCSI, interleave ratios, built-in termination*, and so forth—can be a problem in itself.

The Goals of This Book

The Macintosh Hard Disk Companion is designed to guide you through the technological and practical aspects of your hard disk. We'll start with the basics of data storage (and the concepts behind it), and talk a little about the Macintosh itself. Then we'll move on to the subject of using hard disks in your day-to-day work: what tools and strategies are available for keeping your information organized and optimized.

Next we'll tackle the issue of hard disk security—how to make sure your data won't be lost, corrupted or accessed without authorization. Since even the most savvy hard disk user isn't exempt from something going wrong, we'll cover troubleshooting techniques for the most common hard disk problems. Finally, we'll discuss maximizing and expanding your hard disk system, and take a look at other roles that hard disks can play in the Macintosh universe.

My aim is to increase not only your knowledge about hard disks, but ultimately, your confidence in using that disk as well. Armed with the right information, you should be as comfortable with your hard disk as you are with your Macintosh.

What This Book Is Not About

This is a user-oriented guide. Although it's a solid diagnostic resource, it's not a repair or installation manual. You won't find instructions for disassembling a hard disk, or installing an internal drive in a computer. It also provides only an introductory-level guide to storage device standards for the Macintosh; if you're a programmer seeking in-depth information about SCSI or other Macintosh data pathways, you won't find much here that you don't already know.

What You'll Need to Know

This book assumes you're already familiar with the basics of Macintosh operations: clicking, dragging, menu selection and the like (if you're not, check your user manual). Aside from that, little has been taken for granted. In fact, if you're an experienced Macintosh user you may find some of the information in the early chapters a little too basic for your taste. Even so, it's to your advantage to bear with it and read the introductory chapter: you might learn a few things.

In some instances, I've decided to err on the side of the elementary, simply because the common use of Macintosh terminology is often unclear, redundant, or downright misleading. It's necessary to define even the most basic building blocks of Macintosh data before proceeding to a clear understanding of the more advanced topics. As I say, a little patience will prove worthwhile.

How to Use This Book

Of course, you'll benefit most from this book if you read it from beginning to end. However, many books like these are bought because the user has a specific task in mind. You'll probably find *The Macintosh Hard Disk Companion* useful as long as you own your hard disk, but if you are looking for immediate information, here are a few suggestions.

- **If you're considering purchasing a hard disk,** read Chapters 1 and 2. These cover the basic technology and terminology, and explain some of the features and flaws to look for when shopping for or evaluating a hard disk.

- **If you're overwhelmed by your hard disk,** or if years of regular usage has rendered your hard disk a vast morass of confusion, you'll need to analyze your needs and get organized. Chapter 3 explains the principles behind data management, while Chapter 4 presents several strategies and scenarios for structuring your work.

- **If something's gone wrong with your disk,** or if it is getting cantankerous and unreliable, you'll probably get the most out of Part III and Appendix C. Chapter 2 may also be enlightening when it comes to problems caused by incorrect setup and installation.

  If and when you get to the root of your problems, be sure to read Chapter 5. That's where you'll learn how to take steps to ensure the crisis never happens again...and chances are you'll be very motivated to take those steps.

- **If you've outgrown your current setup,** and are in the market for a higher-capacity drive, check out Chapter 10. That's where I list the main criteria to use when shopping for a drive, and discuss how different kinds of work can require different types of hardware.

  If you're interested in alternatives to hard drives, such as CD-ROM, removable-cartridge, and DAT drives, Chapter 10 discusses these as well.

A Final Note...

Things change. And in the Macintosh world, things change with blinding speed. When the first edition of this book was released in 1989, there were four types of Macintoshes available; now there are more than twenty. Back then, the capacity of the average hard drive was 20 megabytes; now, drives larger than 100 megabytes seem standard.

The Macintosh Hard Disk Companion reflects those changes. But keeping things up to date requires more than the efforts of a single author. I've incorporated suggestions from readers, industry experts, and informed users—and I have every intention of continuing to do so for future editions. If there's any feedback you'd like to provide, please write and let me know.

YOUR

MACINTOSH

HARD

DISK

This section is a guide to hard disk technology: how it works and how to get it started working for you. Chapter 1 explains some of the technical principles behind hard disks and other storage media, while Chapter 2 lays the groundwork for getting your hard disk system up and running.

A MACINTOSH HARD DISK PRIMER

FEATURING:

- → The History of the Hard Disk
- → Memory Types
- → Hard Disk Components
- → Initialization and Formatting
- → SCSI Ports and Disks
- → Interleave Ratios and Access Times
- → Purchase Tips

You probably know already that a hard disk is a means of storing a large quantity of data for ready retrieval, but that's really just a definition of its function. To get the most out of your hard disk, it helps to understand the whys and hows behind the technology.

This chapter introduces you to that technology, to storage devices, and to the Macintosh in general. In it, we'll survey the history of data storage and explore the inner workings of hard disks. Then we'll trace the evolution and the changing, challenge-filled role of hard disks for the Macintosh computer. Finally, we'll look at the SCSI peripheral standard and some of the factors affecting hard disk performance on the Macintosh.

Storage Technology: Past, Present, and Future

The hard disk is just one of a family of machines collectively known as *storage devices*. A computer, no matter how powerful, only processes data. To obtain that data in the first place, and to preserve it afterwards, the computer relies on storage.

In the early years of computing, information was stored on paper that the computer read much like a blind person reads braille. For years, thick stacks of keypunch cards or a reel of ticker-tape-like paper had to be fed to the computer to run even the simplest program.

This was a cumbersome process, so *magnetic medium* devices, the computer equivalent of tape recorders, displaced the paper-storage method. These devices are very similar to reel-to-reel or cassette recorders in that they manipulate *tape,* a thin sandwich of plastic and metallic particles. A magnetic recording head arranges the particles in a distinctive pattern and a similar head reads them. But instead of translating those patterns into sound waves, the computer interprets them as bits of information.

Reels of stored information had a distinct advantage over their paper predecessors: they could store information at a higher density, they could be erased, and they could be reused at will. Many mainframe and miniframe computers still use this technology.

However, reels are limited by their linear nature—to retrieve data, the computer must spool and unspool the tape, which takes time and causes wear and tear. That's why the next generation of magnetic media was devised: the *floppy disk*. These operate on the same principle as magnetic tape, except that the plastic-metallic sandwich is shaped like a platter and encased in a protective covering. Just as a compact disk player can skip from one track to another in seconds, a computer's floppy disk drive can readily access data anywhere on the disk, but with much greater speed (milliseconds as opposed to seconds).

Yet once again, with innovation came limitation. Whereas data tapes could be quite lengthy, floppies were limited to a uniform size. That's why a second approach was developed concurrently with the floppy disk: the *hard disk*. Instead of plastic, hard disks are made of rigid platters of metal or glass. They can store data to a very high degree of density. But because of this density, data loss could be caused by the slightest imperfection on the surface; even a mote of dust can cause data loss. Thus, while hard disk technology was promising, it seemed destined to exist only in isolated environments, far from the dust and dirt of the everyday world.

To make hard disk use more practical, a number of innovations were tried. Most of these involved encasing the disks in "packs," or dust-free removable cases. This kept the platters more or less clean, but still exposed the delicate read/write heads, if only for the time it took to change disk packs. It was at best an expensive, high-maintenance solution to the problem of keeping the hard disk clean.

In the early 1970s, scientists and engineers at IBM began developing what proved to be the most successful strategy. The hard disks and the read/write heads were combined and contained in a single, sealed unit cooled by highly filtered air. Users wouldn't be able to slip disks in and out at will, but dust and other contaminants wouldn't slip in either. This type of storage unit is often referred to by its IBM code name, the *Winchester drive*. Most hard disks used by personal computers today are variations of the Winchester drive.

Impressive as they may be, hard disks aren't the cutting edge of storage technology. The compact disk (CD), write once, read many (WORM) optical drives, erasable optical drives, and digital audio tape (DAT) drives represent yet another generation of storage technology. We'll discuss them in greater detail in Chapter 10.

RAMs, ROMs, and KBs: An Introduction to Memory and Peripherals

Your hard disk may be a means of storing information, but it's not what most people mean when they refer to computer "memory." Just as books have to be read before they're useful, electronic data must be situated in a place where they're "remembered." Memory is the "place" where information is held so that it can be accessed and manipulated by the computer's *central processing unit* (CPU). This place is actually *two* places, commonly known as the *RAM* and the *ROM*.

When you launch a program, that program is loaded into *random access memory*, or RAM. When you open a file, that goes into the RAM too. Since RAM can get filled up pretty quickly, the computer regularly purges and rearranges memory, getting rid of the data it no longer needs.

Yes, but how does it know what it doesn't need to know? That's one of the tasks of the *read-only memory,* or *ROM*. It's the manager of the microprocessor world, a set of rules, instructions and other information that's permanently inscribed. ROM instructions don't disappear when you turn the computer off or trip over the plug. This data is known as *firmware*, whereas the data that gets loaded into RAM from storage devices is known as *software*.

W ARNING

All information in RAM is erased when the power is turned off or interrupted. You can prevent information loss by saving your information to disk regularly.

Most of the ROM's firmware comes into play during the startup, or *booting*, process. In fact, the term *boot* comes from the phrase "to pull oneself up by one's bootstraps," since that's essentially what the computer is doing: it's transforming itself from an inanimate mass to an interactive device that functions in accordance with a number of strict rules. The ROM provides most of those rules; each time you turn your system on, it reinstructs the Macintosh how to act like a Macintosh.

Whether in RAM, in ROM, or on disk, all software is measured and quantified by the same standard. Fortunately, the world of computing is "metric," so you won't have to remember the number of "RAMfeet" in a "RAMmile." The basic unit of data is the *bit*. A bit is only "off" (0) or "on" (1). A *byte* consists of eight bits. Each byte is a binary expression of a number.

You'll often see *KB* (or simply *K*) after a number. That stands for *kilobyte*. Although "kilo" means a thousand (as in kilometers), a kilobyte is actually 1024 bytes, or 8192 bits. The extra bits are there because computers use a base 2, or *binary*, number system, as opposed to our base 10 system, and 2^{10} equals 1024.

A *megabyte* is 1024 kilobytes or 1,048,576 bytes. It is often abbreviated *MB* and sometimes *meg*. Personal computers are beginning to deal in *gigabytes*, which are equal to 1,073,741,824 bytes. At present, a single CD-ROM disk has a raw storage capacity of about 650 MB, or more than half a gigabyte, and gigabyte-sized hard drives are commercially available.

NOTE

> **A byte is a binary expression of a number. It is the smallest**
> ***functional* unit of information.**
>
> **A kilobyte (KB) equals 1024 bytes.**
>
> **A megabyte (MB) equals 1024 kilobytes.**
>
> **A gigabyte (GB) equals 1024 megabytes.**

In Macintosh parlance, any storage device that the computer recognizes as a separate entity is known as a *volume*. A 400 KB floppy disk or a 400 MB hard disk can both be volumes. The larger disk could also be formatted to contain multiple volumes; this process is known as *partitioning* (see Chapter 8). Any physical device designed to provide information to or receive information from the computer is known as a *peripheral*. Hard disks are peripherals, as are monitors, printers, scanners, modems, keyboards, and the like.

One last note about terminology. Technically, a hard *disk* is not the same as a hard *drive*: the former is the physical round magnetic media on which data is stored, while the latter is the unit in which the disk is stored. However, in general usage and in this book, the terms are used interchangably to refer to the storage unit as a whole.

Inside Your Hard Disk

If you're lucky, you'll never need to see the inner workings of your hard disk. All units are sealed to ward off dust and other impurities, and should be opened only for major repairs by qualified technicians in an especially clean environment. That sort of advice is given about a lot of electronic equipment, but in the case of hard disks, it should be taken to heart: most hard disks operate at such precise tolerances that even a highly-informed non-professional can easily do more harm than good. Figure 1.1 shows the inside of a typical hard disk.

Unless it has a storage capacity of 20 megabytes or less, your hard disk is probably a collection of disks, usually called *platters*. Platters are stacked one atop another like records on a multiplay turntable and rotate on a central spindle.

FIGURE 1.1
The parts of a hard disk

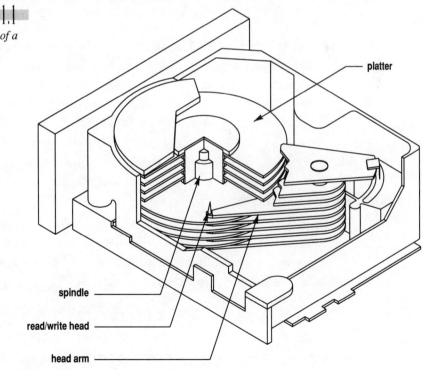

platter

spindle

read/write head

head arm

When you power up the hard disk, an electric motor turns the spindle and the platters start spinning very rapidly. A Macintosh drive is supposed to keep its platters spinning at approximately 3600 revolutions per minute, more than 100 times faster than a long-playing record. It usually takes a few seconds for the platters to reach that speed, which is why it's recommended that you turn on your external hard disk a moment or two before you start up the computer. Disks installed *inside* the Macintosh have circuitry that does essentially the same thing for you.

TIP

Be sure to turn on your external hard disk a few moments before turning on your Macintosh. This will allow the hard disk platters to reach their operating speed.

Why do the platters spin so fast? The faster they spin, the less time the Macintosh must wait for the right block of data to come around. Remember that a hard disk is a mechanical device serving a solid-state electronic one; on the microprocessing level, a tenth of a second is a long, long time. Although 3600 RPM has been set as the standard, many manufacturers are trying to increase disk performance by designing drives with disks that rotate at 4000, 4400, and even 5600 RPM.

Read/Write Heads

The read/write heads of your hard disk are something like a cross between a tape head and phonograph stylus. They're small, light, and suspended on a metal arm, but they don't actually touch the surface of the platter. Instead, they float extremely close to the surface, swinging back and forth to cover the entire surface area.

How close? The distance is usually measured in microinches, or *millionths* of an inch. The average gap is ten microinches, smaller than a single human hair. The head must be that close to the platter surface since any further distance would weaken the head's electromagnetic read/write signals, causing unreliable operation.

Ten microinches is close, but thanks to aerodynamics, the gap between the read/write head and platter is only rarely bridged. The high-speed rotation of the platter creates a layer of air on which the heads ride much as a glider rides an air current.

Neverthless, such close tolerances leave little margin for error. The residue left behind by a fingerprint, by cigarette smoke, or even a speck of dust can cause the read/write heads to touch the platter surface. When this happens, a condition known as a *head crash* usually occurs. The damage from a head crash can range from momentary data loss to the permanent crippling of the drive. For this reason, drive mechanisms are assembled under "clean-room" conditions, in which dust and other air particles are filtered out, and workers wear special gowns. These rooms maintain a level of cleanliness greater than most operating rooms, and these precautions add to the cost of hard drives.

Head crashes are also caused by moving or dropping the drive while it's in operation. Most units have a shock-absorption system that minimizes this danger, but extremes of motion—say, knocking the hard disk off your desk—can cause a fair bit of damage. Many manufacturers advertise *shock ratings* to indicate the amount of sudden movement their drives can safely endure. These ratings are usually expressed as a function of *g*, or unit of gravitational force. If you plan on transporting your hard drive often, you'll want one with a shock rating of at least 60 g's.

The Controller

The *controller* manipulates the read/write heads and passes data to the computer or disk. If you've ever wondered why Macintosh hard disks tend to be significantly more expensive than their PC counterparts, the controller is a large part of the answer: on the IBM and compatible PCs, a hard disk controller board can be plugged directly into the computer's data pathway with an add-on card. Although the Macintosh II and Quadra lines now have a similar design (called NuBus), the configuration of the earlier Macs required the development of another standard (see "What is SCSI?" below). That new standard required newer, more elaborate—and hence more expensive—controller circuitry.

Initialization

Initialization, also called *formatting*, is the process by which your hard disk is organized and mapped, so that data can be stored and retrieved as quickly as possible. An initialized platter is divided into concentric rings called *tracks*, which are further broken down into segments called *sectors* (Figure 1.2). The number and size of the tracks and sectors vary according to a number of factors, such as the density of the platter coating or the limitations of the controller. Currently, the average initialized hard disk platter contains about 600 tracks per inch of surface. The standard size of a sector is 512 bytes, or one half of a kilobyte. Thus a 14 KB file would typically be stored in 28 different sectors. If free space allowed, those sectors would be *contiguous*, with each sector in sequence on a track. But if contiguous space isn't available, the file will be *fragmented*, with sectors scattered around the platter.

All commercially available hard disks come from the factory already initialized, although at some point you may wish to reformat your disk since initialization is more than the neat division of platter space. It also involves identifying unusable or unreliable areas and "walling them off" from future use. These areas can be created by dust motes, manufacturing impurities, or by a jolt that caused a part of the drive to touch the platter surface. The presence of such zones is an almost inevitable consequence of real-world usage and shouldn't be seen as a sign of a defective drive. See Chapter 8 for more information on reformatting your hard disk.

Although the platter space on a hard drive is physically formatted in sectors, the software, or *logical* formatting, defines space in terms of *blocks*. A block is a group of sectors that represents the smallest discreet unit that a drive can read or write to in a single operation. The size of a block depends upon the overall capacity of the drive. Up to 20 megabytes, a block equals one sector (or 512 bytes). From 20 to 60 megabytes, it equals two sectors (1 KB). From 60 to 100 megabytes, it's three sectors per block (1.5 KB).

FIGURE 1.2

*The tracks and
sectors of an
initialized hard
disk*

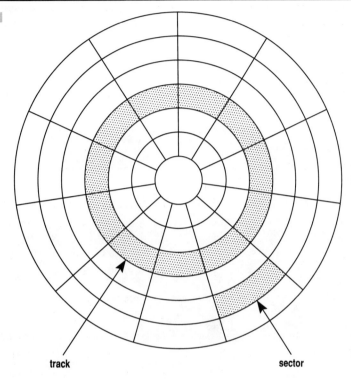

track   sector

The distinction between blocks and sectors is important, since files don't fall
neatly into both measurements. A 2212 KB file will be read into three blocks on
a 40 megabyte drive, even though there will be 860 bytes of empty space in the
last block. On a 20 megabyte drive, the same file would occupy five blocks,
with the last block containing 348 bytes of empty space. This extra unused
space at the end of a file is known as *slack*, and although it might seem like a
waste of platter space, it's a necessary a tradeoff for faster disk performance.
Slack is also the reason why some files seem to grow a little larger or smaller
when copied from one volume to another.

Have you ever noticed that no Macintosh disk is completely blank? Even a
freshly formatted floppy has at least 7 KB occupied, even though no files appear in its directory. That's space taken up by the formatting software: in order

to work successfully with your files, the system needs to reserve some blocks of its own.

Let's take a look at what these blocks include. Although this is information you may never need to use, it could come in handy if you ever need to resurrect a crashed or damaged hard disk.

The *boot blocks* always occupy the first two sectors of each volume. During the startup process, the Macintosh looks to this location for essential information, such as the type of filing system used, whether or not the disk is partitioned, and the maximum number of files that can be opened at once.

The *volume info block* establishes the identity of the volume itself. It includes such information as the name of the volume, the amount of free space available, and the location of the System Folder and other important files.

The *volume bit map* serves as the Mac's directory to the storage space, listing which blocks are available and which are occupied.

The *catalog tree* functions as a counterpart to the volume bit map. While the volume bit map lists only which blocks are occupied and which are vacant, the catalog tree keeps track of which files occupy which blocks. It does this by identifying the length of each file, and the sector in which it begins. When you "erase" a file by dragging it to the Trash Can icon and selecting Empty Trash, the Macintosh doesn't actually erase the file information; instead, it simply removes its entry from the catalog tree. The file is still on your hard disk, but it won't appear in any directory. It will remain there until the drive needs the space for another file, at which point it will be overwritten. Software like the Norton Utilities take advantage of this fact to "undelete" mistakenly erased files (see Chapter 5).

The *extents tree* augments the catalog tree. In the case of a file written to contiguous sectors, the information from the catalog tree—the file length and first sector location—is all the Macintosh needs to know. But if a file has been fragmented, the file's sectors are scattered among blocks throughout the disk. The extents tree keeps track of those dispersed blocks and tells the Mac their location and the order in which to read them.

Macintoshes and Hard Disks

When the Macintosh debuted in 1984, it was a far different machine from the Mac IIs and Quadras of today. The user interface icons, windows, and pull-down menus set new standards for ease of use, but the hardware itself had severe limitations, some intentionally built in by the machine's designers.

The original Macintosh was designed to be the "Model T" of personal computers—a single, utilitarian unit without many options. The idea was to keep the Macintosh from becoming a confusing morass of modifications and permutations. So in order to keep third party developers from tinkering with it, Apple designed the Macintosh as a "closed box" computer. Unlike the Apple II or the IBM PC, the Macintosh lacked *expansion slots*, which allow users to augment the computer with add-on circuitry. When it came to storage devices, users were supposed to be satisfied with the addition of a single external floppy disk drive.

Users weren't satisfied. Personal computer technology was advancing rapidly, and soon 400 KB or 800 KB of floppy storage seemed far from adequate, especially when compared to the IBM PC and compatible computers and their 20 and 40 megabyte hard disks. Soon the Mac's beige box, intended to remain unopened, was being regularly cracked open by third-party "upgraders." By 1985, a number of companies offered *internal hard disks* for the Macintosh.

These early drives, though comparable in construction and quality to other Winchester drives, had the disadvantage of needing to survive in a hostile environment. The interior of the Macintosh was already crammed with hardware, and even well-engineered hard disks succumbed all too often to the Macintosh's lack of air circulation and inadequate power supply. The accessory market soon shifted its efforts to *external hard disks*, which didn't have to be mounted within the central shell and didn't depend on the computer's power supply. Yet these, too, had their drawbacks.

Serial Hard Disks

The first wave of Macintoshes, which had 128 KB or 512 KB of RAM, were built with the expectation that the most advanced accessory would be the addition of another floppy disk drive. So only one external port, a serial port, was provided. That's why the first generation of external hard disks had to, in effect, masquerade as floppy disks (which are serial devices), albeit very large ones. As far as the computer's operating system was concerned, these first serial hard disks were more or less the same as floppies.

These serial disks could store more information than floppies, but the Macintosh couldn't access that information any faster. Data flow remained bottlenecked at the serial port, which could process data at the rate of only 62.5 KB per second. Despite their popularity, these hard disks still had many performance limitations, and in general contributed to the perception that the Macintosh was not a "serious" computer.

SCSI Hard Disks

Fortunately, by 1986 Apple faced up to reality and acknowledged that hard disks were a necessary part of personal computing. With the introduction of the Macintosh Plus, they added a *SCSI* (Small Computer System Interface) port, designed primarily for hard disks and related peripherals. Through this port, the computer could access data from up to seven different devices at once, at speeds several times greater than could be achieved through the serial port. Almost immediately, the Macintosh hard disk industry blossomed. And with the increased power of mass storage, the Macintosh began to make headway into the business marketplace.

Today, every Macintosh in production can access a *daisychain,* or interconnected series, of SCSI devices. Macintosh-compatable serial hard drives are no longer manufactured, and SCSI hard disks are readily available with capacities ranging from 20 megabytes to 1 gigabyte and beyond.

Internal Hard Disks

In 1987, the Mac was fully opened for business. The Macintosh SE (for System Expansion) retained the distinctive size and shape of its predecessors, while adding a single expansion slot and room for an internal hard disk. The Macintosh II, introduced at the same time, was designed with an unabashedly open architecture: there was room under the cover for no less than six expansion boards and *two* hard disks.

These models ushered in a new generation of internal hard disks, as engineers no longer had to make design compromises in order to shoehorn the units into the computer's casing.

Today, the Macintosh family can be divided into three types:

- *Compact Macs.* Models in this group have built-in monitors and cases that are not designed to be opened by the user. "Mac cracking" tools are available for these types, but in general, internal drive installation should be left to qualified technicians. Opening a compact Mac voids its warranty, and it can be dangerous to both the computer and to you. The Compact Mac group includes the Mac Plus, SE, and Classic models.

- *Modular Macs.* The models in this group, which include all Macintosh IIs and Quadras, are often known as "open" Macs, since they can connect to external monitors and accept add-on cards and peripherals. They're designed to be opened by the user; the top or side panel is held in place by only a single screw. By following a manufacturer's instructions, the user can install an internal drive in a few minutes, usually with no more specialized tools than a screwdriver. It's pretty straightforward, but if you balk at the prospect of grappling with the innards of your computer, installation is available at all authorized Apple dealers, and most reputable Macintosh peripheral vendors.

- *Portable Macs.* The models in this line (the Portable, the Power-Book line) are even more densely engineered than compact Macs, so opening them is not recommended. You'll want to make sure that the hard drive you buy was engineered specifically for your portable, and you'll want a professional to install it.

Internal drives are an excellent choice when desk space is at a premium, or when sound needs to be kept to a minimum (internal disks are cooled by the computer's fan). The disadvantage is that they can't be easily transported from one computer to another; many users with both an office and a home system prefer external hard disks, which they can shuttle back and forth.

External Hard Disks

External drives are not physically integrated into the Macintosh and have separate power supplies, cooling systems and control circuitry. We'll discuss their set-up, installation and formatting in Chapter 2.

For the owner of a compact Mac, the external disk is essentially the only hard disk option. But external drives have proven to be popular with modular Mac owners as well. They're easier to transplant from one Mac to another, and easier to remove when something goes wrong. If you work with several different Macintoshes in various locations but need ready access to the same group of files, an external drive, and preferably a portable one (see below), is often the best option.

It's important to note that even though the same external hard disk can be used with most Macintoshes, it can be configured for optimum performance with only one member of the Macintosh family at a time. See "Hard Disk Performance on the Mac" below and Chapter 8.

Portable Hard Disks

A subcategory of external hard drives has emerged in recent years: the portable drive. Although all external drives are portable, these models are especially designed to be lightweight and durable. A typical portable drive weighs under two pounds and can fit inside a shirt pocket. These benefits come at a cost, though. You'll usually pay about twenty percent more for a portable drive than for a conventional drive of similar performance and capacity.

If you opt for a portable drive, look for one that connects to the Macintosh by a cable. Some portable drives connect directly to the back of the Mac, which can make moving and removing the drive awkward. You'll also want one with a "pass-through" port, which allows you to connect other SCSI peripherals (some portables hog the entire SCSI port). Try to find one with a shock rating of at least 100 g's—and keep in mind that even though such a drive is durable, it's not indestructible.

What is SCSI?

SCSI (pronounced "scuzzy") isn't a physical unit or piece of software, but rather a set of rules for ensuring compatibility between devices. SCSI is a complete set of mechanical, electrical, and functional standards developed by the American National Standards Institute (ANSI), an organization that develops and promotes standards to eliminate product incompatibility.

A device that is built to SCSI standards can communicate with other SCSI devices along a data pathway known as a *SCSI bus*. Hard disks aren't the only machines built to SCSI specifications; the Macintosh itself is a SCSI device, and other peripherals such as high-speed printers and backup drives are also available in SCSI versions.

Under SCSI rules, each device can act as an *initiator* or a *target*: the initiator requests that the target perform an operation, such as the reading or writing of a certain block of data. At present, the Macintosh always acts as the initiator on the SCSI bus, although "intelligent peripherals" that initiate commands of their own may be in the wings.

Multiple SCSI devices—up to eight, counting the Macintosh—can be linked to the SCSI bus at once. But only one of those devices can be a Macintosh, which is why shared, or "networked," hard disks must rely on some other connectivity system. The one exception to this rule is the PowerBook 100 (see below).

The SCSI Port

Take a look at the back of your Macintosh. Unless it's one of the earliest models, you'll find the SCSI symbol (Figure 1.3) embossed above one of the larger ports. And unless your Mac is one of the PowerBook models, that SCSI port conforms to a connection standard known as DB-25; you'll note a total of 25 holes, 13 on the top row and 12 on the bottom. This uneven pattern, along with the sloped sides of the port, is intended to discourage accidental upside-down connections. However, it isn't foolproof: given enough obliviousness and force, you can cram an incorrectly-oriented connector into the port, damaging your Mac, your cabling, or both. If it doesn't feel like the right fit, double-check it. Don't force it.

A further note of caution: while the SCSI port may be the fastest way to get data in and out of your Macintosh, it is also one of the easiest means of disabling your hardware, perhaps permanently. That's because SCSI devices aren't the only equipment designed to use the DB-25 standard. Other hardware products are physically capable of connecting to the port, but appearances can be disastrously deceiving. For instance, most IBM PC-compatible computers have DB-25 serial and parallel printer ports, and there are literally hundreds of printers on the market designed to operate with them. But plugging a PC serial or parallel port printer into a Macintosh SCSI port will almost certainly cause circuitry damage to the Mac—and that means hundreds of dollars in repair bills.

FIGURE 1.3

The symbol for
Small
Computer
Systems
Interface (SCSI)

The bottom line is: Don't connect anything to your Macintosh SCSI port unless you're sure absolutely it's intended to work with that port. If the hardware's documentation doesn't tell you, contact the manufacturer directly.

WARNING

Never plug a non-SCSI device into your SCSI port; it could permanently damage your Macintosh. If you're not sure whether a device is a SCSI device, check the device's documentation or ask the manufacturer.

PowerBook SCSI Ports

If your Macintosh is one of the PowerBook portable models—the 100, 140, or 170—you won't find the DB-25 port in back. Since space is at a premium on the PowerBooks, Apple uses the HDI-30 port. It's smaller, but surprisingly it has five more holes than the DB-25 port.

Unlike the slant-sided DB-25, this port is perfectly square, which makes upside-down connections even more of a possibility. Apple connectors guard against this by adding a solid guiding pin on top of the connector. But if you're using third-party cables, confirm which is the top side of the cable before connecting it to the port.

The configuration of the port is the only significant difference of PowerBook SCSI; with the right adaptor cable, you can attach external hard drives and other SCSI devices designed for use with the other Macintosh marketplace. In addition, the PowerBooks have bred a new genre of SCSI products: video drivers. Since the 100, 140, and 170 don't have dedicated video ports, the only way to hook them up to an external monitor is with the SCSI bus, and a number of companies manufacture graphics adapters for just that purpose.

Even though the PowerBook 100 is the bottom-of-the-line portable, it has one capability unmatched by the others: it can use its HDI-30 SCSI Disk Adapter, to connect directly to a desktop Macintosh. When "docked" in this manner, the PowerBook 100 doesn't function as a separate computer; instead, its internal hard drive is accessed directly by the desktop Mac, just like any other SCSI device. Since the PowerBook 100 doesn't have an internal floppy drive, this type of connection is the fastest and most convenient means of transferring information and software from one computer to the other.

TIP

> The PowerBook 100 using the HDI-30 SCSI Disk Adapter is the only Macintosh that can be connected directly to another Mac's SCSI port.

SCSI Ports for Older Macs

If your Macintosh was manufactured before the introduction of the Macintosh Plus, that doesn't mean you can't use SCSI devices. Many hard disk manufacturers have developed after-market SCSI ports that are easily installed by either the user or a qualified dealer. Most take only a few minutes to install and require no special tools or technical knowledge.

Before you buy a SCSI port, however, make sure that it is compatible with your hard disk, and that you're comfortable with its manner of installation. Usually, the manufacturer of a hard disk produces the best port for that hard disk; those made by other manufacturers might not work at all. The typical port is installed through the battery compartment in the rear of the Macintosh.

If you have a 512 Ke Mac (the "e" stands for Enhanced), a port is all you need; your computer's ROM has routines that facilitate the use of SCSI devices. Your machine won't be as fast as a Macintosh Plus, but your hard disk will make a big difference in your computing.

Hard Disk Performance on the Macintosh

Most SCSI Macintosh external hard drives can work with any member of the Macintosh family—the same would go for internal drives, except for the fact that design differences between the SE and Mac II require different configurations. Theoretically, all SCSI hard disks could be 100 percent compatible with any SCSI-ported computer, given the appropriate disk controller circuitry and mounting.

But just because they'll work, that doesn't mean they'll work exactly the same when teamed with any model of Macintosh. The degree of performance depends on a number of factors, particularly the limitations imposed by the computer and the hard disk controller. Primary among these performance factors are *transfer speed* and *access time*.

Transfer Speed

Transfer speed, also known as *throughput*, is the rate at which information is conveyed between the disk and the CPU. Measured in kilobytes per second (KB/sec), it varies with the traffic coordination capacity of the CPU. Like mileage estimates for cars, official transfer speeds reflect optimum performance. However, optimum transfer speed is usually attained only in short bursts—continuous transfer at optimum speed would quickly overwhelm the CPU.

Faster transfer time is one of the benchmarks of the Macintosh family's upward performance curve. The Macintosh Plus SCSI port can only accommodate 312 KB/sec. That's a considerable increase over serial port hard disks (62.5 KB/sec) and over floppy drives (which average around 56 KB/sec), but by current SCSI standards, it's downright slow and pokey. The Macintosh SE's port, operating at approximately 656 KB/sec, is more than twice as fast as that of the Mac Plus. The original Macintosh II's throughput maximum is 1250 KB/sec (or 1.25 MB/sec), again nearly a twofold increase. The Macintosh Quadra 900 represents an even greater leap in SCSI performance, with claimed transfer speeds of up to 4 MB/sec for external drives, and 5 MB/sec for internal drives. These speeds press the theoretical limits of SCSI speed, but optimum speeds don't necessarily reflect real-world performance.

Like the Macs themselves, hard disks and other SCSI products have their own throughput speeds. If a hard disk has a faster transfer speed than the Macintosh it's connected to, the Mac has to enforce a slower speed limit. This is usually done through a process called *interleaving*.

Interleave Ratios

Interleaving slows the effective data transfer rate by deliberately skipping chances to access a sector as it passes by. Because it must wait for the sector to come around again, the read/write head accesses information on disk slower. Since the various members of the Macintosh family have different port speeds, the ratio of sectors encountered to sectors read, known as the *interleave ratio*, varies for each of the models.

IP

> You can think of the interleave ratio as the number of revolutions a disk must make for the read/write head to read one track of data.

On a hard disk formatted with an interleave ratio of 1:1, the read/write head accesses each sector on each track as soon as it encounters the new sector. When the interleave ratio is 2:1, every other sector is accessed during a given revolution, which means that it takes two revolutions to read a track. For a ratio of 3:1, every third sector is accessed each revolution, and it takes three revolutions to read an entire track (Figure 1.4). Since interleaving changes the order in which sectors are accessed, it slows down the amount of time it takes to open, close, or modify a file.

Although it's possible to connect a hard drive with a 1:1 interleave to just about any Macintosh, it won't speed performance and could lead to system crashes and corrupted data. Table 1.1 lists the recommended interleaves for the various Macintosh models. Unless your Macintosh has had a CPU enhancement that includes new SCSI capability, you're unlikely to benefit from an interleave ratio that differs from the standard for your model.

FIGURE 1.4

*Interleave
ratios change
the order in
which sectors
are read—
1:1 (top);
2:1 (middle);
3:1 (bottom)*

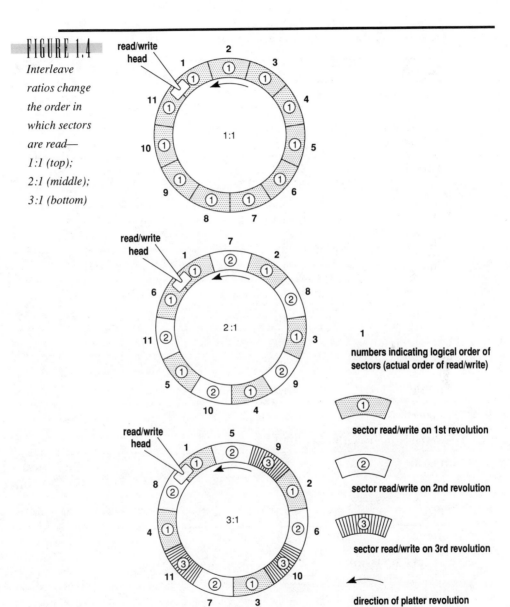

Recommended Interleave Ratios for Macintosh CPUs

Model	Recommended Interleave
Quadra 900	1:1
Quadra 700	1:1
PowerBook 170	1:1
PowerBook 140	1:1
IIfx	1:1
IIci	1:1
IIsi	1:1
IIcx	1:1
IIx	1:1
II	1:1
LC	1:1
Classic II	1:1
SE/30	1:1
PowerBook 100	2:1
Portable (pre-PowerBook)	2:1
Classic	2:1
SE	2:1
Plus	3:1
512Ke	3:1
512K (w/SCSI port)	3:1

Access Times

A common benchmark of hard disk performance is *access time* or *seek time*, the time it takes the read/write heads of a hard disk can locate a given track. Since tracks vary in distance from one another, access time is usually given as an average. Current averages range from 65 milliseconds for older drives to 7 milliseconds and less for the newest, most expensive models. Most drives on sale today have access times between 10 and 25 milliseconds.

Access time is measured in milliseconds and the difference between the slowest and fastest hard disks would be imperceptible except when several hundred sectors have to be located and read (a regular occurrence when launching an application). In this case, a delay of milliseconds is multiplied to the point that it becomes noticable.

When evaluating hard disk speed in real-world terms, don't forget to take into consideration the transfer speeds of both the drive and the computer. Even the fastest drive can only work as fast as the computer it's connected to, and some Macs handle SCSI data more slowly than others. If you have a Quadra 900, for instance, a drive with a 10 millisecond access time will seem positively zippy. But if you connect the same drive to a Mac Plus, it'll probably seem no faster than a 25-millisecond drive.

TIP

When considering a hard disk purchase, don't overlook the factor of your computer's processing speed. Don't pay for performance capabilities that your computer can't use. On the other hand, if you expect to buy a newer, faster Macintosh sometime in the future, a speedy drive can be a good investment.

Before You Buy

If you're in the market for a hard drive, here are a few things to keep in mind:

Used drives are risky purchases. There's no such thing as an odometer on hard drives, so there's no way of knowing for sure just how much useful life is left in one. If you're tempted by the bargain price of a used drive (or if it's part of an overall used computer package), try to find out how long it's been in use, and the conditions under which has been used.

Buy the technology, not a brand name. There are dozens of companies marketing hard drives under a myriad of brand names, but the drives themselves are actually manufactured by only a handful of companies. The retail-oriented companies simply buy the mechanisms in bulk from the manufacturers, and then (in the case of external drives) place them in a case with a power supply, fan, and the requisite ports.

When making a purchasing decision, it's a good idea to weigh the reputations of both the original equipment manufacturer (OEM) and of the company that's selling the drive to you. Among OEMs, Quantum probably enjoys the highest reputation; at one time, they were Apple's exclusive supplier for factory-installed drives. They're my manufacturer of choice, although I've also had good experience with Maxtor, Hewlett-Packard, and Micropolis drives. Seagate is another well-established OEM, although they probably have a better reputation for their high-capacity drives (more than 100 megabytes capacity) than for their more modest models.

When weighing retail companies, take a look at their return policies. Do they offer warranties, technical support, and free and timely replacement of defective parts? Also look at the quality of the components used: Is the power supply adequate? Does it include a circuit breaker to prevent power surges from obliterating circuitry? Is the fan quiet and effective, or noisy and inadequate? Is termination removable? Is it easy to set and reset SCSI addresses? If the terms *termination* and *SCSI addresses* throw you, don't worry; I'll explain them in the next chapter.

Buy for reliabilty as well as performance. Fast access times and transfer speeds are only part of the picture. Another benchmark to look for is Mean Time Between Failures, or MTBF. That's the manufacturer's estimate of how long you can expect trouble-free operation.

MTBFs vary from drive to drive and from OEM to OEM, and the difference can be significant. I once saw a Maxtor drive advertised side-by side with a Conner drive. Their storage capacity and prices were identical, yet the Conner offered only 20,000 hours MTBF, or approximately 2.3 years of constant use. The Maxtor's MTBF was 150,000 hours, or a total of 17 years!

Make sure you get what you pay for. Unscrupulous vendors do exist, and some are not above switching a high-quality drive for one of the same capacity but lesser quality. I once purchased a Macintosh SE from an authorized Apple dealer; when the internal hard disk failed a little over a year later, I discovered that before the Mac had been sold to me, the dealer had removed the factory-original Quantum drive and replaced it with a slower, much less reliable drive—a drive that in fact hadn't been designed to work with the Mac in the first place!

If you have a Macintosh II or Quadra series computer, it's easy to ascertain your internal drive's manufacturer: just remove the top of the case and inspect the drive yourself. Almost all OEMs clearly label their products.

If you own a Macintosh Plus, Classic or PowerBook, the case is not intended to be opened by the consumer, at least not without special tools. External hard drives vary—some make it easy to "look under the hood," while others are hermetically sealed. When physical inspection isn't possible, software can help: each drive has a manufacturer's ID code that is readable by software utilities such as DiskMaker (discussed in Chapter 6).

OPERATING YOUR HARD DISK

FEATURING:

→ **Choosing a Location for Your Disk**

→ **Unpacking and Setting Up Your Disk**

→ **Setting Disk Termination**

→ **Setting SCSI Addresses**

→ **Breaking In Your Disk**

→ **Installing the System Folder**

→ **Custom Startup Screens**

Your computer is essentially a solid state device, but your hard disk is a machine—a sophisticated one with several rapidly moving parts operating to very close tolerances. Yet what's awe-inspiring about today's hard disks is the fact that their reliability belies their complexity. You'll want to handle, install, and use your hard disk with a certain degree of respect, but primarily because of the value of the data stored within. Your hard disk is not fragile, just intricately engineered.

This chapter is designed to help you get started with a hard disk system. We'll examine the details of setup, installation, and connectivity. We'll also look at how best to fit your hard disk into your workplace, and what precautions should be taken for trouble-free operation. Then we'll move on to the software side, demonstrating how to prepare your hard disk for its role at the core of your computing.

Even if you already have your hard disk up and running, you'll probably benefit from reading this chapter. We'll examine several of the concepts you might need to troubleshoot a hard disk problem.

Handling Your Hard Disk

A hard disk is not a box of nitroglycerine, but it's not a brick either. When handling your hard disk, strive for a balance of confidence and caution. Don't get it wet. Don't subject it to extremes of temperature (below freezing or above 100 degrees). Don't place it under a heavy weight. And try to keep it from being sharply jostled or violently shaken.

Unpacking

When removing your hard disk from its packing, try not to mangle the container or the foam padding. Once you've unpacked the disk and double-checked for any stray paraphernalia or documents, set the packaging aside for safekeeping. You may never need it, but if a time comes when you need to transport your hard disk through the mail or by package express (perhaps to return it to the manufacturer for repair), you'll be glad you kept the packaging. You could ship your hard disk in any reasonably padded package, but nothing will be better suited to the task than the original container.

Before you move on to the hardware, take a moment to peruse and fill out any warranty or registration cards that came with your hard disk. Surprisingly, the majority of new equipment purchasers fail to return consumer information of this sort, even when it's clearly to their benefit. It's a good idea to take care of this now, rather than waiting to get around to it.

Transporting

A hard disk is at its most vulnerable when it's operating. If you need to transport your disk, give it ample time to shut down before you move it. Don't just turn off the computer it's attached to; if it has its own power supply, be sure to turn it off as well. Before moving it, wait about a minute for the platters to stop spinning and the read/write heads to return to a position away from the disk data. This is known as *parking the heads,* and all but a few older and third-party disks do this automatically. If you have one of these older disks, consult your manual for instructions on parking the heads.

Once turned off and disconnected, the hard disk is a relatively hardy breed. You can put it in your briefcase, place it in your car's backseat, or even send it through the mail (but be sure to package it well and make a backup of all data first).

Setting Up

Most of the following refers specifically to hard disks of the external, self-contained variety, but the information will be useful to owners of internal hard disks as well. If the documentation that came with your hard disk is complicated, inadequate, or entirely absent, the following should help you on the way to proper installation. For installation instructions, however, you'll have to rely on the manual or the manufacturer. The best way to ensure the correct setup of your external hard disk is to read the instructions. There are too many variations on the process for us to cover here, and since each variation involves direct contact with the computer itself, you'll need to be sure of every step you take.

However, no matter how correct an action might seem, don't force any part or parts. Most computer peripherals are designed to stand up to heavy use, not heavy *abuse*.

Where to Put It?

Most external hard disks are *horizontally oriented,* designed so that the platters spin parallel to the desktop. The majority of these are *zero footprint;* they fit easily under a compact Macintosh without adding to the or amount of room occupied on the desktop. Most compact Macintosh users prefer the under-Mac location, since it raises the Mac screen by a few inches, which many people find easier on the eyes. If you do put your hard disk under the computer, make sure that your unit is designed for such a position, that it has ample vents for circulation, and that the vents won't be blocked by the bottom of the Macintosh.

To see if this arrangement works for you, place the still-unconnected hard disk under your computer. Now fire up the Mac and operate with floppies for a while. If your taste or your workspace doesn't accommodate the added height of the hard disk, no problem; simply place the hard disk elsewhere.

The location of that "elsewhere" is dictated by the length of your SCSI cable. But if you'd like to clear your desktop or put your hard disk in a place where you won't hear its fan, you might look into the purchase of a longer SCSI cable. These can be up to seven meters in length, and they enable you to place the hard disk in a corner, a cabinet, or even a closet. Make sure the location meets the following criteria:

Ventilation Resist the temptation to use the hard disk as a bookend or paperweight; even a sheet of paper placed flat against a vent can impair cooling. There should be at least three inches of clearance on both sides of your hard disk, unless your unit has a special air intake and filtration scheme. Check your documentation to see what kind of filtration system you have.

Most hard disks are designed to be placed on a flat, hard surface. If you must place it on a soft surface such as pile carpeting, first lay down a piece of wood or firm cardboard large enough to cover the unit's base. This will allow air to flow beneath the case.

Cleanliness A hard disk draws air through a series of high-mesh filters. These are more than adequate for filtering out the dust and dirt found in office and household environments, but they cannot deal with high amounts of grease, moisture, or dirt. It is probably okay to store your hard disk under your desk, but not under the kitchen sink.

Accessibility You want your hard disk to be where you can get to it with ease, both to check on its operation and to flip its power switch. Depending on your power supply setup, you might also need to flip its power switch every time you start a computing session. We'll cover power switch strategies in a bit.

Safety Keep your hard disk out of harm's way. This goes not only for the hard disk, but for all your computer system's cords, cables, and connectors. Keep them away from pets, children, vacuum cleaners, and the like.

You can store or transport a hard disk—when it's properly disconnected—in just about any position, but you should operate it only in the position for which it was designed. If you place a horizontally oriented hard disk on its side, chances are it will still work, but not for as long as it might otherwise. Changing a hard disk's orientation puts torque and gravitational strain on the drive's internal bearings and other mechanisms, which can lead to failures.

Keeping your hard disk level doesn't mean you'll have to get out a carpenter's level; any reasonably level surface will do nicely.

Plugging In

If your hard disk will remain under or near your Macintosh, it's probably easiest to plug both of them into the nearest socket. This way you can turn them both on and off by reaching around the back of the units. However, if the hard disk is situated so that the on/off switch isn't easy to reach, you might want to consider a *power strip* setup.

A power strip is a sophisticated extension cord, with multiple outlets, an on/off switch, and in some cases, a circuit breaker. With your hard disk's cord and your computer's cord plugged into the strip, you can leave the units' on/off switches in permanent "on" mode. This way you can simply power up and power down by flicking the switch on the strip.

For many, the best solution is to plug computer, hard disk, printer, modem, and other accessories all into one power strip. With this arrangement, you don't have to spend time searching for on/off switches. No matter how you configure your setup, make sure that the computer and the hard disk don't power up simultaneously: the hard disk needs a few moments to get up to speed before it can be recognized by the Macintosh.

Using Surge Suppressors

Every computer user should have a *surge suppressor* to filter off excess voltage. Surge suppressors increase the reliability of your hard disk and add years to the life of your computer and its peripherals.

AC current, as supplied through the wall sockets of most buildings, doesn't flow at a consistent voltage. The standard flow rate in the U.S., is supposed to be 120 volts, but in reality it often varies plus or minus 10 to 15 volts, depending on the age of the circuitry and the demands placed upon it. When for example, lightning strikes a power pole, a large electricity user goes offline, or a large household appliance turns on, a sudden strain is placed on the system, causing a momentary voltage imbalance that sends surges through local outlets. These have little effect on lights and appliances, but they can cause data loss and even permanent damage in microprocessors and magnetic media.

That's where surge protection comes in. Most surge suppressors are simple plug-in devices that range in price from $15 to $100.

Surge suppressors filter off the excess voltage of a surge, but they won't protect you from brownouts, blackouts, or other abrupt power outages. That's why it's a good idea to save your data regularly. If you want a guaranteed, reliable source of electricity, you might consider buying an *uninterruptible power supply* (UPS), which are more expensive but can render your Mac oblivious to brief power outages. If you want protection from a direct lightning strike, you'll need a *surge arrestor*, available for about $300 from your local power company. It'll protect not only your computer, but any other equipment plugged in to the same circuit.

Most people will find enough security in a straightforward surge suppressor. The problem is that not all surge suppressors do what they purport to do; some are little more than grounding plugs. I've actually seen, on more than one occasion, unscrupulous salespeople sell ordinary power strips as "surge suppressors."

When shopping for a surge suppressor, look for the Underwriters Laboratories (UL) marking of UL 1449 on both the packaging and the product itself. And somewhere on the packaging should be the term "UL Listed 1449 Suppression Voltage L-N 400/L-G 400/N-G 400." These designations indicate that the product has passed UL's surge suppression test for use with personal computers. Be sure to look for the listing and not just the UL symbol, which has been known to be counterfeited.

TIP

> **When shopping for a surge suppressor, look for one with the Underwriters Laboratories seal and the term "UL Listed 1449 Suppression Voltage L-N 400/L-G 400/N-G 400."**

Getting on the Bus: Your SCSI Setup

Most external hard disks come supplied with one SCSI cable and two SCSI ports. That's because each SCSI device, including hard disks, can serve as a link on the SCSI bus, passing on information to and from another SCSI device. A number of SCSI devices linked this way is called a *daisychain*. Up to seven devices can be daisy-chained at once. A SCSI port's capacity to transmit information is greater than the CPU's capacity to process and transmit it, so even a fully-loaded daisychain is usually no slower than a single SCSI device.

On most hard disks, it doesn't matter which port is connected to the computer and which is connected to another SCSI device. But even if you're only hooking up a single hard disk, you're establishing a SCSI bus that must have a clearly defined end. This definition is achieved with termination.

Termination

Daisy-chaining isn't just a fringe benefit of SCSI, it's what the standard was designed for—to overcome the limitation of data port bottlenecks. In order for the SCSI bus to support multiple devices, the last device in the bus must be capped with a terminating resistor, or *terminator*. Internal hard disks are automatically terminated, but most external drives aren't.

Your Macintosh constantly sends and receives signals up and down the SCSI bus, signals that contain commands, status messages, target addresses, and of course, data. Some signals are directed at a specific device, but others of general significance are intended to be read by all the devices in the daisychain (even if only one device is connected). Unless there is a terminator at the end of the daisy-chain, these signals can travel up the SCSI bus and then "bounce back," colliding with other signals and disrupting the entire bus. A terminator safely dissipates the signals.

Most terminators are external, in the form of a short female/male adaptor. If you intend to attach only one SCSI device to your Macintosh, attach it in one of the following ways:

- connect the SCSI cable directly to one device port and place the terminator on the other

- place the terminator between the SCSI cable and the device port

Of the two, the latter is slightly more convenient for users who occasionally daisy-chain another SCSI device. Connecting the SCSI cable to one part and placing the terminator on the other becomes necessary when multiple devices are on the bus—that's when you need to make sure that termination is active only on the last device in the chain. A terminator placed in the middle of the chain effectively cuts off other devices from the bus.

WARNING

> Some external hard disks have internal terminators that can't be deactivated, or terminators that are not removable. Most of these were manufactured in the early days of Macintosh SCSI by companies who assumed that most users would need only one hard disk at a time. If your terminator is one of these, get in touch with the manufacturer; most can at least recommend a means of removing or circumventing the termination. If the manufacturer is no longer around, try taking it to a qualified service technician and hope for the best. Of course, a permanently terminated hard disk isn't obsolete. It'll work fine when directly connected to the Macintosh, or when placed at the very end of a daisychain.

Nearly all terminators are designed to work with almost all Macintoshes. As of this writing, the one exception is the Macintosh IIfx, which implements SCSI in a slightly different manner from the rest. A special terminator (usually black) is provided with the IIfx; it must be placed at the end of the SCSI bus, or none of the volumes will be recognized by the computer. This terminator is incompatible with other Macintosh models.

ARNING

> The Macintosh IIfx requires a special terminator, manufactured by Apple. It will not work with other terminators.

Setting SCSI Addresses

Daisy-chaining is a means of ordering devices along the SCSI bus, but there's another order to the setup: each device has an *address* that serves both as an identifier and as a means of prioritizing data traffic. The address order bears no relation to the physical order, and you can change it without reconnecting any cables.

The SCSI bus has a total of eight addresses—0 to 7—and no two devices on the SCSI bus can have the same address. The address 7 is reserved for the Macintosh itself, and internal hard disks are always set at 0. You can set your hard disk to any of the six addresses in between. When looking for data, the Mac looks at address 7 first, then address 0, then addresses 6 down to 1.

Different drives provide different means of setting addresses. Some come with a preset address that can only be changed with software after the drive is up and running. Others require the setting of switches, and still others have a simple dial or knob on the rear of the unit for changing addresses. And, of course, there are some units that can't be reset at all—a drawback only when you need to daisy-chain two units with the same permanent address.

If you have a choice, it's a good idea to set your main external hard disk to the address 6. Six is the next address after the floppy drive and internal hard disk where the Macintosh looks for system software upon startup. When two or more devices are trying to feed the SCSI bus at the same time, the one with the highest address gets priority. Be sure that no devices share the same SCSI address.

Reset addresses only when the computer is turned off. Or if your system uses software to change addresses, be sure to change them only under the conditions specified by the software. In any case, completely shut down and restart the system before you attempt to access a re-addressed device. Never change a device's address in the middle of a work section. SCSI addresses are read by the Macintosh only once, during the startup sequence. If you change an address in the interim, the computer will remain oblivious; it will blithely send commands and data to wrong or non-existent devices.

Breaking In Your Hard Disk

Your first impulse with a brand new hard disk may be to go easy on it, perhaps by loading only a few applications and files and only adding to them sparingly. Whereas a gentle breaking in period may be appropriate for a new automobile, for hard disks you should take the opposite tack.

It's best to uncover any defects in your hard disk in the earliest phase of use, before the warranty expires. Here's a three-step strategy for ferreting out problems while there's still time to do something about them.

- *Keep the unit running.* If your hard disk has a separate power supply, it can operate (but not read or write data) while the computer is turned off. So long as the noise from the fan doesn't present a problem, keep it running constantly for the first week or so. This can reveal problems with the platter bearings, the exhaust fan, or the drive motor.

- *Copy as much data as possible.* Bad sectors and controller problems are usually discovered while reading and writing data. As soon as you've finished setting up, transfer the applications and files you expect to use regularly to your hard disk. If it's not too much trouble, why not fill up the disk? You needn't struggle to fill up every megabyte—taking up a significant block of storage space can be surprisingly fast and easy.

Instead of laboriously feeding in floppy disks, create a folder. Next, insert into this folder a duplicate of everything currently on the drive. Then open the folder, create another folder within it, and place all the duplicates inside that one. Now, select the folder containing the duplicates and duplicate it. Repeat the process for as long as possible; your Macintosh will tell you when it reaches the limits of its memory. Be sure to discard these folders and their contents before getting down to work, however: the multiple versions of files and applications could cause the system to crash in confusion. If this copying process causes any complications (such as a system malfunction or incomplete copying), the hard disk may be defective. See Chapter 6 on troubleshooting problems.

- *Make the hard disk drive the startup device.* You'll want to do this anyway, since nowadays even a modestly equipped System Folder can take up more than 1.4 MB (the capacity of a high-density floppy). Your Macintosh probably reads and writes the contents of this folder more than any other software, so its presence on your hard disk ensures a workout. System installation and startup designation is discussed below.

Getting the System Running

Now that your hard disk is properly situated, installed, and connected, it's time to see if the computer recognizes the drive. If your drive comes preformatted with a resident System Folder, all you need to do is to make sure everything is turned on. The computer should boot automatically (make sure no disks are in your floppy drives). If, on starting up, all you see is the Macintosh's request for a disk icon, then your hard disk doesn't have a valid System Folder. Keep the hard disk running, but boot up from a floppy. When the desktop appears, note that the hard disk icon looks different from the floppy disk icon. Some hard disk manufacturers provide different icons, so yours may look different from the standard icon (Figure 2.1).

FIGURE 2.1
*The standard
hard disk icon*

On the other hand, if you had to boot from a floppy and a hard disk doesn't show up on the desktop, shut down the Macintosh. Check the power cord and SCSI cable to make sure they're securely connected. It's important to do this with the computer switched off. Often the Macintosh doesn't recognize SCSI connections made after startup. If you make SCSI connections with the computer on, the Macintosh might send data to the wrong address, which can cause system crashes. If securing the power cord and cable doesn't do the trick, see Appendix A.

If you have a serial hard disk, watch out for instances when a floppy disk replaces the hard disk icon. This indicates that the Mac has confused the drive with a floppy. Although rare, subsequent performance problems can occur. Whenever the Macintosh displays an incorrect icon for any hard disk, immediately save all data, shut down, and restart.

Installing the System Folder

In Chapter 1, we discussed the role of the ROM in running the Macintosh. But the ROM provides only part of the Mac's operating system: the rest must be loaded into RAM at the beginning of each session. This software usually makes up the bulk of the System Folder contents—it's the first software you should install on your hard disk.

Apple has released several versions of the Macintosh System software since 1984. Unfortunately, it isn't safe to assume that the latest version is the best for you. The best System Folders are a often a mix-and-match collection of system components, custom-configured to match the needs of the user and the limitations of the machine. We'll take up the subject of System software in detail in Chapter 4.

You may eventually choose to upgrade the System Folder resident on your hard disk, for the moment the best version to install is probably one you've been successfully using with your floppies. One way to determine if your System Folder will meet your short-term needs is to examine the System Folder icon. Does it have an image of a miniature Macintosh in the middle, as in Figure 2.2? This symbol is called a "blessed" folder: it means the system files within the folder are sufficient to operate the computer. If you rebooted on another system and removed vital files from this folder, the "blessing" would be absent. The miniature Macintosh image has been a feature of all Finder files since System 6, and it's a sign that the software is at least recent enough to work with your hard disk.

FIGURE 2.2

The "blessed"
System Folder

system folder

Another way to determine if your System Folder meets your short-term needs is to read the Get Info entries. If your active System Folder does not display the "blessed" folder symbol, use the Get Info command to determine version number. Open the file and find the file named System. Click on it once to select it (Figure 2.3), then choose Get Info from the File menu. An information box similar to the one in Figure 2.4 should appear. Get Info boxes exist for every visible file on the Macintosh and they are storehouses of useful information.

Note the version number. If it's Version 3.1 or earlier, *do not use it.* Such Systems are remnants of the *Macintosh File System (MFS),* a file management approach long since abandoned by Apple. The *Hierarchical File System (HFS)*

FIGURE 2.3

Selecting the
System file

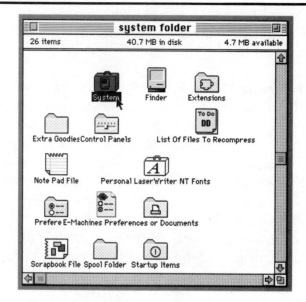

FIGURE 2.4

The Get Info
box for a
System 7 file

has supplanted the MFS version. Unlike its precedecessor, the Hierarchical File System is capable of handling the multiple nested folders generated by a hard disk system. If your system is an MFS version, replace it with an HFS version, which you can obtain at an Apple dealer or through Macintosh user groups. The HFS system is discussed in more detail in Chapter 4.

After you've checked the System file, make sure that the Finder file with the same icon is present. The Finder can be omitted if certain options are selected on one of the more recent System files, but for now you should play it safe and include it on your hard disk.

Once the System Folder has passed the test, copy it as you would any other file by selecting its icon and dragging it over to the hard disk icon. The folder won't disappear from the floppy, but a duplicate will be created on the hard disk. Double-click on the hard disk icon to confirm its contents, then shut down.

Now, while holding the mouse button down, start the Macintosh back up, once again making sure that the hard disk is turned on first. If the floppy disk wasn't automatically ejected upon shutdown, it should eject itself now. If it doesn't, wait until the startup is completed, select the floppy, and choose Eject from the File menu. Now shut down and restart again, and your Macintosh should be up and running from the hard disk alone. If it isn't, see Appendix C.

System 7 Versus System 6

In 1991, the Macintosh system software took its biggest leap forward yet with the introduction of System 7. This new System version was far more than an incremental improvement or expansion of the previous versions. The new system changed the Macintosh interface considerably, and added a number of new features. But for all its sleekness and versatility, System 7 may not be for everyone.

For one, System 7 is extremely RAM-hungry. System 6 introduced the Multi-Finder (see Chapter 3), a feature that expends at least a megabyte of RAM at all times. In System 6, this option could be turned on or off. System 7 keeps it on permanently. Other features of System 7, such as the TrueType font management standard, use up additional RAM. Although Apple claims System 7 can run on a minimum of 2 megabytes of RAM, in reality you'll want at least twice that much memory before trying to do any meaningful work.

Another consideration is software incompatibility. Although practically all applications will eventually be compatible with System 7, upgrading your software can be both inconvenient and expensive.

In general, you'd be better served with System 6 if:

- *You have a compact Macintosh with less than 4 megabytes of RAM.* If you have an SE/30 or Classic II, you might consider additional RAM a small price to pay for the capabilities of System 7. Otherwise, you're better off with System 6.

- *You can't afford to upgrade the software you already own.* If your copies of Microsoft Works 1.0 and MacPaint 2.0 do everything you need them to, why go to the expense of buying newer versions?

- *You truly don't need the extra features of System 7.* The networking, file management, and type manipulation features of System 7 are pretty nifty, but your System software is truly obsolete only when it no longer does the work you need it to do.

Why *would* you want to upgrade to System 7? To answer that, peruse the System 7 features listed in Chapter 4.

The Startup Sequence

Making your hard disk the Mac's startup device requires more than depositing a System Folder on it. The disk must occupy the proper place in your computer's startup sequence.

When the Mac is switched on, it displays the Disk Requested icon (Figure 2.5) and looks for a startup disk. First it searches the "native" internal floppy drive that is sold with the computer (not the optional third-party internals). Next, it looks in the second internal or the external floppy drive. If the Macintosh finds a floppy disk in any of these locations and the floppy disk does not contain a System Folder, it ejects the floppy. However, if it finds a System Folder in one of those locations, it will begin to boot up. Make sure the floppy drives are empty—or at least not occupied by disks containing System Folders—when you want start up from a hard disk.

FIGURE 2.5

The Disk
Requested icon

If the computer cannot find a System Folder in any floppy drive, it starts searching the SCSI devices, starting with SCSI 0 and then SCSI 6 on down in descending address order. Again, the search stops as soon as a System Folder is found. At this point, booting up begins. If you have only one SCSI device, and it is set at any SCSI address other than 7 (the address for the Mac itself), this device becomes the default startup device. If, however, two or more units are in the daisychain, you'll have to establish a hierarchy—you must give the startup unit of your choice the higher address. (As mentioned before, SCSI address priorities bear no resemblance to the physical order of devices in the daisychain.)

Users working with System 4.2 or later have another option: the program called Startup Device. This program, accessed through the Control Panel desk accessory, enables you to change SCSI priorities without resetting addresses. First, open the Control Panel, click on Startup Device (or Startup Disk under System 7). and then click on the icon corresponding to the drive you want (Figure 2.6).

FIGURE 2.6

Designating
startup device
via the Control
Panel

Why all this effort to ensure that the Macintosh boots off of the same System Folder every time? Speed and consistency, for the most part. You can operate your hard disk with a floppy-based startup file, but the time spent reading and writing from the floppy will slow your work considerably. And even if there is a System Folder on another hard disk in the daisychain, it may lack a number of the elements (most notably fonts) that were used to create your files, elements needed to accurately reproduce those files when reopened. Remember, not every system configuration works on every Macintosh. To keep chances and unpleasant surprises to a minimum, it's best to boot your system from the same System Folder each time you operate your Macintosh.

Custom Startup Screens

As the bootup process begins, the screen display changes from the Happy Mac icon to the startup screen. Usually the screen shows a stylized version of the Mac and the "Welcome to Macintosh" message. This screen is automatically written into the boot blocks of each startup disk. This image can be modified or replaced by another image. This is a very helpful feature when working with a hard disk. With a customized startup screen, you can tell at a glance whether your Mac accidentally booted from the wrong System Folder.

One easy way to create a custom startup screen is with SuperPaint, a paint/drawing program from Silicon Beach Software. SuperPaint operates much like MacPaint or other graphics programs, but it can also convert bit-mapped images into the Mac's startup screen format; just choose Save or Save As from the File menu, then enable the StartupScreen option (Figure 2.7).

Note that *StartupScreen* is one word with each *S* capitalized. Once saved, you'll need to give that precise name to the file, and then place it in your System Folder. One of the boot block commands directs the Mac to search for a document by the name StartupScreen only. The SuperPaint application does not have to be resident on the disk for the customized startup screen to be displayed.

Another popular software program with the ability to produce startup screens is Adobe Photoshop. After creating a Photoshop file, you can make it your initial screen by saving it as a Pict Resource under the Save As command. (Figure 2.8). Again, be sure to save the file as *StartupScreen* and place it in the System Folder.

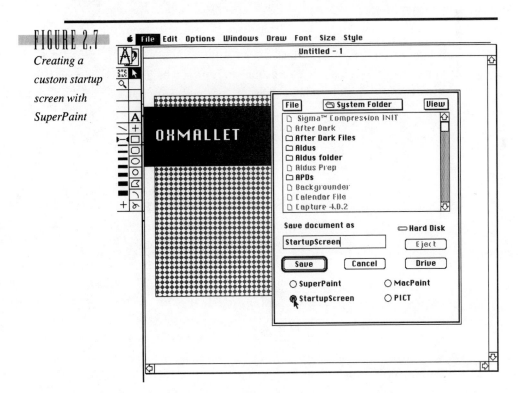

FIGURE 2.7

Creating a custom startup screen with SuperPaint

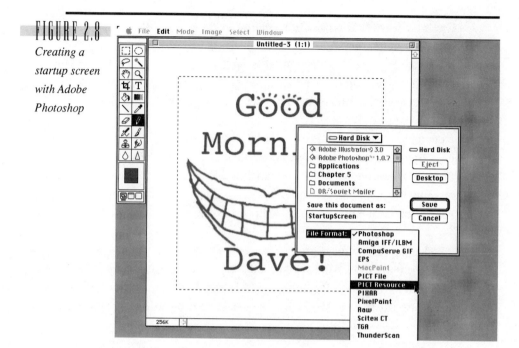

FIGURE 2.8

*Creating a
startup screen
with Adobe
Photoshop*

Custom screens can also be created with utility programs such as ScreenMaker, and ready-made screens are also available. Both can be obtained commercially, through electronic bulletin board systems, or through user groups.

WORKING

WITH

HARD

DISKS

In this section, we'll explore the elements of effective hard disk usage, from the basics of the data structure to performance-enhancing software options. Chapter 3 defines and discusses applications, documents, and related resources. Chapter 4 details numerous approaches to organizing data on your hard disk. Chapter 5 assesses the task of keeping your hard disk safe, not only from accidental loss, but also from virus corruption and unauthorized access.

MACINTOSH DATA: TYPES AND TOOLS

FEATURING:

→ File Types

→ Data and Resource Forks

→ MultiFinder

→ Options for Storing Documents

→ File Compression

→ Compacting the Desktop File

Applications, and the documents they generate, will doubtless make up the vast majority of the data stored on your hard disk. But there are other types of data, and although their roles are limited, their impact on your computing can be significant.

The well-managed hard disk uses all data types in a configuration that adds up to an optimum work environment for the individual user. There's no one "right" way to organize data, but any systematic approach must first take the user's needs into account—and the approach should change when those needs change.

This chapter introduces you to the tools and resources you'll use in organizing your hard disk. I'll start with an overview of the Macintosh data structure. Then, I'll explain how to transfer files of various data types to a hard disk. Finally, I'll look at the various means to manipulate and store data, including folder variations, file compressors, and the use of the Finder and MultiFinder.

An Overview of the Macintosh Data Structure

Because the differences between data types on the Macintosh are often apparent only to the computer, the related terminology has become somewhat blurred. One often hears "application" used interchangeably with "program," or "file" as synonymous for "folder."

A clear understanding of the different data types wasn't really necessary in the early days of the Macintosh, when performance and storage technology were severely limited. But now there are numerous storage options and variations, and a knowledge of how the computer uses and interprets information can give you a better perspective on both choosing and managing your hard disk.

Figure 3.1 shows the three discrete levels of data: the volume level, the file level, and the fork level. *Volume* refers to any element of storage medium that has a single identity and root directory, such as a floppy disk, a hard disk, or other storage device, such as a CD-ROM or WORM drive. These devices usually contain only one volume, but with the Macintosh, volume recognition isn't hardware-dependent. A single storage device can be broken up into multiple volumes. On hard disks, this division is known as *partitioning*. With partitioning, the computer treats the disk like several small but separate disks, each with its own desktop icon and directory. The reasons methods behind partitioning are discussed in more detail in Chapter 8.

When a volume is online and accessible to the computer, it is called a *mounted* volume. Inserting a floppy or booting up a SCSI device are means of mounting a volume. You can tell that a volume has been mounted when its icon appears on the desktop.

File Types

If volumes are the libraries of the Macintosh world, *files* are the books on the shelves. However, Macintosh files can be much more than simple storehouses of information. Below, I will discuss several different types of files. Together they cover the entire spectrum of the Macintosh's operations and abilities.

FIGURE 3.1

*The three levels
of Macintosh
data*

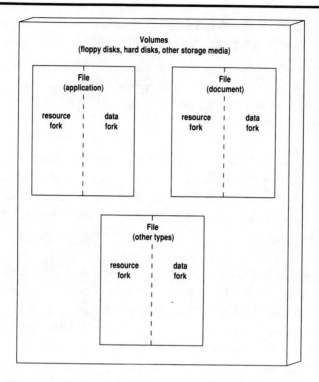

Applications These are programs that allow you to perform tasks, such as word processing, numerical calculations, or desktop publishing. Most allow the work accomplished to be saved in another file. Some applications, however, perform tasks that are less apparent to the user. The Finder, for example, is an application that's constantly running whenever you use your Macintosh. It displays and updates the desktop and icons, and it translates your clicking and dragging into meaningful commands for the System file to read. (The System file itself is not an application, but the software portion of the operating system.) When you launch an application by clicking on an icon like those in Figure 3.2, you're actually using one application, the Finder, to load another. As the Macintosh system becomes more sophisticated, more of these *meta-applications*—applications that manage other applications—will appear. Alternatives to the Finder have become more popular; they're explored in more detail in Chapter 9.

FIGURE 3.2

Some examples of application icons

 Adobe Illustrator® 3.0

 Adobe Photoshop™ 2.0

 Globe

 Norton Utilities

 TeachText

Documents These are the products of the applications, the files which contain the work you've done. They have their own distinctive icons (Figure 3.3) and can be opened by double-clicking. In Mac jargon, documents are "opened" while applications are "launched.")

Before document can be opened, an application capable of reading it must also be present on a mounted volume. In fact, when you open a document, you

FIGURE 3.3

Document icons

 Read Me

 Table of Contents

 Newsletter Spring Issue

 Scan of Sheldon

Tony's typing test

generally launch its parent application as well. In the past, only the parent application could read and edit a document; if you wanted to transfer text or graphics, you had to use the Clipboard. Now, many applications can either *convert* or *import* files created by another application. As Macintosh software becomes more feature-laden, chances are that most word processing or desktop publishing applications will be capable of importing a text or graphic document, and spreadsheets will be able to import any numerical document, regardless of the document's parent application.

Resource Files These files store user preferences and customization information. They're usually created, updated, and filed away automatically by the application, and often are unreadable by the user.

For example, the word processing application Microsoft Word creates a number of resource files to perform different tasks (Figure 3.4). The Hyphenation file stores the correct hyphenation of often-used words, while the Main Dictionary has a similar list of correct spellings. The Temp file provides temporary storage for handling long or complex documents, the Glossary file holds frequently-used text for easy access, and the Settings file contains the user's default choices for menus and formatting. You can't open and peruse these files directly, but Microsoft Word opens, reads, and modifies them every time you use that application.

Resource files are usually placed in one of two locations: the home folder of the application or the active System Folder. I recommend that you keep track of

FIGURE 3.4

Resource files of Microsoft Word

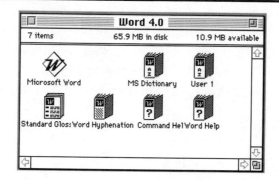

which applications create Resource files and where the files are stored. Whenever you need to work on a different disk or system, copy them along with the applications.

Desk Accessories Also known as DAs, these are programs that can be incorporated into the System file, which enables them to be accessed from within an application. They all have the same suitcase icon (see Figure 3.5). Once installed, they are launched via the "Apple" menu. Under System 6, you use an application known as Font/DA Mover, which comes bundled with all System software disks from Apple, to install and remove DAs. The use of Font/DA Mover is discussed in the next chapter.

Under System 7, no special installation software is necessary. However, you'll need to follow these steps to successfully access desk accessories:

1. Double-click on the DA's suitcase icon. This will open a window containing the suitcase's contents (Figure 3.6).

2. Drag the contents of the suitcase (but not the suitcase itself) from the window into the System Folder. A dialog box will inform you that the desk accessory should be placed in the Apple Menu Items folder, and ask if you want it to do so.

3. Click OK. The desk accessory will then appear on the Apple menu, and the suitcase window will be closed.

If, in the future, you wish to remove the desk accessory from the Apple menu, simply relocate it from the Apple Menu Items folder, which is located within the System Folder.

DAs were originally intended to be simple, accessible tools—extensions of the Macintosh's computer-as-desk metaphor. Some of the most common DAs—the Alarm Clock, the Calculator, the Calendar—are still simple and small, but others now offer features and capabilities to rival full-fledged applications. Word processors, spelling checkers, graphics programs, and spreadsheets are

FIGURE 3.5

Desk Accessory

icons

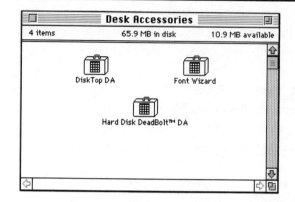

FIGURE 3.6

Opening a DA

suitcase under

System 7

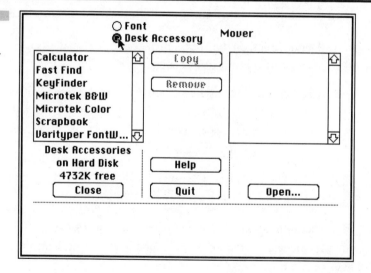

all available in DA form. Not only have programmers transcended the limitations of DA size (they generally cannot occupy more than 32 KB of memory), they've managed to circumvent Apple's limitation of 15 DAs per System file. Now, utility programs like Suitcase can make up to 500 DAs available at one time.

The distinction between DAs and applications is becoming blurred with time. Since the advent of MultiFinder, a Macintosh with enough RAM can run multiple applications simultaneously. And according to Apple, true multitasking on the Macintosh is one of their goals for the future. MultiFinder and multitasking are discussed later in this chapter.

Fonts These files aren't programs, but instruction sets displaying and modifying a particular type style. There are two kinds of fonts:

- *display fonts* govern the bit-mapped display of a typeface both on the screen and on a dot-matrix printer
- *downloadable fonts* are used with laser printers to translate the choppy bit-mapped font into smooth characters via Postscript, a page-description language for laser printers like the Apple LaserWriter

As Figure 3.7 illustrates, the difference between display font text and downloadable font text can be quite pronounced.

The display font icon is similar to that of desk accessories (Figure 3.8, left). Like DAs, they're incorporated into the System file either by means of the Mover application for Systems 6 and earlier, or through the double-clicking

---

FIGURE 3.7

LaserWriter output of display font text (top) and downloadable font text (bottom)

Twas brillig, and the slithy toves
Did gyre and gimble in the wabe;
All mimsy were the borogoves,
And the mome raths outgrabe.

Twas brillig, and the slithy toves
Did gyre and gimble in the wabe;
All mimsy were the borogoves,
And the mome raths outgrabe.

procedure for System 7 (see above section on DAs). Generally, a properly-installed font is available in every application that uses fonts, although some older applications require further steps in order to make the fonts accessible from the main menu.

Downloadable fonts (Figure 3.8, right) are not part of the System file. In order to work with the LaserWriter and similar devices, they need to be part of the System Folder. Simply place them in the System Folder—place them in that folder only, not in a subfolder—taking care that you don't accidentally rename them. If while processing printing for a PostScript device, the System cannot find the downloadable font, it will instead rely on the display font and create a bit-mapped version of that font.

An exception to this rule is presented by TrueType fonts, which use a single file for both screen display and printout (Figure 3.9). A TrueType font can be distinguished from a PostScript font by its icon, which displays three "A"s, as compared to the single "A" on PostScript files. TrueType can be used with either System 7 or System 6.0.7.

Icons for display fonts (left) and downloadable fonts (right)

TrueType (left) and PostScript (right) font files

Because of their ability to produce near-typeset quality characters, downloadable fonts are expensive, whereas most display fonts cost little, are shareware, or are free. For example, Adobe, the leading PostScript font manufacturer, sells its downloadable fonts but makes the display versions available to user groups and electronic bulletin boards for free duplication. You probably don't need downloadable fonts unless you have a PostScript device—and even most of those have a number of fonts in ROM. So even with a PostScript device, you may not need many external font files for crisp, readable text output. However, if your work includes graphic design or desktop publishing, extra fonts may be a worthwhile investment.

Drivers These are the programs that allow the Macintosh to control a device. A *device*, in Macintosh parlance, means a piece of equipment or part of the computer that transfers data in and out of the machine. Devices include floppy drives, hard disks, scanners, modems, keyboards, and printers. The video screen is also a device on the Macintosh II and Quadra Lines, although it is not considered a device on compact Macintoshes (due to their direct use of Quick-Draw routines). Drivers are not accessible by the user.

A number of drivers are built into the ROM; others are incorporated into the System file along with fonts and DAs. However, some drivers, such as printer drivers, must be made available by the user, usually by placing their icon (Figure 3.10) into the System Folder. In the case of printer drivers, you must place the icon in the System Folder and then select it from the Chooser desk accessory. In the case of System 7, drivers should be placed in the Extension folder which is nested in the System Folder.

NOTE

In System 7, if you try to place drivers within the System Folder, a dialog box will appear, asking if you want to move the drivers to the Extension folder. Click Yes and the drivers will be moved to the Extension folder automatically.

FIGURE 3.10

Examples of driver icons

Drivers can work as "nested" programs; that is, one driver may be built upon another driver. In Figure 3.10, the SerialPrinter file is an application-specific driver written to manage a generic serial printer, while the Diablo 630 file is a driver for a specific serial printer. When you select SerialPrinter in Chooser, the Diablo 630 is presented to you as a selectable option. However, the Diablo driver would be useless without the serial driver file. This is why it's necessary to keep track of which combinations of drivers your hardware requires, and to store, install, and transfer them as a unit.

INIT Files   INIT (short for INITial) files are files which, when placed in the System Folder, will launch install and activate themselves automatically. Figure 3.11 shows some examples of INIT file icons. Often, an INIT file will remind you that it's installed by adding some sort of notice to your startup screen, either a graphic symbol or textual statement.

The INIT file is a useful file format for utility programs that you'll want to have in the background at all times. Because their features are automatically put into action, you'll never forget to "turn them on." A laser spooler, a network communications system or a debugger are examples of INIT files.

Some INITs pop up as another menu in the Finder, some are accessed by way of the Apple menu, and some are virtually invisible to the user. If you have a file that doesn't look like a document, yet can't be opened by double-clicking, chances are it's an INIT.

FIGURE 3.11
*A few INIT
icons*

DiskDoubler™ INIT

Suitcase™ 2.0

TypeAlign Startup

Sigma™ Compression INIT

Init

 **WARNING**

A word of caution is appropriate for INIT experimentation: because it modifies your system's startup sequence, a buggy, bad or incompatible INIT installed on your hard disk could make it unable to boot. When in doubt, try out the INIT on a floppy-based System Folder first. Just make sure the floppy is placed in the floppy drive before you power up the Mac.

 TIP

INITs are automatically loaded in alphabetical order. If for some reason you want to them to be launched in sequence, simply add a letter to their name. For example, change "LaserSpool" to "ALaserSpool" or "ZLaserSpool".
To deactivate an INIT, just remove it from the System Folder—it won't be launched the next time you start up.

CDEVs CDEV (short for Control Device) files are a subcategory of INIT files. They are accessed only through the Control Panel selection under the Apple menu, but are automatically launched by placing them in the top level of the System Folder. Figure 3.12 shows some of the more common CDEVs.

The Control Panel was originally just another Desk Accessory. As options increased, however, Apple realized that different users needed to control different aspects of their system. The Control Panel DA was then rewritten to encompass CDEVs, which now appear in a scrolling field to the left of the Control Panel box (Figure 3.13). Clicking on an icon will cause the options controlled by that CDEV to be displayed in the main window of the box.

CDEVs are a popular format for utilities affecting operations (such as Stepping Out II, a screen enhancer, or the Adobe Type Manager font display program). They're installed and removed in the same fashion as INITs, but take care not to rename them—if you do, they may not be recognized by the Control Panel. Apple bundles many CDEVs with System software, but there's no need to load ones that don't pertain to your setup. Compact Macs, for example, don't need the Monitors CDEV, which manages color and shade settings for the modular Macintoshes. And only the Mac Portable and PowerBooks need the Battery CDEV.

FIGURE 3.12
CDEV icons

ClickChange™

SoundMaster

The GuardDog

Stepping Out II

Easy Access

FIGURE 3.13

*The Control
Panel, with
scrolling CDEV
field*

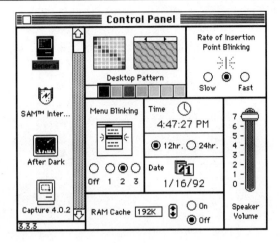

Using Suitcase

As I've already noted, there are two ways to install fonts and desk accessories in the System file: by way of the Font/DA Mover application (for System 6 and earlier), and by manually moving them in and out of the file (System 7). Fortunately, there's a third, more convenient way: with Suitcase, an INIT that provides simple installation and deinstallation under both Systems 6 and 7.

Once installed, Suitcase places itself at the top of the DA portion of the Apple menu. When you call it up, it lists all currently active "suitcases" (both display fonts and desk accessories), as shown in Figure 3.14. These are suitcases that have been activated with Suitcase itself; suitcases that have been installed in the usual manner won't show up in the Suitcase window. For this reason, it's a good idea to clear out the DA and font suitcases from your System file, and then reinstall them with Suitcase.

To install a suitcase, first select the suitcase's "set." *Permanent* will ensure that the suitcase is loaded every time you boot your Macintosh from the current volume, while the suitcases in the *Temporary* set will be removed as soon as you shut down. You can also create sets of your own, with the New Set command in the upper-right corner. Once the set has been specified, you add the

Suitcase is a
utility that
manages both
display fonts
and desk
accessories

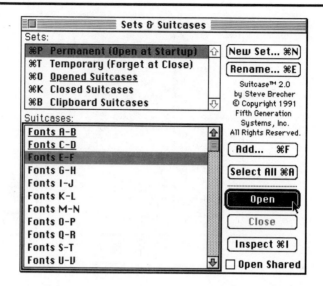

suitcase by clicking on Add and selecting the display font or DA from the dialog box. The suitcase name will subsequently appear in the Suitcases field and will be underlined to indicate that it is open. If you've designated it as part of the Permanent set, Suitcase will find and load it again the next time you start up the Mac.

To close a suitcase, you don't need to remove it from its set: just select it and click on the Close button. Its name will remain in the Suitcases field, but it will no longer be underlined.

The flexibility offered by Suitcase sets can really come in handy, especially if you're a graphic designer, desktop publisher, or otherwise work with many fonts. The suitcase "sets" allow you to group fonts according to project, and load all relevant ones at one time. This capability is not only convenient, but it also increases your Mac's performance. Since an abundance of fonts can bloat the System file and fill precious RAM, Suitcase offers a quick way to stream-line the system when you need maximum RAM, such as when you work with a scanned image or large document. In addition, Suitcase will inspect font files for evidence of corruption, and will notify you when a two or more fonts have conflicting ID numbers (a problem that can cause printing mishaps).

IP

Sometimes it's hard to remember exactly how a given font looks. That's why Suitcase offers a special option under the Fonts subset of the Preferences menu. Select the "font menus show font names in their own typefaces when modifier key is" option, then select Pressed. Whenever you hold down the modifier key (⌘, shift or option) while selecting a font menu from within an application, the fonts will show their own faces on the menu. This special menu takes longer to draw on screen than a conventional list of font names, so you'll probably want to use this option only when you need to refresh your memory.

Choosing the Right File Type

The advance of technology has increased the Macintosh's capabilities, but it has also brought an array of often-confusing options. DAs and INITs can now perform tasks that at one time required the use of an application. When choosing software, which is the right format for any given job?

Ideally, you should choose software on the basis of its features, not its format. But given the constraints of your system (and your pocketbook), format itself can become a feature. If your Macintosh has many megabytes of RAM, you'll probably work under MultiFinder, in which case the limitations of a DA or INIT may outweigh its benefit.

On the other hand, if your RAM resources are more modest or if you work with memory-hungry applications such as HyperCard, MultiFinder may not meet your needs. Convenience may be an important factor—even with MultiFinder, an application must be located and launched in order to be available. In contrast, DAs and CDEV-type INITs are always just a menu selection away.

Introducing the Fork

One of the most important concepts to grasp is that of *forked data*. Essentially, forking is the process of storing a file in two files. As another glance at Figure 3.1 will indicate, the fork is the final level of information organization. Though they are fundamental to Macintosh technology, forks are invisible to the casual user. But an understanding of them is essential when you need to retrieve lost or garbled data.

To put it in a nutshell: every file—applications, documents, etc—is in fact two files, a *resource fork* and a *data fork*, both stored under a single file name. Either fork can be empty, but an empty fork still exists as an entity as far as the Macintosh is concerned. Both forks collaborate to launch a file.

The Resource Fork

Stored in the resource fork (sometimes called the "resource file") are all the *resources* required by the file. What are resources? Generally speaking, resources are the building blocks of Macintosh programming—the elements that build a file. Icons, menus, dialog boxes, fonts, and programming code are all resources. Resources are broken down into *resource types*, which are stored in the fork and arranged by function in logical groupings. Resource types are identified by distinctive four-letter codes; each resource in the type is in turn identified by a *resource ID* number.

Why is all this programming broken up into so many discrete units? There are two primary reasons. The first is has to do with memory management: because the data is so fragmented, it can be loaded into RAM more efficiently than if it were large chunks of code. The Macintosh has highly sophisticated firmware in ROM known as the Memory Manager, which uses this flexibility to great advantage.

But the second, perhaps more significant reason why resource codes are so fragmented has to do with the user interface. The resource approach gives Macintosh software a standardized look and feel—it's a rare application that deviates from the familiar arrangement of pull-down menus, dialog boxes, and scrolling windows.

With many operating systems, the programmer has to build the "world" of the program practically from scratch. When a pull-down menu is called for, the programmer must design the menu right down to the typeface and write a code that draws it on the screen. If the program is later translated into, say, Italian, the programmer must write the code all over again. What happens if the Italian versions of the commands are too long to fit into the original menu box? The menu code itself would have to be rewritten, which means that code would have to be modified throughout the software.

Fortunately, this isn't true for the Macintosh programmer. All he or she must do to create a new menu is redefine the MENU resource (the four-letter code for that resource type) with its own ID number. The definition would not only describe the menu and every item on it, but also specify what other resources are to be accessed when a particular menu item is selected. With the resource codes redefined and stored in the resource fork, the Macintosh then takes over from there, displaying the menu and initiating the commands.

Since all this can be done without writing a single line of code, even a non-programmer can make menu modifications. Want to market an Italian version of your Mac program? Just type in replacements to the English words in the resource definition fields. If the menu must be widened to accomodate Italian words, you can modify the menus, too.

The ROM routines that create and manage these resources are collectively called the User Interface Toolbox, or more commonly, the *Toolbox*. A Macintosh programmer could bypass the Toolbox and build an application entirely from scratch, but the application would be slow, incompatible with other applications, and difficult for users to master.

You can use applications such as ResEdit to explore and modify the file's resource fork. I'll explain the whys and hows of doing so in Chapter 7.

The Data Fork

More mundane but just as important as the resource fork is the data fork. As the name implies, the data fork is the storehouse where the data that's manipulated by the program is kept. This data is broken down and saved as numeric code.

The process works like this: say you launch a word processing application by double-clicking on its icon. If it was designed to industry standards, the application should open with a document screen labeled "Untitled." But "Untitled" isn't a document just yet; it's the more-or-less empty data fork of the application.

If you type the word *Macintosh,* then save the document, the application works with the Toolbox to create a new file (which you're then requested to name). This new file is still controlled by the application, but has its own data and resource forks. The data fork contains only the letters *M,a,c,i,n,t,o,s,* and *h,* while the resource fork contains a "recipe" of sorts, a list of all the resources you used while typing that word—the font, font size, letter spacing, position in the document, and so on. The resource fork also contains information about which application created it, which is why opening a word processing document simultaneously launches the word processor.

The separation between data and resources is the main reason why formatting changes can be done easily on the Macintosh, even with huge blocks of text. Instead of loading the text into RAM in order to alter its appearance, the Macintosh simply changes the rules by which the text is displayed. An application's data fork is useful because an application can use its own data fork as a storage area while are working on a document. This fork is copied to the document data fork only when you answer yes to the "Save changes?" dialog box.

One fringe benefit of the fork structure pertains to data retrieval. When the resources in a file's resource fork have become garbled, the file is usually unreadable by the system. But an "unopenable" document still has an intact data fork, and the information it contains can often be salvaged. I'll survey tools for extracting data from data forks in Chapter 7.

Making the Transition from Floppies to Hard Disks

If you've already installed a working System Folder on your hard disk, the next step is to transfer your applications and documents from your collection of floppies, so you can do most of your work with the hard disk alone.

If you're new to hard disks, all those megabytes of storage space can seem awfully tempting. You might feel an understandable impulse to fill your hard disk up with every piece of software on hand. But a bit of advice is in order: don't copy software to your hard disk just because you have one. Copy the software because you need it. And only copy software when you need it.

There's an old saying about nature abhorring a vacuum. Your new hard disk is one of those vacuums, and chances are it'll fill up before you know it. Most well-used Macs develop a voracious appetite for storage; that's why the capacity of drives on the market gets bigger every year, making those first-generation 5 MB drives little more than curiosities. The more files you load, the sooner you'll be faced with choices between which files get stored on the hard drive and which don't.

Of course, only you can decide which applications and files you'll need at your fingertips, and when you'll need them. It helps to take a cold, hard look at your floppy collection before you begin transferring in earnest. You can start by dividing your files' data into three categories.

We'll be referring to these categories throughout this chapter and the next, as we discuss volume-based and file-based storage strategies.

Work Files These are the applications and documents you use regularly—the ones that justify the Mac's presence in your life. You might be surprised how little of your software actually falls into this category—perhaps only a word processor, a spreadsheet, and a few games you're addicted to. But since you're defining these categories to suit your purposes, you might consider as work files everything that lets you use your Macintosh the way you want to use it.

Reference Files Reference files are those you probably won't use often, but which you should have on hand anyway. For instance, you may never need to take another look at the invoices you've sent to customers, but if a customer refers to last April's order while making this month's order, it's a lot easier to go to the hard disk for the order than to search through floppies.

Reference files are also the type that benefit from centralization. If you have a spreadsheet to project the profitability of several investments given a number of different scenarios, you would want all the investment files on the same hard disk as the spreadsheet, rather than scattered across several floppies. You can do serious number-crunching without a hard disk, but the flexibility and ease of making speculative analyses are severely impaired.

Archival Files Archival files comprise the remainder of your software, the files that might come in handy someday, although there's no telling when "someday" might be. This category might include little-used applications, documents ready for storage, exotic fonts, and other electronic bric-a-brac.

Another possible archival file is any file that might overwhelm your hard disk by virtue of its size. A scanned image or HyperCard stack can easily occupy a megabyte or more of disk space. Yet size can be a criteria for keeping a file *on* your hard disk, as some files are too large to fit on a floppy disk.

Managing Applications

Of all file types, applications are probably the easiest to manage. They require no special installation, can be stationed anywhere on a hard disk, and can be renamed with impunity. Yet there are a few general principles to keep in mind when loading applications on your hard disk.

- *Watch for duplicate versions,* as two copies of the same application on one hard disk—even if they're different versions—can cause system hangs, crashes, and lost data. If you have multiple versions of the same application, copy only the latest one. However, having multiple versions of an application on separate SCSI volumes should present no problem, as long as there is only one copy on each volume.

- *Keep track of resource files and drivers.* Many applications create or require dependent documents—dictionaries, user preferences settings, device drivers, and even companion INITs and DAs. Be sure to transfer to your hard disk every dependent document necessary to produce your normal working environment within an application. Unlike applications, dependent documents may need to have a certain title and be in a certain folder in order to work. Consult your software manual if it has a section on hard disk installation. Once again, try to avoid having multiple versions of a dependent document on the same SCSI volume.

- *Be prepared for your hard disk to introduce certain changes to your files.* When a document is transferred to a volume with another System, elements such as spacing, columnization and alignment may be affected. If you created your document with a font that isn't present in your hard disk's System Folder, the application may automatically convert all text into another font, which will cause changes in formatting. The accurate placement of page elements is probably crucial in your documents, so make sure all the necessary fonts are installed in your hard disk before you transfer files there. Then open a few documents under the new System file to see what changes, if any, occur. If you don't want to save any changes made during the transfer, you can still retain the integrity of the original document by choosing not to save changes upon closing. The Save Changes dialog box governs both System- and user-initiated modifications.

WARNING

> Changes created by the new System vary in degree from the
> obvious to the invisible. In some cases, when you close a
> transferred document, you may be asked if you want to save
> changes, even if you made no changes and no changes are
> apparent. In these situations, give the document close scrutiny
> to ensure its acceptability, then save the changes. If you don't,
> the Save Changes dialog box will continue to appear every
> time you close your document.

Loading Non-Copy-Protected Files

With a few rare exceptions, any application or other file that can be copied from
floppy disk to floppy disk can easily be loaded onto a hard disk as well. You
use essentially the same procedure:

1. Click on the floppy disk icon to select it, then drag it over the hard
   disk icon.

2. A dialog box similar to the one in Figure 3.15 should appear. Note
   that it lists the number of files to be transferred and this number
   decreases during the process. You can cancel the transfer procedure
   at any time by clicking the Cancel button. However, this doesn't actually cancel the entire procedure; it stops the copying in midstream,
   and any files already copied to the target volume will remain there.
   Take the time to delete any files created by a cancelled Copy command, since they may have not been completely duplicated.

Copying icon by icon can be tedious as well as disorganizing, since it may
separate an application from its documents. In practice, you'll probably prefer
to transfer larger groups, either folders or entire floppy disks.

The Copy
dialog box

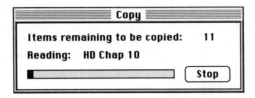

Copy
Items remaining to be copied: 11
Reading: HD Chap 10
[Stop]

NOTE

Copy-protected applications and some commercial applications such as PageMaker 4.0 cannot be copied to the hard disk by simply moving its icon there. These applications require you to copy separate resource files to the System Folder.

Moving all of a floppy's files into a folder and then copying the folder to the hard disk is probably the most convenient means of transferral. If that's the method you choose, be sure to open the new folder and see if it contains a System Folder. If it does, drag the System Folder into the Trash (and don't forget to select Empty Trash afterwards). Many floppies are startup disks, so it's important to police your hard disk for System duplication. Of course, transfer any resource files, INITs, DAs, and the like before deleting the System Folder.

Transferring a floppy without putting all its files into one folder requires an interim step. Here's how to transfer a floppy to the hard disk:

1. Drag the floppy disk icon onto the hard disk icon.

2. Under System 6, a dialog box like that in Figure 3.16 will appear. If you select OK, the floppy's directory information will be changed during the copying process, and the copied disk will appear as a folder on the uppermost, or root level, of the hard disk.

   Under System 7, this message does not appear; instead, the copying will begin without a dialog box.

FIGURE 3.16

*A dialog box
for copying a
floppy to a hard
disk*

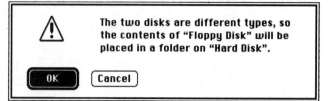

The two disks are different types, so the contents of "Floppy Disk" will be placed in a folder on "Hard Disk".

[OK]   [Cancel]

WARNING

> **If you are not running System 7, and if for some reason your Mac does not present this dialog box, the Mac may have confused your hard disk for a floppy—which could mean that it will erase the hard disk! Stop the operation immediately by turning off the power or pulling the plug on the computer! That's a sign that somehow file types have been confused or misidentified, and havoc can result.**

3. Drag the floppy disk icon to one of two places: the hard disk icon, or the open root level window of the hard disk (the window that opens when you double-click on the hard disk). If you try to copy the icon to a preexisting folder on the hard disk, you will probably be unsuccessful—Systems 4.0 and later won't let you do this. No matter how you copied the floppy, you should probably then delete any System Folders from the copy on the hard disk.

No matter how you've made the transfer, it's a good idea not to start transferring other floppies until you've done the following:

- *Eject the floppy.* But don't just cause the drive to eject the disk. Make sure a dimmed version of its icon is present on the desktop before you eject it. There's a quick though scary shortcut for ejecting a floppy icon: drag it to the Trash. The disk will not be erased, just ejected.

- *Examine the copied files.* See if the application and document icons have been changed into default icons. The default icons are displayed in Figure 3.17, but you should note that some of the more modest applications don't display custom icons to begin with. If you find that *any* icon has been *changed* to a default icon, or that a file name has been changed, you should immediately delete not only the changed file, but all files that were transferred along with it—that is, with the same copy command. Do not attempt to launch or open an altered file and investigate why your file icons were changed; by so doing, you will damage your System Folder.

- *Launch an application or two and look for glitches, incompatibilities, or System-file-related changes.* Now's the time to find about them. Open a few documents and see if you can spot any changes there as well. If an application's menus do not reflect user settings or other custom information, double-check to see if all resource files are in order and in their proper place.

If a test launching fails, it may indicate that the application is copy-protected. Some copy-protected applications cannot be transferred at all, others are transferred in garbled form, and still others demonstrate their copy protection only when the user attempts to launch the copy. These types of software require a separate approach to hard disk transfer.

Loading Copy-Protected Files

The issue of copy protection remains hotly contested. Software developers defend its use as a necessary means of protecting their financial and intellectual investment. Users deplore it as an major inconvenience.

FIGURE 3.17
Default icons for applications (left) and documents (right)

Application   Document

In the Macintosh world, the issue has more or less been decided in favor of the user. In fact, nowadays hardly any Macintosh software is released with copy protection. Although, copy protection may be on its way out, many users still find themselves with a necessary application or two that incorporates some sort of protection scheme.

In general, copy-protection falls into five categories:

- *Key disk software* can be copied freely but will only run when the original or "key" disk is placed in a floppy drive. Some of these are programs demand the key disk not just upon startup, but also at random times during a work session. Software of this type can probably be copied to your hard disk, but since you'll have to use the floppy anyway, it's hardly worth the bother.

- *Uncopyable software* either can't be copied, or else the copied "duplicate" version will not work (or at least not work very well). You're limited to working directly with the floppy.

- *Semicopyable software* can be transferred to either a floppy or hard disk, but only a limited number of copies can be transferred, and of those, only a few are copyable.

- *Serialized software* requires the one-time entry of a serial number before the application will run. You're limited to working directly with the floppy.

- *Random quiz copy protection* is also a frequent tactic. With it, each time the application is launched, the user is asked to provide information from the manual, such as "Type the last word of the first paragraph on page 36." This method of copy protection is most often seen in games.

For the most part, each of these copy-protection tactics applies only to applications, not to documents created with them.

If you are a registered owner of an application that uses copy protection, you can often get a nonprotected upgrade from the publisher for a small fee. The main exceptions are game manufacturers, most of whom have no plans to abandon copy protection in the near future.

Copy Protection and the Law

The microcomputer software industry has made many millionaires (and a billionaire or two) since taking off in the 1970s. So it's understandable that software companies seek to protect their copyrights to the fullest extent of the law. Unfortunately, most national and international laws regarding copyrights and intellectual property were written for static printed media, not interactive, changeable electronic media. Statutes will eventually catch up with the Information Age, but for the present the legal issues implied in software ownership are still somewhat fuzzy for the average consumer: what industry figures call "software piracy" is often an act of innocence or ignorance.

Only a lawyer could fully explain all the implications of software law. But from a user's standpoint, you should know a few main principles that (unless otherwise stated by the manufacturer) apply to most of the software commercially available for the Macintosh.

- You have a right to preserve and transfer all files and applications. Even if your software is copy protected, it's okay to duplicate it for purposes of convenience, safety, or just to protect your investment. That includes backups and hard disk transfers.

- You may duplicate freely, but you cannot use your duplicates in a situation that would legitimately require you to purchase another copy of the software. In other words, you can make a backup of a program for your office computer, and the co-worker who shares your office computer can use the backup program at work. Your co-worker, however, cannot be using your backup version on another computer while you're using the same program on your home computer. Software designed for multiple users and software sold under a "group user" or "site" license are exceptions to this rule.

- Your documents are your property. Copyright laws apply to applications and other programs, not to the documents created with them. If you use a graphics program to create artwork, you're free to copyright that artwork in your name, and you can sell it or give it away as you see fit. You cannot, however, distribute copies of the application you used to make the artwork, even if your intent is for the application to be used solely to view your artwork.

There is one important exception to all of the above rules: *shareware*. Shareware was developed as a means of distributing software without the hassles of marketing and retailing. If a program has been designated as shareware (this is usually noted in the "About..." portion of the Apple menu), you're encouraged to give away copies to anyone who might need one. Each new user is asked to voluntarily become a registered user by sending in a fee to the developer. I will discuss several shareware applications in this book.

No matter what the distribution method of software, there are compelling reasons beyond compliance with the law for being a registered, legal user. Legitimate users get more than software—they get documentation, technical support, and free or inexpensive upgrades when the product is improved. Given the growing ability and complexity of Macintosh application, it's getting harder and harder not to be a registered user.

Spliced Applications

There's a third type of application, one that isn't exactly copy protected but can't be easily transferred from floppy to hard disk. Usually it is called a spliced or merge application, and it exists in two states: unassembled and assembled.

Spliced applications are packaged and sold with the software spread across several floppy disks; at least one of the disks also includes an "installation" program, which reassembles the segments of the application on a hard disk or other storage device. Spliced applications may be used because the application itself is too large for a single floppy, or because effective installation (with the supporting resource files in all the right places) involves more than simply dragging icons. PageMaker, for example, now requires four floppy disks to contain all its features and attendant files.

If you have a spliced application in unassembled form, try to install it on your hard disk directly from the original floppies by launching the installation program and following the prompts. Avoid making a floppy-to-folder copy of each of the disks. You'll save time and space that way, and you might save yourself a system crash. If you use the floppy-to-folder method, you will have to launch the installation program from the hard disk, which may be difficult because of assumptions it makes about floppies and drives.

If you have already assembled a spliced application on another storage device, you can transfer it by simply daisy-chaining your hard disk to the device and copying over all files. It's the floppies that present the biggest problem when transferring spliced applications: a failure of any floppy in the set to transfer can render the entire program unusable. Moreover, floppy-by-floppy copies onto other floppies don't always produce a working duplicate set. In these instances, the user is in the odd position of using a hard disk as a backup for a floppy! If you must do this, be sure to back up your hard disk regularly with an effective backup program. The most capable ones will preserve all data in floppy-sized chunks, regardless of file size or copy protection scheme. Backup programs are discussed in Chapter 5.

MultiFinder: New Windows on Your Work

Having a hard disk doesn't just eliminate the time you formerly spent juggling floppies. It opens up new work horizons, since much advanced and innovative software requires the space and speed of a hard disk. In fact, nearly all of the latest Macintosh software is written for hard disk-based systems; they'll barely run on floppies, if at all.

Foremost among this class of hard-disk-dependent software is the system software itself, which, with the inclusion of MultiFinder, increased the productivity of the Macintosh. MultiFinder lets you work with several applications at once, switching back and forth between them with the ease of a single mouse click.

The capabilities MultiFinder offers are often referred to as "multitasking," but it's not multitasking in the strictest sense. Although multiple applications can be open at any one time, only one application can be "active," i.e., exploiting the processing power of the Macintosh CPU. When not active, an open application is held in suspension. In contrast, a true multitasking system (such as UNIX) allows work to be completed "in the background": for instance, a graphic can be rendered automatically while a word processor is also being used. Under conventional System software, the only real background processing to be found is in the PrintMonitor, which can process printing commands without interrupting your work. It does so by "stealing" CPU time during moments when the active application is idle—those fractions of a second when a key isn't being pressed, or a mouse moved, or the screen display doesn't need changing.

NOTE

Under System 6, MultiFinder is an option; you can turn it on or off at will (although you do need to restart the system before the change takes effect). With the introduction of System 7, MultiFinder was incorporated into the Finder itself, and became a permanent part of its operations. Although Apple retired the term "MultiFinder" in System 7, I use it here to refer to the technology, which remains essentially the same under both System versions.

An Introduction to MultiFinder

Like the Finder, MultiFinder is an application that opens, manages, and manipulates Macintosh files in accordance with your commands. When you launch an application with the Finder, the application is simply read into the RAM. Since only one application can run at a time, the Finder is only concerned that there's adequate available memory, and any unused RAM remains unused.

In contrast, MultiFinder not only reads the file into RAM, it confines the application to a designated portion of the total available memory. This frees up the remainder of the RAM for other files. MultiFinder keeps the files carefully segregated, expanding or contracting the various regions as necessary. The Finder is always the first of the applications launched, so normal operations (the desktop, etc.) are always just a mouse click away.

I've already mentioned that MultiFinder doesn't give you true multitasking capability. But since you can activate an application simply by clicking on its window, you can use MultiFinder to perform several meaningful tasks at once.

If you're equipped with System 5 or System 6, you can enable MultiFinder by selecting Set Startup from the Special menu. Notice that the dialog box contains several options, as shown in Figure 3.18; after you select MultiFinder, you can choose what files, if any, you'd like to have opened automatically upon startup. This is a useful feature if you use a particular application each time you start up the Mac. Under System 7, Set Startup options are not available.

N O T E

The System 7 MultiFinder does not allow you to reconfigure its startup options to open a particular file or application automatically. You are taken straight to the desktop on startup.

FIGURE 3.18
*Enabling
MultiFinder
and other
startup options*

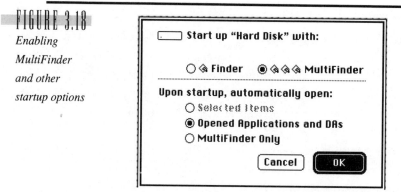

Start up "Hard Disk" with:

○ ⬧ Finder   ◉ ⬧⬧⬧ MultiFinder

Upon startup, automatically open:
   ○ Selected Items
   ◉ Opened Applications and DAs
   ○ MultiFinder Only

[Cancel]   [OK]

If you want to see the familiar desktop setup whenever you start up your Macintosh, choose the MultiFinder Only option; MultiFinder will be active, but only the Finder will be automatically launched. To open each work session with a particular application launched or document opened, select the desired icon before opening Set Startup. You'll find the name of the file in the same location as the phrase *Selected Items* is in Figure 3.18; that's the button you'll want to select.

If you'd like to go directly to a frequently used work environment (say, a word processor with a spell-checking DA), you can select Opened Applications and DAs. But you'll first have to shut down and restart the Macintosh under Multi-Finder in order to keep the applications and DAs open while switching back to the Finder.

The desktop of a Macintosh running under MultiFinder looks the same as that of any other Mac, with the exception of a miniature version of the active application's icon that is displayed in the upper-right corner of the screen (Figure 3.19). Not only is this is a helpful identifier, it's also a button (System 6) or a menu (System 7). Under System 6, clicking on this icon will make another loaded application the active one; the icon will change to indicate which application is active. If three or more applications (including the Finder) have been loaded, they will be activated in alphabetical order.

FIGURE 3.19

Interface
modifications
under
MultiFinder
(System 6)

icon indicating currently active
application (click to change)

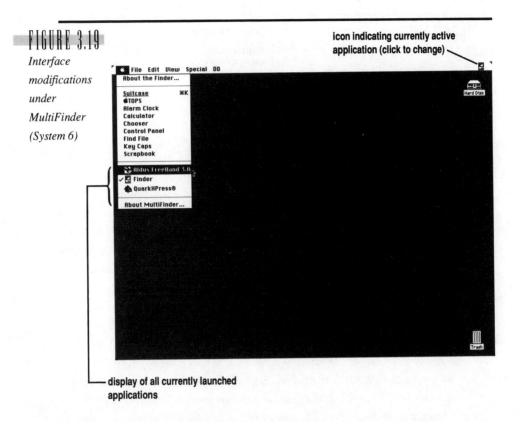

display of all currently launched
applications

Under System 7, the right-hand corner icon is a pull-down menu (Figure 3.20).
Clicking on it displays not only a list of launched applications, but also a set of
Hide and Show commands, which are important tools for combatting clutter.
MultiFinder, with its multiple applications running in a myriad of open windows, seems to breed clutter. But when the Hide command is selected, all open
windows pertaining to that particular command are hidden, just as if the application had been closed. Selecting the Show command restores the opened windows. When you want to focus on a single open application, you can select
Hide Others when that application's window is active. All other windows will
be suppressed.

FIGURE 3.20

System 7's
active-application
icon features
pull-down menu

System 6's clickable icon is convenient, but its limitation to alphabetical order can make it inefficient—why activate HyperCard when you're trying to shift from Adobe Illustrator to QuarkXpress? The easiest way to shift active applications is to simply click on the desired window, but sometimes that window is obscured by others. That's why a third method exists: under the Apple menu, the loaded applications are listed below the DAS. The active one has an adjacent checkmark, and you can activate another by selecting it.

Once you've experimented with MultiFinder and feel comfortable with its features, you'll want to try it in your day-to-day work. If you don't need to shift rapidly from one application to another, you may find MultiFinder unnecessary. If you need to work with several large applications, you may find your computer's RAM insufficient to load more than two applications at once. Some programs written before the advent of System 6 can't be loaded under Multi-Finder because they make assumptions about RAM that MultiFinder cannot manage.

Options for Storing Documents

You create, save and store documents because you want to preserve your work, and you can choose from a number of formats for saving your documents. You preserve disk space if you choose wisely. The first step in selecting a file format is an analysis of your requirements: do you only want to store the information contained in a file, or do you need to store it in a specific form?

Normal Mode

Unless you've selected other options, most applications automatically save your work in normal mode. If you store a document this way, it will look more or less the same when you reopen it (although using a different System can cause changes). Normal mode is the most memory-intensive format. It is the best choice for work data, for documents in an unfinished state, or for documents you want to open, consult and perhaps borrow from quickly.

You can always save a new document in normal mode and save it later in another format. Usually, if you try to save a document in a different mode with Save As, the original document it usually not changed; instead, a copy of the document is saved under the new format, often with a slightly modified name. You'll have to return to the Finder, throw away the old document, and give the new document the correct name.

Text-Only Mode

Many applications dealing heavily with words, such as page layout programs and word processors, offer the option of saving only the text in a document. In these files, all formatting information—fonts, headers/footers, pagination—is discarded.

Along with the advantage they offer in saving space, text-only files are useful for transferring documents larger than the Clipboard can handle from one application to another. Some text-only files can also be transferred to other operating systems, such as MS-DOS or UNIX.

The text-only format can be useful for storing your archival data, but take care to use it only when you're sure that the words alone, and not the formats, are worth saving. Otherwise, you may save disk space but lose a lot of time in laborious reformatting. And just how much space can be saved is a function of how full the resource fork is: an elaborate five-page document may be half the size in text only mode, whereas a hundred-page document with few format variations may stand to lose only a few kilobytes.

Other Modes

Depending upon the parent application, document files can also be saved in a variety of other modes. Experiments and experience will help you make the most of these options, but bear in mind that just because an application can save a document in one format doesn't mean that it can read the resulting file.

- Word processors often let the user select a format that changes the parent application. Microsoft Word documents, for example, can be saved as MacWrite documents. Another common option is the *Interchange format*, which can pass text and formatting data among incompatible applications. If you want to open a WriteNow file in Microsoft Word, you'll need to convert it to an Interchange file first.

- Graphics applications can often import, export and convert documents in a number of formats. For example, ImageStudio can save files in MacPaint format, in Encapsulated PostScript format or Tagged Image File Format (TIFF). Choosing any of these is more an act of modification than preservation, since the resulting document will be radically different from the original, and suitable for different uses. Unless you need to use multiple applications on the same graphic file, you're probably best off saving in normal mode.

- Spreadsheets are applications that can generate multiple document types: text files, charts, graphs, and the spreadsheets themselves. When saving such files, you may be faced with the option of linking or unlinking. Linked documents draw their raw data from the spreadsheet; they change to reflect changes in the spreadsheet. If you don't want a linked document to change with the spreadsheet, either unlink it or save it in the format of another application.

File Compression

Document format options can be used to save disk space, but if you're looking to maximize your disk space, you'll want to use a file compression utility. These programs squeeze most files (applications and DAs as well as documents) down to a bare minimum of space, but they do have drawbacks.

There are two main types of file compressors available today: archive utilities, which work as stand-alone applications, and "on the fly" compressors, which automatically compress files during the course of the user's regular work. Archive compressors weren't created with hard disk optimization in mind; they were created to save money on phone bills. Electronic bulletin boards often allow users to transfer, or *download,* files via modem. But even with high-speed modems, downloading a single, modest-sized application could take an hour or more. Compression programs such as StuffIt, PackIt, and MacArc can cut that time drastically. The file is compressed before it's placed on the bulletin board. Once downloaded, the file must be decompressed, usually with another copy of the same utility, before it can be used.

Compressors can significantly reduce a file's size, but they cost the user time spent in compressing and decompressing a file. A one megabyte file can be squeezed to less than half its normal size, but it may take two to five minutes (dependening on the processing power of your computer) to restore it to an operable condition. For that reason, compression is usually useful primarily with archival data, where preservation is more important than accessibility. However, if you have a relatively powerful Macintosh (such as a Mac II series, PowerBook or Quadra), and if the majority of your files are small- to medium-sized, you may benefit from an "on the fly" compressor such as DiskDoubler (see below).

How Compression Works

Although the particulars may differ, the basic principle behind compression software is the same. Sometimes a description of a file takes up less space than the file itself. The typical compression utility first analyzes a file determines what information can be safely discarded. For instance, if a graphics file contains a large amount of white space, the utility may discard the color information about those areas, and make a general note that an area should be displayed as white if there is no color information available.

Once the file has been reduced to its essentials, the computer substitutes the standard eight-bit code for graphics and characters with codes of varying lengths, assigning the shortest ones to the characters that show up most often in the file. For example, in an English-language text file, a compression utility might replace the eight-bit code for the most prevalent character (usually the letter "e") with a three-bit one. This encoding process is what achieves the greatest compression effect, especially in text files. Some decompression standards go a step further, substituting short codes not only for characters but for common words, such as *the* or *and*. As I noted in Chapter 1, the byte is the basic unit of data acknowledged by the Macintosh; when dealing with an uncompressed file, the computer identifies letters, numbers and other characters by their unique ASCII code, each of which occupies a single byte. When the file is decompressed, the utility substitutes the longer, Mac-readable ones for the shorter codes.

The difference between an eight-bit code and a three-bit one might not seem that big, but it adds up: a good compression utility can reduce a text file by about 50 percent. Most applications and graphics files don't compress as well, since they rely less on text or other repeating characters.

Working with StuffIt

Of the current archive-type compression utilities, StuffIt (shown in Figure 3.21) is the one you'll encounter most often. If you plan on downloading files from bulletin board or electronic mail systems, you'll probably need a copy. It offers three choices of compression methods: RLE (which is automatically used if the file is under 25K), LZW and Huffman. The respective advantages of these depend upon the characteristics of the file itself, but you can instruct the application to simply select the one most appropriate for the task. StuffIt has the added advantage of being able to open and convert files that have been compressed with PackIt.

StuffIt saves one or more files in an archive, which is much like a folder but can be opened only from inside StuffIt. When you launch StuffIt, you begin work by either opening an existing archive or creating a new one; either way, the contents of the archive folder will be displayed in StuffIt's main window. Once the archive folder is open, you can add, compress, uncompress, rename, or delete any or all files. If the archive is especially large, you can even break it into segments small enough to fit on individual floppies.

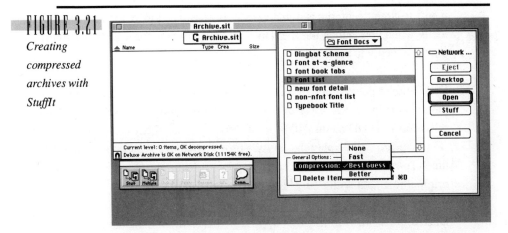

FIGURE 3.21

Creating
compressed
archives with
StuffIt

The archive arrangement is convenient, but it can lead to confusion since you can't tell the Finder to determine the contents of the archive; you must open the archive with StuffIt to inspect it. For that reason, try to name and populate archives on a logical basis. For example, keep business correspondence in an archive titled "Business Correspondence.sit." (All StuffIt files are automatically given the ".sit" suffix.) You can add new files to a document at any time, but you can't transfer a compressed file from one archive to another. You'll have to decompress it first.

There are three versions of StuffIt, each of which are not 100% compatible with the others. StuffIt Classic is the shareware version, which has many of the features of the commercially-available StuffIt Deluxe, including virus detection and the ability to view the contents of an archive folder without uncompressing it. The third version, StuffIt 1.5.1, is an earlier shareware version that is still in use on many BBSs; it only opens archives created by either of the other two versions if they were saved as StuffIt 1.5.1 archives. Only StuffIt Deluxe includes Magic Menu, an INIT that allows the utility to function on the fly, much like DiskDoubler.

Working with DiskDoubler

DiskDoubler is the most efficient and easiest to use of the "on the fly" category of file compression utilities. Once you use DiskDoubler to compress a file, you won't need to decompress it to access it; decompression is done automatically when you launch the file. DiskDoubler will automatically recompress the file when you are done.

DiskDoubler places another menu category, named "DD," on the Finder's menu bar (Figure 3.22). When a file or folder is highlighted, selecting Compress from the DD menu will begin the compression process. A status window (Figure 3.23) will display the utility's progress, and let you know just how much space is being saved. A file compressed with DiskDoubler retains its original icon, but with a tiny "DD" in the lower-left corner.

DiskDoubler pretty much lives up to its name: although the amount of disk space saved varies file to file, the overall effect of the compression is to double the number of files you can place on your hard disk. However, it's unlikely that you'll want to compress every file on your drive. Applications and fonts compress only minimally, and it's usually not worth the hassle to decompress them every time you want to use them.

Another thing to keep in mind is that even though a file compressed by Disk-Doubler retains its icon (in a slightly modified form), the file is treated by the Macintosh as belonging to DiskDoubler, not the application with which it was created. This can cause confusion when trying to open a document from within

FIGURE 3.22

DiskDoubler's
DD menu

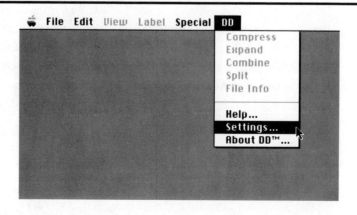

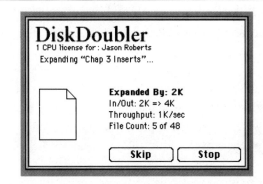

FIGURE 3.23

*DiskDoubler's
status window
appears during
compression
and
decompression*

an application. For example, QuarkXPress (a desktop publishing program)
might not recognize a compressed Xpress file, and therefore might not list it in
the Open dialog box. In such a cases, you'll need to return to the Finder and
decompress the file before proceeding.

File Compression Cards

The problem with on-the-fly compression utilities such as DiskDoubler or Stuff-
It Deluxe is that they take time to work—the larger the file, the longer it takes
to compress and decompress it. That's why some manufacturers offer a hardware solution, in the form of compression cards.

Most compression cards are of the NuBus configuration, designed to fit into
members of the Macintosh II and Quadra families. Once installed, they supply
dedicated processing power to a compression utility, intercepting the process
before it's passed to the Macintosh CPU. In most cases, a compression card
will make the compression process all but invisible to the user. These cards
aren't cheap, but they're often more cost-effective than the purchase of an additional hard drive. If much of your work involves large graphics files, a compression card can be an intelligent investment.

Compacting the Desktop File

One of the largest files on your hard disk may be an invisible one. It's called the Desktop file, and although you can't see it without a utility program (such as ResEdit), it usually resides on the root level of each volume. It's essentially a list of all the information the Macintosh needs in order to accurately represent the contents of every file on the volume: the icons, the type ID of files, instructions on where to find the application needed to launch a document, and so on. It's read whenever you open a folder or double-click on an icon.

The more files and folders you have on your hard disk, the bigger the Desktop file—and since much of the information isn't automatically purged, it can grow even bigger with time. In fact, the bigger it is, the longer it takes the Macintosh to read it, and it can become so big that normal operations start to slow down. This shows up most often on hard disks of 80 megabytes or more, but it's not uncommon on drives of lesser capacity.

Fortunately, you can compact the Desktop file by holding down the Option and Command keys during startup. This command will prevent most INITs from loading. A dialog box will appear, asking if you want to proceed with a desktop rebuild. Doing so will not affect operations in any way, but the display formats of some folders may be changed, and some custom icons may be replaced with default versions.

 TIP

To compact the Desktop file, hold down the Option and ⌘ keys during startup.

ORGANIZING YOUR DISK

FEATURING:

- → Hierarchical Filing System (HFS)
- → Folder Navigation
- → Folder View Formats
- → Sorting Folders and Files
- → Searching for Files

In the previous chapter, we looked at the factors involved in creating, modifying, and managing data on the Macintosh. Now we'll turn from general concepts to practical principles, detailing a number of elements and approaches to hard disk organization. Although this chapter presents specific scenarios, you're encouraged to create your own customized strategy, drawing from any or all of the following.

We'll begin by covering the topic of navigating your hard disk's directory and the methods for locating a file quickly. Next, we'll turn to folders—format options, display features, alternatives, and related information and advice. We'll also review alternative data locations, such as on the desktop and on partitioned volumes. Finally, since files can get lost on even the most thoroughly organized hard disk, we'll look at a few of the available high-speed file search-utilities.

Folders, Files and Conceptual Piles: Making Sense of Macintosh Document Organization

As anyone who has used one knows, the Macintosh organizes and manages files in a manner that mirrors real life. Instead of directories, the Mac uses "file folders", whose icons are shaped roughly like manila folders. The topmost level of data isn't the root, but rather the desktop. And files aren't deleted, they're thrown into the "Trash." This file cabinet metaphor makes it easy to learn how to work with the Macintosh, but the metaphor only goes so far. A real-world file folder can hold only so many pieces of paper, but a Macintosh folder can not only contain hundreds of documents, but "nested" folders (folders within folders within folders) as well. Similarly, while a hard disk may be roughly analogous to a real-world file cabinet, today's high-capacity drives (such as CD-ROM drives) can contain more information than a roomful of filing cabinets. That's why special skills are needed to easily and consistently manage your data in a manner that doesn't cramp your working style.

In the following pages, I'll help you develop those special skills. We'll look at the general principles behind file management and at specific choices you can make to keep your files from becoming little more than computerized heaps of information.

Prehistory: the Macintosh Filing System (MFS)

In Chapter 2, I mentioned that System files previous to Version 3.2 should not be used because they contain the outmoded Macintosh File System (MFS) rather than the Hierarchical File System (HFS). Here's why: MFS was created with the expectation that all Macintoshes would be work with only one or two floppy disk drives and that all floppy disks would hold a relatively limited amount of information—about 400 KB apiece. MFS created folders that weren't really folders. All files and folders placed in other folders didn't actually exist on other organizational levels—they were still on the same root level. Their individual file icons were simply replaced by the folder icon. In other words, MFS folders were a convenient way to designate a group of files, but the organization was only cosmetic. The difference between representation and reality was most apparent when one tried to open a file from within an application. The Macintosh desktop may have seemed uncluttered (top), with files neatly grouped in folders, but in the application, the user still needed to scroll through every file on disk (bottom). The folders were nowhere in evidence.

The Hierarchical File System (HFS)

With the advent of double-sided floppies, serial port hard disks, and finally SCSI buses, MFS soon became unmanageable. HFS replaced it in 1986. HFS creates folders in true nested subdirectories. Under HFS, users can navigate through volumes from within an application and do so far more rapidly because files are stored in a useful folder structure.

HFS has its drawbacks, however. A misplaced file can be difficult to find. And the proliferation of folder levels can lead to "over-organization," with files tucked away so deeply in the hierarchy that simply locating one becomes a tedious process.

Because a disk's file system is active whenever a volume is mounted, you'll want HFS not only on your hard disk, but also on any reasonably full floppies you use regularly.

There are a number of ways to determine which file system is present on disk:

- Check the Finder file; if it's Version 5.0 or earlier, it features MFS.

- If a disk does not contain a Finder file, try seeing if folders disappear when the Open command is selected from within an application. If they disappear, MFS is present.

- In every open folder window, there are two closely spaced lines right under the space where the column headings are displayed. On an HFS system, the space between the lines is filled with one pixel on the far left, below the number of the items. Under MFS, the space is entirely clear (Figure 4.1).

FIGURE 4.1

*HFS folders
have an extra
pixel in the
upper left-hand
corner (top) to
differentiate
them from MFS
folders (bottom)*

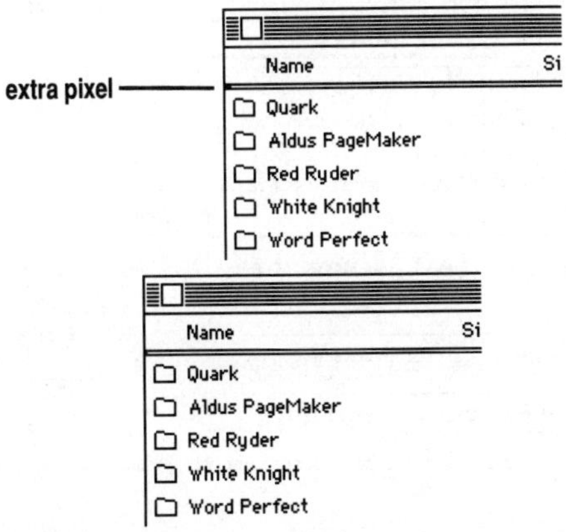

extra pixel ——

Name	Si
Quark	
Aldus PageMaker	
Red Ryder	
White Knight	
Word Perfect	

Name	Si
Quark	
Aldus PageMaker	
Red Ryder	
White Knight	
Word Perfect	

If you want to convert an MFS disk to HFS, first make sure that the Macintosh is started with an HFS System file. Make a backup of the disk's contents (and make sure the copy is a functional one). Then select the disk and choose Erase Disk from the Special menu in the Finder. The disk will be reformatted for HFS. Complete the task by copying all the files back to the disk, and dispose of the duplicates on the hard disk.

Navigating in the Macintosh Environment

In this section, we'll discuss the basics of getting around in your Macintosh's work environment—locating, opening, closing, saving, and copying files—with a minimum of delay or confusion. Unless otherwise noted, the principles presented here apply to both System 6 and System 7.

Opening and Saving: the Standard File Dialog Box

Take a look at the two dialog boxes in Figure 4.2. Both are actually versions of the same standard *File dialog box,* a Toolbox feature that most applications use, often with minor modifications. The first time you save a document, and every time you choose the Save As option, you'll likely see some version of the first box. Every time you try to open an existing document from within an application, chances are you'll see a variation of the second.

FIGURE 4.2

Variations of
the standard
File dialog box
are used for
many tasks,
such as saving
a document
(top) or
importing one
(bottom)

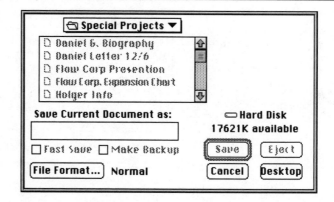

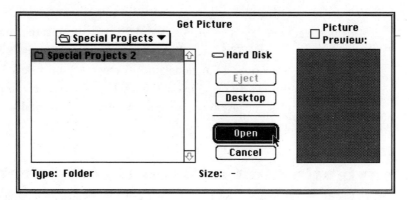

The File dialog box is located next to the Finder and is the main portal through which you'll navigate your hard disk. The HFS has features that may not be obvious to the casual user. Let's take a look at a few.

Path Name Navigation

When you save a document, where is it stored? Unless you specify otherwise, it'll be stored in the folder from which you entered the application. The sequence of nested folders in which a file is stored is known as the file's *path*, or *path name*. It is displayed whenever you click on the folder name field, located directly above the folder contents field (Figure 4.3).

FIGURE 4.3

Clicking on the folder name field displays the current path name, in descending order from current folder to volume root level

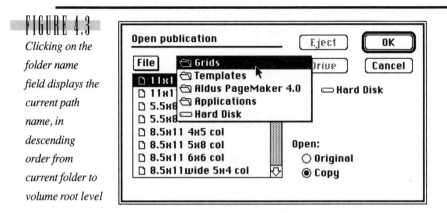

This path name field is more than a box; it's also a menu. You can move up the hierarchy by any number of levels by simply selecting the target level. To navigate down the hierarchy, double-click on any folder in the folder contents window. If necessary, you can scroll the contents window to locate the desired folder. With these tools, you'll be able to save or seek a file anywhere on any currently mounted volume on your system, without first quitting your current application. To shift the search to another mounted volume, click on the Drive button.

System 7 takes the process a step farther. Instead of stopping at the volume level, the path goes all the way to the root level of the Macintosh, the level on which the Finder maintains the desktop. This makes it easier to search multiple volumes mounted on the same Mac, since you don't have to click the Drive button. (Figure 4.4)

By the way, there's a shortcut to climbing back up the hierarchy: clicking on the name or icon of the current volume will automatically move you one level up the hierarchy. Path names are listed in descending order, from current folder to volume root level, but in this book, "up" will always refer to the direction of the root, or highest level.

Under System 7, clicking on the folder name field displays the path name down to the desktop level

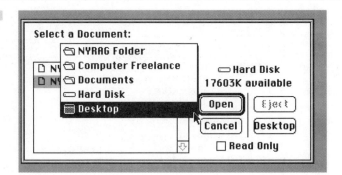

In a Save or Save As dialog box, only the folders can be opened, whereas in the Open dialog box, both folders and files are accessible. However, the Open box can be misleading. Sometimes, files that the application cannot recognize are not listed at all, so don't panic if a folder containing valuable data appears to be empty. Furthermore, the files that can be selected are not necessarily ones that belong to the application you're in at the moment. For instance, the Open dialog box in Microsoft Word will list all MacWrite documents as selectable, even though selecting one will actually start a time-consuming conversion process instead of opening the original file directly. Also, some utility applications will prevent files from appearing in dialog box lists. For example, if you use a file compression program such as Disk Doubler, don't panic if a file doesn't show up in the Open dialog box; it may just be compressed in a format that the parent application is unable to read. You can use the Finder to take a look at the actual folder and find the file.

Don't panic if a file fails to turn up in the Open dialog box; it may just be saved in a format unrecognizable to the application you're presently in. If in doubt, use the Finder to inspect the folder directly.

All path name navigation can be done before the Save or Save As button is selected; once the path name is set, all files will be saved to that locale. Designating a "home" for a file as you create it is the most efficient way to go, but it does have its limitations. In most cases, you can't use the standard File dialog box to relocate a file once you've saved it, nor can you create a new folder, or rename a file or folder (some application File dialog boxes allow you to do this). To do those tasks, you'll need to return to the Finder, or use a Finder augmentation program like Directory Assistance (see Chapter 9).

Field Navigation

Since folders can hold numerous files and folders, the folder field can become imposingly long. You can scroll up and down the field until you find the file or folder, but fortunately, there is a shortcut that makes the task easier.

The contents of the field are always listed in alphabetical order, with the first file or folder automatically selected whenever the dialog box opens. You can skip down the list by typing a character or two from the keyboard: the first file beginning with those characters will be selected. In other words, typing *h* will select the first file starting with "h" or "H" (the function ignores upper and lower case). However, don't pause too long between characters: typing *j* and *o* in rapid succession should select "Job File," but a pausing too long between characters could select "Orientation Notes" instead.

The Macintosh tries to match these keystrokes as closely as possible, but it does allow a margin for error. If you type *z* and a file or folder beginning with that letter does not exist, it'll select the file whose name starts with the closest letter before the keystroke, such as "y" or "w" or "v." Numbers, spaces, and other nonalphabetic characters precede letters in the folder field, so any one of those keystrokes will send you to the top of the list.

Using Default Features

One of the things that makes the Macintosh so helpful for beginners is its use of *defaults*: whenever a choice needs to be made, the computer either presents an automatic option or makes the safest course the easiest to take. As such, an unnamed document will be saved as "Untitled," or an attempt to throw away an application will prompt an "Are you sure?" message before the task is completed.

To the experienced user, such default functions may seem unnecessary and un-welcome. But defaults can also be useful shortcuts in a number of circumstances.

- **The double border default.** In dialog boxes that offer more than one choice, the option button with the thick double border (as in Figure 4.5) can be selected by pressing the Return key. Even if none of the buttons has a double border, the Return key will usually select one option or another; experimentation will reveal which.

- **The field selection default.** Most dialog boxes which allow the user to enter text or numbers automatically highlight the contents of one field. To change the contents, you don't have to select, delete, or backspace over it—just start typing. This can be a tricky feature, since an accidental keystroke can make major changes, and Undo doesn't work in dialog boxes. If an accident of this sort happens, don't try to restore everything to its original condition; just click on the Cancel option and open the dialog box a second time.

- **The "Save changes" default.** When you've completed work on a document, you don't need to save and close it before quitting the application. The Quit command will open a "Save changes" dialog box (in which "Yes" is usually the double-bordered default choice) for each open document. Whether or not you choose to save the changes, the document will be closed automatically.

- **The tab default.** When a dialog box has multiple boxes for data entry, pressing the tab key will usually advance the cursor to the next user-accessible box. Try it the next time you issue a print command; the Print dialog box will appear with the Copies box selected, but pressing the tab key, either before or after making an entry, will move the cursor to the From box. Pressing the tab key again will move it to the To box. This function cycles through all the boxes; when the cursor is in the last box, the next press of the tab key will return the cursor to the first. However, applications do not employ this method consistently.

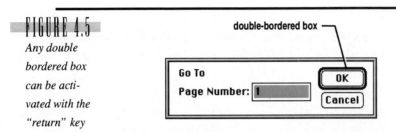

FIGURE 4.5

Any double bordered box can be activated with the "return" key

double-bordered box

Go To
Page Number: 1
OK
Cancel

These are just some of the more common default features of the Macintosh, and they may be missing from applications that depart from the standard user-interface guidelines. With experience and experimentation, you'll discover more of these default actions.

Working with Folders

Folders are more than a means of conveniently grouping files— they're one of the best tools for structuring your Macintosh work environment. The first step in using folders to your advantage is gaining an understanding about their features. Let's take a look at the most important ones.

Folder windows remember their place on your screen. To see how this works, double-click on a folder to open it. Click and drag on the title bar area to move the window anywhere on the screen. Then close it and click it open again; until you reposition it, the window will continue to open in the location you specify. With this feature, you can work with multiple folders without getting lost in the clutter of overlapping windows.

Folder windows have two sizes. Click on a folder, and then move the size box (the lower right corner of the window) to make the window as long or thin, large or small as you like. This size is the *set size* of the window. The folder window will take this form every time you open it. Of course, you can change the set size at any time.

But the window has another size, *full size.* Clicking on the zoom box in the upper right corner will expand the window to a width of nine inches and a depth roughly equivalent to the depth of your monitor's screen. For all compact Macintoshes, full size is the equivalent of full-screen size. On modular Macintoshes with large monitors, full size does not fill the entire screen.

Windows remember their View format. There are seven different ways that a folder window can display its contents. When a folder is created, its window displays it contents "by Icon." However, the order in which the files are displayed can be changed by selecting another format from the View menu while the folder is open and active.

N O T E

> View formats are probably one of the most underutilized features of the Macintosh. Even experienced users often prefer only one format, which they apply uniformly to all folders. But each format has its own distinct advantages, and when used in combination with each other, they can greatly add to the clarity of hard disk organization.

View by Icon

The Icon view (Figure 4.6) displays all files with full-size icons. This format is useful if you need to easily identify applications and documents at a glance. The large icons also make it easy to select and drag files with the mouse.

However, the format takes up a lot of screen space and is best used with folders that have relatively few files. What's more, since the icons can be arranged in any manner, the folder can easily become cluttered and icons can get "lost" by being placed too far below the main grouping. You can tidy up such a folder by selecting Clean Up Window from the Special menu. You can scroll around to find it, but often it's easier to simply change the folder format to View by Name.

TIP

If you have System 7, you can rearrange the files in an Icon view window into name, size, kind, label, or date order. Press the Option key while opening the Special menu; the Clean Up Window command will change to reflect the view format used *prior* to the Icon view format. For example, if the window was in View by Name format prior to its current View by Icon format, pressing the Option key will change the Clean Up command to Clean Up by Name, and the command will not only tidy up the window's contents, but will alphabetize the files as well. To sort an Icon view window in size, kind, label, or date order, simply select the desired view format, reselect the View by Icon format, press the Option key, and select the Clean Up command.

View by Small Icon

This format is a variation of the View by Icon format. Icons are one-quarter the size of the latter format, and the file names are listed to the right of rather than beneath the icons. Small icons can fit more densely into a window, but this leads to their disadvantage: the miniature versions of many icons are difficult to distinguish from one another (Figure 4.7). This may not be a problem if you're familiar with the names of your applications and documents. But if such is the

FIGURE 4.6
*The View by
Icon folder
format*

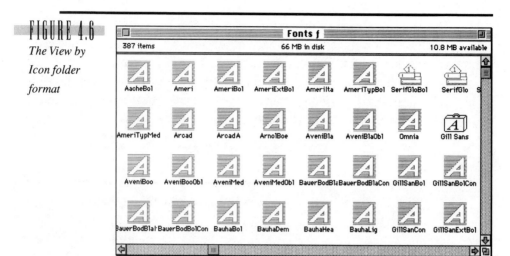

case, why not use an even more compact view format? View by Small Icon is
most useful for folders whose contents need to be arranged in a custom,
idiosyncratic fashion, such as a "Prioritized projects" folder.

View by Name

Under the View by Name format (Figure 4.8), icons become so small as to be
unidentifiable. As a result, application-specific icons are replaced with default
icons for their file type: all applications share the same icon, as do all documents. All files and folders are listed in a single column in alphabetical order.
You can drop one folder into another, but you can't change the order of files
and folders without changing file names and the reordering won't take place
until you close and reopen the window. As in the standard File dialog box,
numbers, spaces, and symbols appear before letters in the file list.

Since icon standardization could lead to confusion, the View by Name window
has a "Kind" column, which lists the parent application of a document. This
way, you'll know which application you're launching when you open a document. But since the Kind column is limited to 18 characters, the entry is often

FIGURE 4.7

The View by Small Icon format; note that many of the icons are difficult to distinguish

Fonts f					

387 items 66 MB in disk 10.8 MB available

AacheBol	Ameri	AmeriBol	AmeriExtBol	Amerilta
AmeriTypMed	Arcad	ArcadA	ArnolBoe	AveniBla
AveniBoo	AveniBooObl	AveniMed	AveniMedObl	BauerBodBla
BauerBodBlaIta	BauerBodBolCon	BauhaBol	BauhaDem	BauhaHea
BauhaMed	BenguBol	BenguBoo	BerkeOldStyBla	BerkeOldStyBlaIt
BerkeOldStyBolIt	BerkeOldStyBoo	BerkeOldStyBoolt	BerkeOldStyMed	BerkeOldStyMedI
Black	Bodon	BodonBol	BodonBolIta	BodonIta
BookmBol	BookmBolIta	BookmMed	BookmMedIta	BVelBld
BVelItl	BVelNor	Cart	CasloOpeFac	CentuOldStyBol
CentuOldStyReg	CheltBol	CheltBolIta	CheltBoo	CheltBooIta

FIGURE 4.8

The View by Name format; note that the icons have been replaced by standard default icons

Fonts f					

387 items 66 MB in disk 10.8 MB available

Name	Size	Kind	Label	Last Modified
AacheBol	35K	system extension	Cool	Thu, Jul 16, 1987, 9:57 AM
Ameri	50K	system extension	Cool	Sat, Dec 31, 1988, 11:30 PM
AmeriBol	50K	system extension	Cool	Sat, Dec 31, 1988, 11:30 PM
AmeriExtBol	48K	system extension	Cool	Sat, Dec 31, 1988, 11:30 PM
Amerilta	50K	system extension	Cool	Sat, Dec 31, 1988, 11:30 PM
AmeriTypBol	45K	system extension	Cool	Wed, Jun 24, 1987, 4:13 PM
AmeriTypMed	45K	system extension	Cool	Wed, Jun 24, 1987, 4:13 PM
Arcad	27K	system extension	Cool	Tue, Oct 9, 1990, 9:25 AM
ArcadA	27K	system extension	Cool	Tue, Oct 9, 1990, 9:24 AM
ArnolBoe	65K	system extension	Cool	Mon, Mar 20, 1989, 10:48 AM
AveniBla	33K	system extension	Cool	Mon, Mar 6, 1989, 5:01 PM
AveniBlaObl	45K	system extension	Cool	Mon, Mar 6, 1989, 5:02 PM
AveniBoo	32K	system extension	Cool	Mon, Mar 6, 1989, 5:02 PM
AveniBooObl	42K	system extension	Cool	Mon, Mar 6, 1989, 5:02 PM
AveniMed	32K	system extension	Cool	Mon, Mar 6, 1989, 5:02 PM

longer than the column width, as indicated by the trailing ellipsis (…). You can see the complete Kind entry by selecting the file and choosing Get Info from the File menu.

In addition to the file name and parent application, View by Name also displays the file's Size and when it was Last Modified. In System 6, the Size column does not display the size of folders; in System 7, it does.

Not only does this format display more file information than either of the Icon view formats, its inherent orderliness and compactness can make for a very neat desktop. Yet you do need to take a few precautions. A file or folder can be selected not only by clicking on its icon, but by clicking anywhere in the adjacent horizontal band area (on any of the category entries and all spaces in between). However, since the icons are very close together, casual clicking can accidentally select and start dragging a file or folder, which can then be inadvertently dumped into another folder. If you're dragging from one folder to another, don't release the mouse button until you're sure that none of the target folder's subfolders are highlighted.

System 7 adds another useful feature to the View by Name format. The miniaturized folders are accompanied by a small triangle to the left of the file icon (Figure 4.9). When you click on the triangle, it will rotate 90 degrees and the contents of the folder will "spill" temporarily into the currently active level. Files in folders are distinguished from files in the current level by their indentation. Clicking on the triangle again returns the display to normal. This feature makes inspecting folders less cumbersome since you don't have to open an new window every time you want to see what's in a folder.

View by Date, Size, Kind, Color, and Label

Each of these four formats is a variation of the View by Name format. The data categories, the default icons, and the automatic organization remain the same; only the organization criterion varies. As with View by Name, you can determine the window format by looking for the underlined the category heading (Figure 4.10).

View by Date rearranges the folder contents in order of date last modified (as opposed to date created, which is recorded in each file or folder's Get Info box). The modification date is drawn from the calendar setting in the Control Panel.

*Under Sys-
tem 7, clicking
on the triangle
next to a folder
(above) will
cause its
contents to be
displayed
(below)*

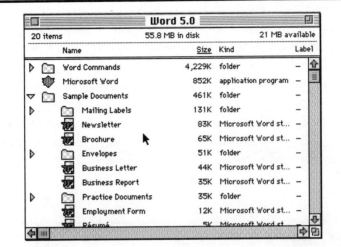

*The View by
Date, View by
Size and View
by Kind
formats; note
how the
category
heading of the
main criteria is
underlined.*

View by Size displays files in order from largest to smallest, as measured in number of kilobytes, with folders bringing up the rear. If two or more files are the same size, they will be listed alphabetically. This format is useful for folders with applications you want to be readily accessible; since most applications are larger than documents, they are placed at the top of the folder window.

View by Kind lists folder contents in order of type—applications, documents, or folders—with documents placed first, then applications, and finally folders. The files and folders are in alphabetical order.

I P

> Because the file type order can be customized, the View by
> Kind format can be a versatile organizational tool. If you want
> to change the order of a folder's contents, just empty the
> folder, and refill it in the desired sequence. Or you can simply
> create a new folder, transfer the folder's contents, and re-
> name the new folder after discarding the old, emptied folder.

View by Color (System 6 only) is an option for those Macintoshes that have a color monitor. This option won't show up in the View menu unless the Monitors CDEV in the Control Panel is set for 16 or more colors. Although color-capable Macintoshes can display up to 256 colors at once, only eight colors are reserved by the system for file and folder designations: orange, red, pink, light blue, dark blue, green, brown, and black. You can color-code an icon by clicking on it, and then selecting color from the Color menu in the Finder (Figure 4.11). Until you change their color, all files and folders will be displayed as black. In the folder window, the order of organization follows the order on the Color menu, with files and folders of each color arranged in alphabetical order.

FIGURE 4.11

Assigning colors from the Finder's Color menu (System 6)

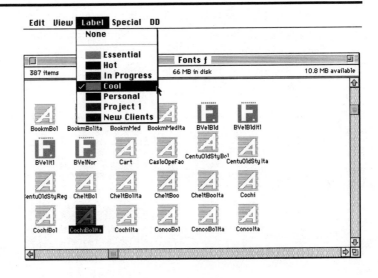

If your computer can employ the View by Color format, you'll find it to be one of the most useful of folder formats, enabling you to group applications, documents, and folders together in any combination, based on any criteria. On the other hand, the format also requires constant updating; you'll need to color-code files and folders as they are created.And the subtleties of such organization will be lost if you need to transfer your work to a black-and-white Macintosh. Interestingly enough, the View by Color format will work on a Macintosh II with a nongrayscale black-and-white monitor, but all of the eight colors will be displayed as solid black, and only the computer will be able to differentiate them.

View by Label is the System 7 variation of View by Color. It's essentially the same as color-coding, but includes the option of assigning custom labels to each color (Figure 4.12). You can change the labels by selecting Labels from the Control Panels menu (under the Apple menu), and then typing in the terms you want associated with each color.

One advantage of the View by Label format is that you're not limited to factory-preset colors. If you want to pick an entirely new color, double-click one of the pre-set colors; you'll see a color wheel displayed (Figure 4.13), a representation of the full spectrum of available shades of that color. Use your mouse to move the

FIGURE 4.12

Assigning colors from the Finder's Labels menu (System 7)

FIGURE 4.13

Using the color wheel to add a new color label to View by Label format (System 7)

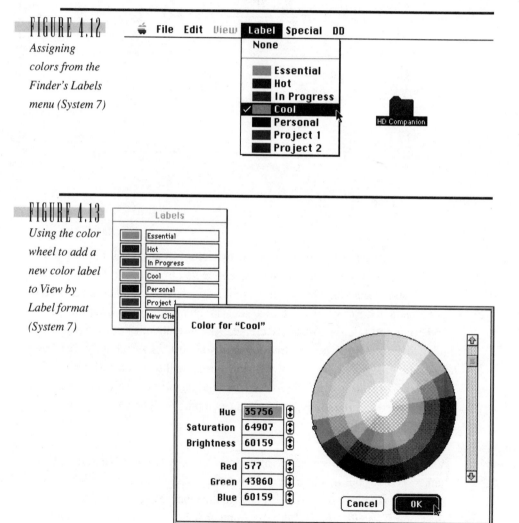

selection circle around on the wheel, either by manipulating it directly or by adjusting the hue and brightness controls. When you are satisfied with the new color, click OK.

Storing on the Desktop

Folders aren't the only place where files (or other folders) can be placed. Another especially useful location is the desktop of the Macintosh itself—the home base screen, with the Trash icon in the lower right-hand corner and your hard disk's icon in the upper right (Figure 4.14). Although you may at first feel a bit uneasy about placing important data near the Trash, it can be very useful, as you'll soon see.

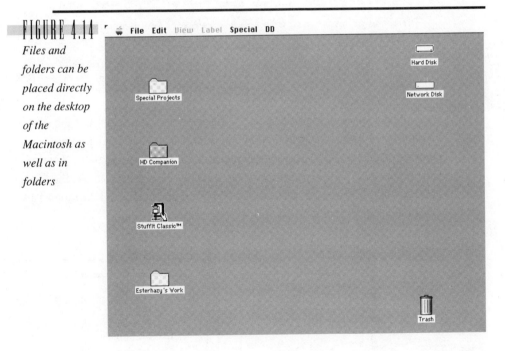

FIGURE 4.14

Files and folders can be placed directly on the desktop of the Macintosh as well as in folders

To place a file or folder on the desktop, just drag it from its folder to a vacant spot. You'll notice that no matter what the view format of its previous home, the file's icon is automatically displayed in full size. Although the Clean Up command on the Special menu won't help, you can arrange any number of icons on the desktop in any way you wish, and then shut down with confidence. Upon rebooting, the icons will appear right where you left them (if they don't, it's probably because the hard disk isn't the current startup volume).

TIP

> You can use the desktop as a location for the applications you use most often, or as a means of giving top priority to projects that demand special attention. And under System 6, if you *really* want to make an application or document as prominent as possible, you can use the MultiFinder's Set Startup feature to launch the application or document automatically upon booting up.

As far as the HFS system is concerned, the desktop is simply part of the startup volume's root level; a look at this level with any standard File dialog box will show the desktop's contents incorporated into the scrolling list field. You can't use the File box to place a document on the desktop; you need to use the Finder to place it there. However, System 7 dialog boxes recognize the desktop as a valid file location (Figure 4.15).

FIGURE 4.15

System 7 dialog boxes have a button to navigate directly to the desktop level

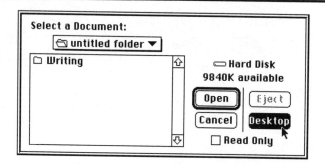

ARNING

> If your machine is on a network that allows others to access
> your hard disk, keep in mind that files on your Mac's desktop
> will also appear on *their* desktop when they mount your drive.
> If, for example, both you and a co-worker have a folder
> labeled "Today's Work" on your respective desktops, the
> moment she accesses your drive, she'll have two "Today's
> Work" folders on her desktop. Needless to say, this can lead
> to some confusion, not to mention a loss of privacy.

Cleaning Up and Closing Up

With icons in a folder, or multiple folder windows on the screen, it often seems
like the rule is "the more, the messier." Try these shortcuts to keep things more
tidy and less tiresome. You'll find that order breeds simplicity, and your hard
disk will be more efficient, as well as easier to use.

Managing Icons

Icons and small icons are placement-sensitive; unlike the other folder formats,
they can be arranged in any order on the monitor's screen. And when that order
gets disorderly, you may have to resort to one of the following quick clean-ups.

*To tidy things up, select the Clean Up Window command from the Special menu
in the Finder.* If the command reads Clean Up Selection instead, that's because
an icon inside the folder is currently selected; deselect it by clicking elsewhere
on the desktop and try again. The Clean Up command will align icons or small
icons on an invisible grid, moving them from their present position to the
nearest grid coordinate. If an icon is not visible in the current window configuration, it'll be moved into any open space in the window. This command is useful for minor reorganization, and you may want to select it from time to time
just as a helpful habit.

To maximize folder organization, hold down the Option key while selecting the Clean Up command from the Special menu. When invoked, this command will redraw the entire window's contents in a new, close formation. Icons will be rearranged into a rectangular block, with no gaps between them. This command is especially useful for thoroughly disorganized windows, and should be used whenever you change the icon format.

Keep in mind, however, that the Clean Up commands organize the folder *window*, not in the folder itself. As such, the icon organization is based on the size and shape of the folder window; for example, if the window is long and skinny, the icons may be placed in single file. If you're dissatisfied with the results of the Clean Up commands, resize the folder window and try again.

To move or delete multiple objects in a single folder, hold down the Shift key while clicking on the icons. You can select as many files and folders as you want, relocating or disposing of them as a group. As long as you keep these two keys depressed, you'll be able to scroll and resize folder windows while maintaining your selections. If a wrong file or folder is included in the group by mistake, just click on it a second time to unselect it.

Closing Folder Windows

Locating a particular file often entails plunging into the depths of your hard disk's folder hierarchy, requiring you to open a half-dozen or more folders before reaching your goal. Of course, when you are finished working with the file, you need to close all the folders that you opened. You could do this by clicking on each folder window's close box; fortunately, there are less-tedious alternatives.

To close each folder window one at a time, just press the Command (⌘) and W keys simultaneously. The active folder will close and the next folder in the path will become the active one. You can repeat this command until all nested folders are closed. If you make a mistake, pressing the ⌘ and O keys will reopen the last folder closed.

To close all the windows at once, hold down the Option key while closing any one window (either by clicking in the close box or pressing ⌘-W). All windows will be closed, including the root level window for the hard disk itself. This is the quickest method, and the only method available when you have a number of open windows from unnested folders.

Mass Volume Searches, or "I Know It's in Here Somewhere"

Even the most thoroughly organized hard disk can sometimes lose files in a labyrinth of path names and nested folders. If you have at least a vague notion of the whereabouts of the file you want, you can try searching for it with the Finder. But if you don't know the file's general location, its type, or even its name, you'll find the Finder little more than a time-consuming desperation effort. Fortunately, a number of programs have been developed to search an entire storage volume very quickly. Let's examine two of the most popular of these utilities: Find File and GOfer.

System 6: Working with Find File

Find File from Apple Computer was included as part of the System software package in versions prior to System 7. Although it has the advantage of being free, it has limited search capability. It can search only for file and folder names, and cannot differentiate an entire file name from a simple string of characters.

To use Find File, select it from the Apple menu. A window will appear (Figure 4.16); to initiate a search, type the desired name or characters into the "Search for" field. If you want to search another hard or floppy disk, click on the Hard Disk icon until the desired volume appears. Finally, click on the symbol that looks like a pedestrian "Walk" sign, or simply press the Return key. The program will begin searching from the root level. As the search continues, it will display the names of all the files and folders that match the "Search for" criteria. When the search is over, the Macintosh will beep and the crosswalk-like "Stop" symbol will be selected.

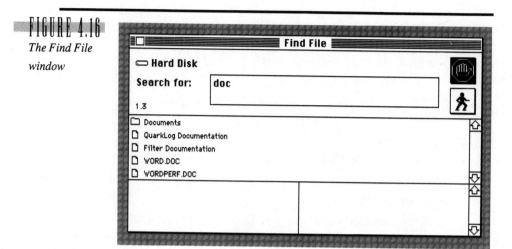

FIGURE 4.16

The Find File window

Fortunately, you don't have to wait until Find File has finished searching the entire volume before you can monitor the results of the search. As each criteria match is made, the file name is added to the scrolling field in the center of the window. You can inspect any of the files by first clicking on the "Stop" symbol. This won't end the search; it'll just freeze it until you click on "Walk" again.

You don't have to stop the search to examine a file. Just click on the desired name. This will fill the bottom two portions of the Find File window. The left box contains the file information usually found in the Get Info box—file type, dates created and last modified, and file size. The right box contains the path name of the file. You can use this path name as a "road map" to the file or folder. But if you want to extract the file permanently from its present hiding place, select Move to Desktop from the Find File menu. This will automatically transfer the file from its current location to the desktop. (The desktop shouldn't be confused with the root level of the hard disk.)

The other command on the Find File menu, Search Here, is used to start the search at any level and in any folder. After you select the command, the standard Open dialog box appears. Select the starting folder for the search and press the Return key. Selecting the command while one of the files is selected will inform you of the other folders and files located in the selected file's home folder.

TIP

> You can instruct Find File to work in the background. Taking care not to hit the close box (which will cancel the search), click on another open window. Find File will continue to search and will beep when it is complete.

System 7: Searching with the Finder

Apple retired Find File with System 7, favoring instead to make the Find command an integral part of the Finder itself. You can initiate the search for a file whenever the Finder is active, either by selecting Find from the Edit menu or by pressing ⌘-F. The dialog box seen in Figure 4.17 will then appear.

When you type all or part of a name into the Find field, the Macintosh will search all of the volumes on your desktop, starting with the startup volume. When it finds a match, the Finder will open the folder in which the match resides and highlight the icon. If it's the right file, you can launch it by double-clicking on its icon or pressing ⌘-O. To continue the search, type ⌘-G. The folder will be closed, and Find will seek another match. If no match can be found, you'll get both an alert beep and a notification message.

The Find command can perform more sophisticated searches, based on criteria you specify. Click on the More Choices button to display the expanded Find

FIGURE 4.17

*The Find
command's
dialog box
(System 7 only)*

Find

Find: Nowinski

[More Choices]   [Cancel]   [**Find**]

dialog box (Figure 4.18). Note that instead of a single text-entry field, the dialog box offers a number of pull-down menus. Use the top left menu to establish the type of search you want: by name, size, kind (i.e., documents, applications, or aliases), label, date created, date modified, version number (e.g., PageMaker 4.0, QuarkXpress 3.0), comments entered in the Get Info box, or whether a file is locked.

Once you have chosen the main search criterion, the selections on the top center pull-down menu will change to reflect your choice. For example, if name is the main search criterion, the selections on the center menu change to enable you to specify that you're searching for a file whose name contains, starts with, ends with, is, is not, or does not contain the text in the text field (Figure 4.19). However, if you search by date created, the items on the menu change to search

FIGURE 4.18

*The More
Choices level of
the Find
command*

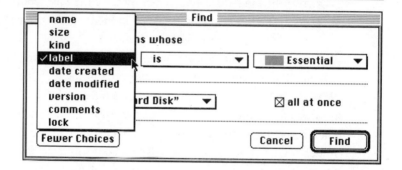

FIGURE 4.19

*The search
criteria can be
further limited
by selections in
the middle
pull-down menu*

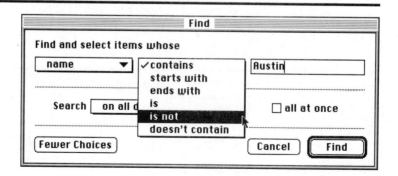

for files whose created dates are the same, are before, are after, or are not the same as that specified in the text box.

If you'd like to wait until the end of the entire search to view the results rather than having each match displayed individually, mark the "all at once" box. The Finder will not open individual folders, but will highlight all matches on the root-level of the searched volume. This not only eliminates the need to reissue Find Again commands (⌘-G), but it's also useful for performing increasingly narrow searches. Once the original Find command has selected the matches meeting the original search criteria, you can return to the Find window and launch another search, based on more specific criteria. Choose "selected items" from the Search pull-down menu (Figure 4.20), and the new search will be limited only to those items.

Although System 7's Find command is more powerful than Find File, it still has limitations. You can't automatically move a file to the desktop, or preview its contents before opening it. And since the search matches are not listed in a single, easy-to-read field, it's hard to ferret out duplicate files. For those reasons, you might want to keep another search utility, such as Fast Find, on hand.

Working with Fast Find

If System 6's Find File or System 7's Find don't quite meet your needs, you might want to look into Fast Find, which is part of the Norton Utilities for the

FIGURE 4.20

Limiting a
search to
selected items
lets you narrow
your search
criteria

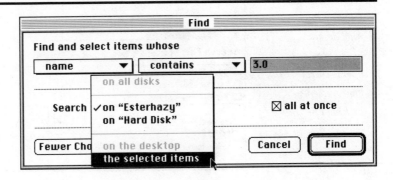

Macintosh package. Fast Find looks and works a lot like Find File, but it has more options and greater speed.

The Fast Find dialog box (Figure 4.21) looks and operates in much the same manner as Find File. However, Fast Find can search every volume mounted on your Macintosh, even those that are accessed over a network. You can search any combination of volumes by holding down the Shift key while clicking on their icons. To search all volumes, type ⌘-A.

Fast Find also enables you to search less than an entire volume for those times when you have a general idea of where a file resides. To limit the search to a folder, type ⌘-S and select the folder. Then, to return to searching on the volume level, type ⌘-S again.

To start the search, click on the running man button or press the Return key. Note that the horizontal bar beneath the volume icons fills as the search progresses; the little running man icon stops when the search is complete. Adjacent to the horizontal bar, Fast Find lists the total number of matches it has encountered. As with Find File, clicking on a file name will display information about its location and dates of creation and modification. However, Fast Find will also let you preview or open a file without having to locate its icon in the Finder. To preview a file, click on the magnifying glass icon (or type ⌘-F).

FIGURE 4.21

The Norton Utilities' Fast Find desk accessory offers several improvements on Find File

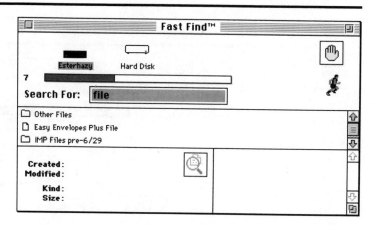

A new box will be opened, displaying the contents of the file in plain ASCII characters (Figure 4.22). You won't be able to see formatting or graphics, but you can use this command to confirm the contents of text files. If you want to open the file itself, type ⌘-O.

Working With GOfer

GOfer from Microlytics, Inc. is a fast, versatile, easy-to-use search utility. It can search not only file names, but also a file's contents, a specified text string, keywords, or combination thereof. Furthermore, it can locate files containing text that matches a very specific set of parameters. For instance, you can instruct GOfer to identify all word processing files that contain the words *Chrysler* and *Chevrolet,* but only when they are mentioned in proximity to the word *Buick.*

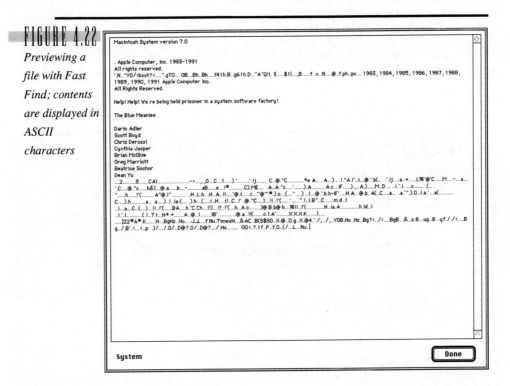

FIGURE 4.22

Previewing a file with Fast Find; contents are displayed in ASCII characters

Macintosh System version 7.0

. Apple Computer, Inc. 1983-1991
All rights reserved.
`.N..˚YO/<boot?<....".gTO... OB...Bh...Bh....f41h.B..g61h.D..˚A˚Q!!. !|....$1|...,B....f. x..N....@..f.ph..pc... 1983, 1984, 1985, 1986, 1987, 1988,
1989, 1990, 1991 Apple Computer Inc.
All Rights Reserved.

Help! Help! We.re being held prisoner in a system software factory!

The Blue Meanies

Darin Adler
Scott Boyd
Chris Derossi
Cynthia Jasper
Brian McGhie
Greg Marriott
Beatrice Sochor
Dean Yu

System   [Done]

Once installed, the GOfer DA can be accessed from within any application. As Figure 4.23 shows, it has many of the same features as Find File; however, the three buttons along the top of the window open dialog boxes which allow you to customize the search. The What option sets up the object of the search: what is to be located, in what context, and whether to find only exact matches or allow matches that GOfer considers to be "close". The Where option enables you to save search time by specifying exactly where GOfer should look; you can direct GOfer to search in any combination of folders, or focus the search to include or exclude files of a certain type or those created by a certain application. You can even limit the search to only text or data forks. The How option lets you decide how you want the search results displayed, and when the Mac should beep to notify you of the search results.

Once you have defined the search criteria, GOfer works extremely fast—it takes about one minute to search one megabyte of data. The Where option further speeds the search since it prevents you from having to search the entire hard disk for a file. Unfortunately, GOfer does have a serious shortcoming: it can't search for file and folder names alone. Even when you're sure of a file name, you must wait for GOfer to search for matches in the text of files.

FIGURE 4.23

The main window of the GOfer desk accessory.

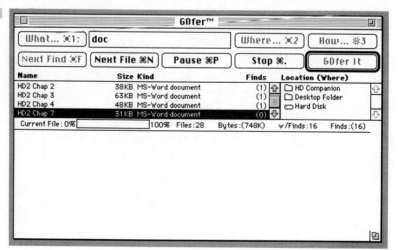

Searching for file names, however, happens to be Find File's greatest strength, so installing both Find File and GOfer on your hard disk will cover all of your volume search needs.

TIP

GOfer also offers a major fringe benefit: it can display the contents of a file's text fork, and this text can be cut and pasted from one application to another. Since you can do this without leaving one application or launching another, GOfer can be a useful text-only alternative to the Clipboard.

Cleaning House with Volume Searches

Mass volume search utilities are useful not only for locating misplaced files, but also for weeding out the redundant, the obsolete, and the otherwise superfluous. Keeping only one version of a file has three main benefits: it saves space, it eliminates confusion on your part, and it guards against confusion on the part of the Mac (which can lead to system crashes). Here's a brief rundown of the software most likely to proliferate on a hard disk:

- Duplicate system files are a likely cause of operational glitches. Such duplicates often result when an entire startup disk is copied onto a hard disk. Use Find File or another search utility to extract files named System, Finder, Clipboard, ImageWriter, LaserWriter, or any related duplicate files.

- Desk Accessories and Fonts can often be found in multiple versions, since the act of installing them in the System file itself creates a copy. Once properly installed, the individual icon of the desk accessory or font does not need to be present anywhere on the hard disk (with the exception of downloadable fonts, which need to be placed in the System Folder). Look also for excess versions of the Font/DA Mover application.

- Temporary files are often created by applications (such as Microsoft Word) for a multitude of reasons, most notably to store as-yet-unsaved document changes and free up RAM. Once the changes have been saved by the user, these "temp" files are usually drained of their contents but not deleted from the Finder. Although most take up virtually no storage space, they do add to disk clutter and confusion. You can often find these discarded files in the System Folder. Temporary files usually display the default document icon, and have a title that indicates their parent application, such as "Word Temp 1" for Microsoft Word file.

WARNING

Before you permanently delete *any* file, however, make sure that you can do without it. In the case of a duplicate file, make sure that the one retained is the correct version. Two or more documents can share the same name, and the most-used copy of an application may not be the one with the most features. When in doubt, open the documents for perusal, and check the Get Info boxes of the applications for version numbers.

PROTECTING YOUR DATA

FEATURING:

→ **Archiving Files**

→ **Backup Utilities**

→ **Undelete and File Saving Utilities**

→ **Viruses and Remedies**

→ **Data Encryption**

→ **Hardware Security**

In this chapter, we'll turn to the issues of data preservation and security—how to ensure that your data is safe from accidental loss, unauthorized access, and corruption by "viruses" and other damaging software.

We'll begin by looking at using both floppy and hard disks in conjunction with your primary hard disk, both as a means of preserving your software and of backing up your complete work environment. We'll survey different preservation strategies and evaluate some of the more important features of backup software.

Next, we'll examine viruses and other rogue software: how to detect them, how to guard against them, and how to remove them from your system. Then we'll turn to an even thornier subject, human intrusion. We'll look at the strategies (and psychology) behind choosing and using passwords, and look at access-limiting software. Finally, we'll see how to protect your hard disk, as well as its contents, with hardware security systems.

Archives, Backups, and the Inevitable

It's important to note the distinction between archiving software and backing up your hard disk. Archiving consists of simply making sure that all files exist in duplicate form in a location other than the hard disk. Backing up ensures that all functional aspects of your hard disk are preserved along with the data: the System file setup, hierarchical organization, folder formats, etc. Archiving requires no special software but does require a systematic, disciplined approach; backup provide a more automatic, straightforward procedure.

Which is the right tactic for you? For the most part, it depends on the tasks for which you use your Macintosh. If you work with only a handful of document, database, or spreadsheet files over the course of a month, you may not need to invest in backup software. But if you regularly produce numerous new or updated documents, chances are you'll find a backup program to be an excellent investment.

No matter what your needs, there's a hard truth that can't be overemphasized: *data preservation is a necessary part of owning a hard disk.* It is as important to using a computer as adding oil and brake fluid is a necessary part of owning a car. As you have seen, a hard disk is not a solid-state unit, and at some point, it will stop working. Even if you have used your hard disk for years without incident, it's just a matter of time before it fails.

To be honest, preserving your data can be a hassle. It takes time, it takes money—if not for special software, then for floppy disks—and it rarely produces any visible benefit. It all seems to add up to wasted effort. Besides, you probably bought a hard disk just so you wouldn't have to juggle dozens of floppy disks.

But take a moment and consider the effort that went into creating the data stored on your hard disk. Unless you can afford to do it all over (if that's even possible), you can't afford to do without a data-protection scheme. At the risk of sounding overly pessimistic, I recommend that you think of it as insurance against the inevitable.

When and How Often?

Your data preservation schedule should be built around your work schedule. Still, the rule of thumb is, "If you can't afford to lose it, save it." Here are a few tips about saving documents.

- Save the document you are working on to your hard disk any time your work is interrupted for a more than a few minutes or if you need to leave your desk. Most programs recognize the ⌘-S keystroke combination for saving documents, and some have an auto-save option that automatically saves the document before a specified period of time. If you work under MultiFinder, you may wish to take the added precaution of saving a document every time you switch from one launched application to another.

- As an extra precaution, save an important document to a floppy disk as soon as it's completed. This is especially recommended for time-sensitive documents (such as a report you must submit the next day), since problems have a way of occurring when you least have time to deal with them. One good way to do this is to take a single floppy disk, label it something like "Current Work," and keep it in your floppy drive. Save the documents you work on to this disk as well as to the hard disk. By the time the disk fills up, you should have archived or backed up your hard drive, so you can safely trash the floppy's contents and start anew.

- Schedule regular back up sessions for a time when the task won't have to compete with other duties. Many people schedule their backups as the last agenda item on Friday, but all too often the task is put off in favor of last-minute obligations. It's better to schedule your backups as the first item on your least hectic weekday morning.

Archiving with Floppies

Most floppy disk-based archives consist of two parts: commercial data (applications, DAs, etc.) and personal data (your documents, folders, and custom resource files). This is a practical distinction to make, since each data type presents a separate challenge. Commercial files tend to take up more storage space, but since they are relatively static, they usually need to be archived only once. Personal files are usually smaller, but since they change more often, they need to be archived frequently.

Commercial Data

The best way to start your archive is by gathering the master floppies of your commercial data, the disks the software was packaged on. Run each disk briefly in the Mac to make sure that it has not been damaged or inadvertently erased.

To these, add disk copies of software without source disks—programs down-loaded from bulletin boards, shareware programs, and the like (Figure 5.1). Once these files have been copied, make sure that all your commercial software is clearly labeled and arranged in some useful order, such as alphabetically or in order of importance. You may also want to note as well which disks contain startup files.

Finally, copy your System Folder, configured to your preferences, to a fresh disk. Since it's easy to have a System Folder—or even a System file—that greatly exceeds a floppy's capacity, you may need to split the folder's contents over more than one disk. The System file itself can be shrunk by making a copy on the hard disk, and then using Font/DA Mover to purge it of Fonts and DAs, which you can then copy separately to a floppy disk. Don't forget to throw away the System duplicate on the hard disk when you have finished.

Personal Data

How you approach your personal data archive depends on three main factors: how much data you'll be dealing with, your organizational choice, and whether you have a file compression utility (discussed in Chapter 3). Any one of these factors can affect the others, and you should give your archive strategy a bit of careful consideration before proceeding. The better your plan fits your needs, the easier it will be to maintain.

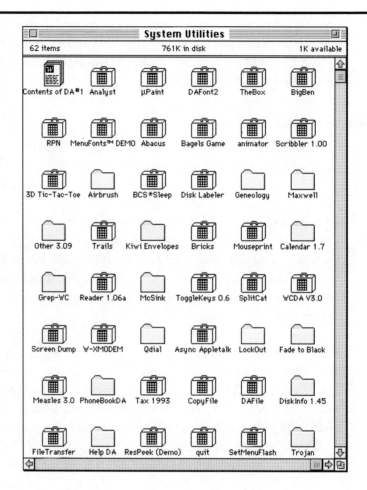

FIGURE 5.1

A floppy disk archive with commercial data; this one stores System preferences and related utilities

In choosing a strategy, keep in mind that the goal of archiving is to make your files available in the event of a mishap, not to replicate your hard disk's contents (that's what backups are for). You could simply copy every folder onto a floppy, but in a time of crisis, you could find yourself frantically juggling dozens of disks, trying to find a vital file.

You can categorize your data by subject, client, or project, and dedicate specific floppies for each category. This option is probably the easiest for locating specific files, but it uses significantly more floppies than other methods since the disks won't be consistently filled to capacity. It's also much more time-consuming since you'll need to update many disks. If this is the best viable approach for your data, you can reduce your floppy consumption through the judicious use of a compression utility (Figure 5.2).

For most users, the most efficient archive method is to organize files by date of creation. That way, you need to add only one new floppy at a time to the archive, with no need to update the previous archive disks. This take a little more time to set up at the start, but it's usually worth it; when used in combination with file compression, this method is probably the best use of your time and resources.

To establish a date-based archive, first consider just how difficult it'll be to organize your file on such a pattern, and then determine just how specific your archive needs to be. If you have, say, 50 megabytes of data on your hard disk, the task of placing them all in strict chronological order is far more daunting than if you have only 15 megabytes. And depending on your ability to locate files, you may be able to organize on the criteria of a single distinction: every file created up to now, as opposed to all files created in the future. Using a "librarian" utility such as DiskQuick (see next page) can make this location task easier.

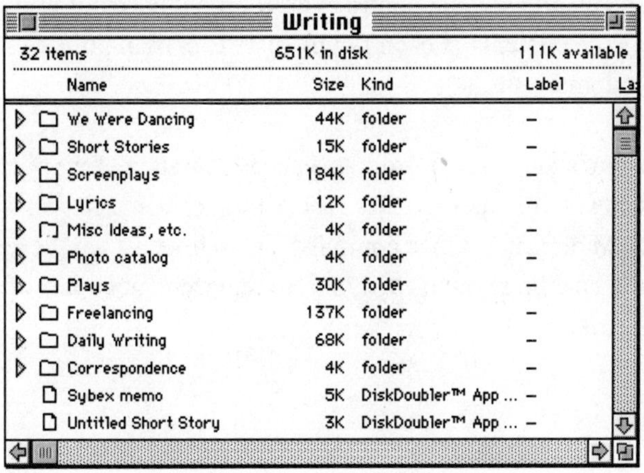

FIGURE 5.2

A floppy disk archive of personal data; note that two files have been compacted with a compression utility

Writing				
32 items	651K in disk		111K available	
Name	Size	Kind	Label	La
▷ ☐ We Were Dancing	44K	folder	–	
▷ ☐ Short Stories	15K	folder	–	
▷ ☐ Screenplays	184K	folder	–	
▷ ☐ Lyrics	12K	folder	–	
▷ ☐ Misc Ideas, etc.	4K	folder	–	
▷ ☐ Photo catalog	4K	folder	–	
▷ ☐ Plays	30K	folder	–	
▷ ☐ Freelancing	137K	folder	–	
▷ ☐ Daily Writing	68K	folder	–	
▷ ☐ Correspondence	4K	folder	–	
☐ Sybex memo	5K	DiskDoubler™ App ...	–	
☐ Untitled Short Story	3K	DiskDoubler™ App ...	–	

Once you've determined your archive standard, start by plowing through the folders on your hard disk, temporarily changing the view format of each folder window to View by Date. Take care to organize each folder by date last modified, not the date of creation. Copy your personal data to floppies, giving each disk a name that indicates the time period of its contents.

After you've finished the initial archive, you'll need to decide on a means of updating your archive. The best way is probably to move each new or modified file to a special folder and rearrange them in chronological order only after the transfer to a floppy has been made. If you need to restore your hard disk's contents from your date-based archive, be sure to load the floppies in strict date order, from earliest to latest. That way, the latest versions of files will automatically replace earlier versions; you should expect to see the "Replace existing file" dialog box quite often.

No matter what archival approach you take, sorting, shuffling, and copying a myriad of files is a tedious process—one only too conducive to oversight, error, and neglect. That's why archiving is recommended primarily for the user who has either a small amount of files or a large amount of discipline and free time. For the rest of us, it is more practical to streamline the process with backup software or hardware.

Using Librarian Utilities

Whatever strategy you choose, you'll probably find it useful to have a catalog listing the contents of each floppy disk. Librarian utilities such as DiskQuick do this automatically.

DiskQuick and similar programs act as "curators" for your archive, listing the contents of your archive disks according to such criteria as file size, creator ID, or RAM demands. Once compiled, an archive list can be appended or modified at will, enabling you to easily locate replacement copies of software when disaster strikes.

DiskQuick can keep track of the contents of your hard disk as well as your floppy-disk archive, and tag certain files for regular updating. The utility can also establish and maintain different storage reports, generating different files according to different standards. If your data is saved on a multitude of floppies, a volume librarian can be well worth the expense.

Backing Up Your Hard Disk

Archives require no specialized software, but their usefulness is limited. When it comes to hassle-free data preservation, backups beat archives hands down. Not only do backups save volume structure as well as file contents, their automation speeds up the process, enabling you to keep track of duplicates and restore lost data with a minimum of fuss and effort.

There are two classes of backups: floppy-based systems, which preserve your data on floppy disks; and hardware-based systems, which store data on another mass storage volume. The former is cost-effective but time-consuming, the latter expensive but efficient. The appropriate backup method for you depends on a number of factors: your budget, the value of your data, your work habits, and your degree of dedication to preventative maintenance.

Choosing Backup Software

There are many backup software packages offering a wide range of performance and features. A careful choice will go a long way toward making the process tolerable. Many manufacturers bundle their hard disks with a free backup program , and Apple includes an adequate one, HD Backup, with each System package (Figure 5.3). But as with many things, you get what you pay for. When evaluating backup software, you should look for at least some of these features:

- **Volume management.** Good backup software will work with floppies, other hard disks, and removable media storage (see Chapter 10). If floppies are used, it should calculate the number of disks necessary for the job, and prompt the user to insert new disks. It should evaluate each backup disk and halt the proceedings when

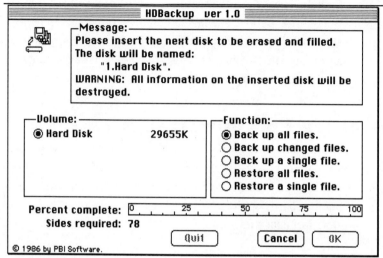

FIGURE 5.3
*Apple
Computer's HD
Backup utility*

something is amiss. The software should also rename or reinitialize floppies when the need arises, and automatically perform minor desktop and directory repairs.

- **Selective protection.** The user should be able to specify precisely which files should be backed up and in what fashion. A good program will identify all files that have been modified since the last backup, and copy those files that meet specific criteria. It's also desirable to have the flexibility to specify individual files when restoring damaged files from the backup.

- **Copy verification.** The backup utility shouldn't just make copies— it should test those copies to confirm that the new copy is an accurate reproduction. If a file is too big to fit on a single floppy disk or other storage volume, the software should be able to safely segment the file into smaller pieces, and splice them easily and accurately.

- **Speed and versatility.** Some backup software packages are feature-laden but slow, while others are swift but spartan. Most programs can back up 100 KB and 300 KB of data per minute, but some companies claim that their programs can handle nearly a megabyte per minute. Many backup programs also allow you to save files in various formats, from text-only to full compression and encryption.

- **Automation.** A good backup program can be set to initiate a backup at regular user-specified intervals. This minimizes the effect of human forgetfulness or procrastination, and also makes it possible to perform the backup at a time when the computer isn't used, such as late at night or after business hours. When automation is an option, make sure that the program provides adequate notification features in the event of an unsuccessful backup, including the information you need to proceed.

One popular program that meets all of the above criteria is Retrospect by Dantz Development. Retrospect can function not only as backup software, it can also compile and restore archives. It can read and write to nearly all storage formats, and it offers file compression and password protection. In fact, you can use Retrospect to back up *any* volume accessible from your Macintosh, including network file servers and drives on other networked Macs (Figure 5.4).

Floppy-based Backups

If you've chosen to back up your hard disk onto floppy disks, take a few precautions before plunging into the task. Calculate the number of floppies you'll need, allocating one double-sided volume for each 740 KB of data, or one high-density disk for every 1.25 MB of data. That's not the maximum capacity of either disk, but you don't want to fill every byte of space.

Fresh disks are preferable to used ones, but the latter will do fine as long as they're reliable and properly formatted. You don't need to reformat a used floppy, but make sure you delete its contents, rename it, and relabel it appropriately.

FIGURE 5.4

The Retrospect program can back up any volume directly connected or networked to your Macintosh

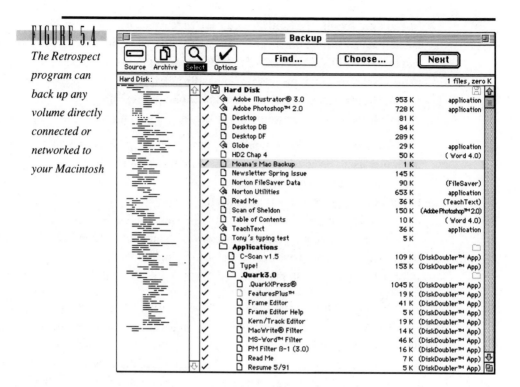

Make sure that the copy protection shutter is disabled. Test each floppy by copying, opening, and deleting documents in its directory while keeping a watch for unexpected results. It's tempting to retire marginal floppies to backup duty, but remember, your files are only as safe as your floppies are dependable.

Hardware-based Backups

Even with the best backup software, copying the contents from a hard disk to a stack of floppies is a bulky, cumbersome process. If your budget allows, you may want to take a look at the hardware options that can make the job of backing up data much easier and faster.

One obvious, but expensive, hardware solution is simply to buy another hard disk of the same capacity and add it to the SCSI daisychain. This will do the job, but it could prove problematic: if your storage needs to expand, you'll need to match each new volume with a companion backup drive. A more cost-effective solution would be to purchase a *removable media* device, which can backup all your storage volumes as your system grows. Removable media drives store data on some sort of high-capacity module, such as Digital Audio Tape (DAT) cassette, a large floppy-like disk, a CD-ROM disk, or a WORM drive. Each method has its own critics and champions. And since cost, features, and performance are all factors to be weighed when shopping for such devices, it's hard to declare any one format clearly superior to the others.

Some removable-media mass storage devices are designed especially for backup purposes. Others represent stand-alone alternatives to the hard disk, and a few are forerunners of the devices that may one day replace hard disks. The issues involved in making the proper choice for your system are discussed in Chapter 10.

Complete Backups

The backup process usually begins with a comprehensive copying effort, a foundation which later backups will update and augment. This takes time, but when done, it's easy to maintain. You'll want to do this once and do it right, so approach it with all the thoroughness you can muster.

If your backup program provides the option of excluding files, you may want to bypass much of your commercial data, since it's already stored on its original floppies. But before you do, run them from the original floppies to confirm that the files are functional and intact. Make sure you open the copy protection shutters on the floppies so that you don't unintentionally alter the files.

When deciding which data should go into the backup, remember that your startup System Folder and many of your applications may be modified according to your preferences, and should thus be preserved in their current incarnations. And don't forget to back up the software that may not have a proper source disk: shareware and public domain programs, the INITs, files, fonts, DAs, and other sundry programs that most Macintosh owners acquire almost without effort.

Unfortunately, the only sure way to test a complete backup is to use it to recreate your hard disk's contents, a task recommended only for those with ample spare time and a spare hard disk. Most backups use some form of file compression. You might compare the files on the floppies with those on the hard disk, watching for omissions and irregularities. If your backup application is capable of partial restorations, you should restore a file or folder or two, just for practice and self-assurance.

NOTE

> When your full backup has been completed, label the floppies clearly, set them aside from your other disks, and just let them be. Don't change any volume, file, or folder names. Don't attempt to open the backup files with any application other than the backup utility. And don't add to or diminish the contents of any of the floppies; a seemingly innocuous change could confuse the backup program and render your data reserves unreadable. You can, however, safely make direct disk-to-disk copies of your backup volumes, if you want an extra measure of security.

Incremental Backups

Once the basic backup of your entire hard disk has been completed, there's no need to go through the whole process again. All but the most primitive backup programs follow the initial session with incremental backups, in which, only the files that have been added or changed since the last session are added to the backup. If the "last modified" date of a file has changed, the backup software adds its to the backup.

The incremental strategy significantly speeds up later backups, but that's not all it offers. A full-featured program like Retrospect can catalog and store previous versions of files; if you want to retrieve a version of the file other than the latest version, you can do so.

The advantage of this soon becomes apparent. Say that you back up your data daily. Say also that for the past three days, you've made changes to an important file, but now you realize that you prefer the version from three days ago. With an incremental backup program, you can retrieve that copy of the file, as well as the versions from the later two days.

ARNING

Because incremental backups involve the modification of previously backed-up files, they can cause their own problems. If the new version is corrupted, or if the updating process is incorrectly executed, the resulting file can be garbled and unusable. Nonetheless, incremental backups are far more convenient than starting from scratch every time you back up your hard disk.

Restoring from a Backup

No matter what your backup strategy, the moment of truth comes when you must retrieve your data. A full-featured backup application should offer three restoration options: mirror restoration, second-volume restoration, and file-specific restoration.

A *mirror restoration,* when correctly executed, recreates the contents of the volume as if the hard disk never malfunctioned in the first place. The directory structure is recreated, and files are placed in their original location. This is the restoration option of choice when a disk itself has been successfully repaired following major damage or data loss.

A *second-volume restoration* copies the contents of one volume into the sub-directory of another volume. For example, the backup files of a 20 megabyte hard disk could be restored into a folder of an 80 megabyte drive. The files could then be accessed as normal. Once the 20 megabyte drive is repaired, the files could be transferred back in "mirror" form.

The final option is *file-specific restoration,* in which individual files or groups of files can be selected and recreated. This is the best approach when time is limited and you need access to only a few vital files.

You should note that none of the options are mutually exclusive. You should be able to perform them in any combination, and at any time.

Planning for Maximum Security

Whether you have used a floppy- or hardware-based system, chances are you now have a collection of disks or other removable media. Since the safety of your data rests in a large part upon the safety of this collection, you may want to take a few extra steps to minimize the possibility of mishaps.

- **Isolate your backups from your other data.** This is particularly true with floppy-based systems. Don't place your backup floppies in the same area as the disks you use for other tasks. Otherwise, you run the risk of one your backups disks being accidentally used for something else, like shuttling data between computers, especially if you're not the only one working with your Macintosh.

- **Enable the copy-protection tab.** In the upper right hand corner of every Macintosh-compatible floppy disk is the copy protection tab, a sliding plastic square (Figure 5.5). When the tab is slid down (so that you cannot see through the square window), the data can be read from and written to the disk. When placed up, the drive will only read data, but will not write changes to disk.

- **Store them away from the workplace.** Perhaps you want to guard against more than mechanical malfunction—perhaps your data is too valuable to risk being destroyed by fire, theft, or other catastrophe that affects your entire workplace. Consider storing your backup disks in another secure location entirely, such as your home, another office, or even a safe. Some people assign a briefcase or other carrying case just for floppies; carrying it back and forth whenever an update is needed. Floppy disks are remarkably tolerant of temperature and environment, but keep them away from extremes of heat and moisture, and from significant magnetic fields, such as those generated by refrigerators, microwave ovens, or other major appliances. If you decide to purchase a safe for storing your disks, you'll find that many manufacturers specify which models are particularly suited to the storage of magnetic media.

Preventative Software

Regular backups are the most thorough insurance against data loss, but they have one drawback: they can only restore your data to the condition it was in at the time of the backup. Even if you back up your data every day, your data remains unprotected for a 23-hour period—ample time for disasters to occur. Files can become unreadable for no apparent reason, your Mac may simply refuse to acknowledge your hard disk, or you might throw away a file and then realize how important it is—or rather, was.

Fortunately, preventative utilities, designed to work *transparently* (that is, in the background, while you do your normal work) fill this critical gap. One software package, the Norton Utilities, dominates this field. This set of programs is is so

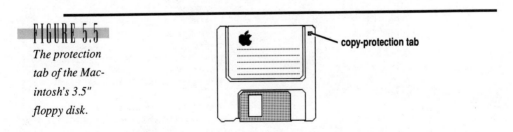

FIGURE 5.5
*The protection tab of the Macintosh's 3.5"
floppy disk.*

copy-protection tab

useful that I strongly recommend them for every single Macintosh hard disk user. We'll explore the Norton Utilities in more detail in the next chapter, but for now let's focus on those utilities devoted to rescuing damaged or deleted files. (Sum II also includes an "unerase" feature; it is discussed in Chapter 7.)

Working with Norton Utilities' UnErase

The Norton Utilities' UnErase (Figure 5.6) does what its name says: it actually "unerases" files after you have emptied the Trash. It's even possible to delete the entire contents of a hard disk, and then make the files reappear. (But don't do this without taking the proper precautions!)

UnErase takes advantage of the fact that the Macintosh doesn't *really* erase most files; instead, it just erases the file's identity from the Volume Information Block, and declares that the space occupied by the file is available for use by other files. Until that space is actually overwritten, the file's data is still on the disk. UnErase pieces together the erased Volume Information Block data, usually based on clues in the file itself.

FIGURE 5.6

The Norton Utilities' UnErase feature can literally restore files that have been deleted

Name	Data	Rsrc	Modified Date	Type	Creator	Recoverability
Photoshop		1K	12/08/92 18:07	fdrp	MACS	Excellent
Ponde		27K	7/18/90 10:01	LWFN	ASPF	Excellent
Prese		43K	3/20/89 10:49	LWFN	ASPF	Excellent
QuarkXPress®		1K	1/09/92 18:36	adrp	XPRS	Poor
QuoruBla		40K	2/14/90 12:08	LWFN	ASPF	Excellent
QuoruBol		39K	2/14/90 12:08	LWFN	ASPF	Excellent
QuoruBoo		38K	2/14/90 12:07	LWFN	ASPF	Excellent
QuoruLig		37K	2/14/90 12:07	LWFN	ASPF	Excellent
QuoruMed		38K	2/14/90 12:07	LWFN	ASPF	Excellent
Read Me		1K	1/12/93 15:04	HAMd	HAMw	Poor
Read Me		1K	1/12/93 15:03	HAMd	HAMw	Poor
Read Me		1K	1/12/93 15:03	HAMd	HAMw	Poor
Readme.asc		1K	12/18/92 10:16	HAMd	HAMw	Excellent
Readme/Edit		1K	12/18/92 9:59	HAMd	HAMw	Excellent

Norton UnErase™

UnErase » 27K selected

Hard Disk   Hard Disk   View File   Get Info   Sort

UnErase is an valuable utility, but it isn't a panacea. It can only rescue a file that hasn't been overwritten. The less free space is you have on your hard disk, the more likely it is that your Macintosh has completely obliterated the file by writing new information to the old file's blocks. Even if the file hasn't been overwritten, there is no guarantee that UnErase will be able to recover the file. The utility relies upon information contained within the erased file itself to reconstruct the file; that information is rarely sufficient for the task. Therefore, you should use a *file information saver* to increase your chances of recovering erased files.

File Information Savers

File information savers aren't stand-alone utilities. They work in the background, intercepting information regarding erased files and storing it away for later use by recovery utilities.

The most popular and powerful file information savers are FileSaver, part of the Norton Utilities, and Shield, part of the Symantec Utilities for the Macintosh II (SUM II). Once installed, these utilities (and others like them) work in the background; you won't see any evidence of them except the occasional appearance of a special icon.

Configuring FileSaver

FileSaver is an INIT that is automatically installed during the general installation process of Norton Utilities. If you would like to take advantage of its protection, use the Norton Install utility or drag a copy of FileSaver to the volume's System Folder. (If you are using System 7, the Macintosh will place the file in the Control Panel's subdirectory for you.) When you reboot, the FileSaver window can be opened from the Control Panel's menu (Figure 5.7).

After you have installed FileSaver, you must configure and activate it. You have the following configuration choices:

- **Save Finder's "Get Info" comments.** If turned on, this feature will protect the information entered into a file's Get Info box. Normally, that text is lost whenever the desktop is rebuilt.

FIGURE 5.7
*The FileSaver
control panel*

- **Save Format Recover and UnErase info.** Since format recovery and erased file retrieval are two of the most important powers of the Norton Utilities, you'll want to select this option.

- **FileSaver.** This button switches protection on and off. Although you'll want to leave FileSaver on, this option allows you to disable it temporarily while retaining your user settings.

- **How many files?** The slide bar lets you specify the number of erased files you want FileSaver to keep track of; you can set it from a minimum of 0 to a maximum of 500. The larger the number, the more hard disk space FileSaver will need to store file information, and the longer it will take to periodically update that file. Note that the prospective size of the file changes as you move the slider up and down. Unless you have a extremely large number of files on the volume, a selection between 200 and 400 will probably be adequate.

You can also opt to hide the FileSaver icon during the startup process, but it's a good idea to keep it displayed. That way, it's easier to keep track of which volumes have protection, and which don't.

Once you're satisfied with your user settings, click on the Save button. After a short pause, FileSaver's special file for that volume will be created. Then, if you would like to extend the same protection to another online volume, click on the Drive button until that volume's icon appears. Click Save again and that volume will be protected as well.

Working with FileSaver and other portions of the Norton Utilities is discussed in further detail in Chapter 7.

Configuring Shield

Shield, the file protection component of SUM II, works similarly to FileSaver. Its protection is broken down into three parts, and you can choose to enable any combination of them. You can also specify exactly how Shield should update its information.

Use the SUM II Installer utility to install Shield, making sure that both Deleted File Record and Volume Restore Record are checked during the process. Then, reboot your Mac and select Shield from the Control Panel menu (Figure 5.8). Aside from "Show icon at startup," you'll find three configuration options:

- **Volume Protection Active.** This selection acts as a sort of security guard for your hard disk, intercepting some types of viruses and overriding potentially damaging operations that can be triggered by corrupted or damaged software.

- **File Recovery Active.** This is Shield's "undelete" feature. Keep it active if you want to increase the likelihood of retrieving erased files. If this option is disabled, the names and locations of files will not be recorded when the Trash is emptied.

- **Volume Recovery Active.** This is Shield's directory recovery feature. If you select it, make sure you also set the Volume Save options.

FIGURE 5.8

The Shield

control panel

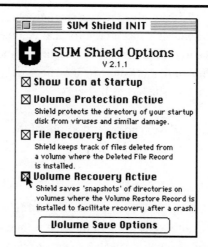

The Volume Save Options window is a dialog box that enables you to control when and where the Volume Restore file will be saved (Figure 5.9). Although the default choice of "Update Record on Shutdown" is adequate for most users, you can also change this setting to one that better fits your needs.

- **Save the information about this volume on another volume.** This option creates a second copy of Shield's Volume Restore file to a specified volume, which is a good insurance policy in case damage to the first volume renders the original Volume Restore file unusable.

- **Update the file with a keystroke command.** With this option, you can set a "hot key" consisting of ⌘, Option and a third character that when pressed simultaneously will instantly update the Volume Restore file.

- **Update at Specified Intervals.** You can instruct Shield to update the Volume Restore file at regular, specified intervals. When the specified time has elapsed, Shield produces a warning sound and suspends your current activity while the Volume Restore update is underway. During the update, the Shield icon appears on the screen.

This is the most thorough means of protection, but it can slow down your normal operations.

One final note: Shield can interfere with the installation of certain programs, including Aldus PageMaker and Persuasion. For that reason, it's a good idea to remove the Shield INIT from your System Folder and reboot before proceeding with any installation that requires the use of a special installation program (as opposed to the simple copying of files from floppy disk to hard drive). But after the installation is completed, don't forget to return the INIT to the System Folder and reboot before proceeding!

Working with Shield and other portions of SUM II is discussed in further detail in Chapter 7.

Automated File Savers

Another useful utility is the automated file saver, which seeks to overcome human carelessness and unexpected events by saving a file in the background without waiting for the Save command.

FIGURE 5.9

The Volume Save Options dialog box

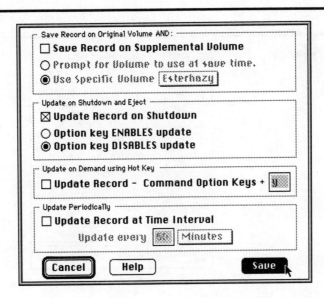

Working with NowSave

NowSave (Figure 5.10), part of the Now Utilities package, is a CDEV that performs a simple task: it silently issues a Save command at regular intervals when you are inside of an application. You can set the interval to be set in terms of minutes, keystrokes or mouse clicks, and you can set different intervals for different applications.

The main drawback to an autosave utility like NowSave is that it completely overwrites the original file; once a new version has been saved, there's no way to return to a previous version. Sometimes an automatic save can be unwelcome: you could be experimenting with a graphic file, or rewriting a passage, and finally decide that the original version was better. In recognition of this, NowSave allows you to configure it to turn itself off if a file's name begins with, matches, contains, or doesn't contain a specified text string.

Working with Last Resort

Strictly speaking, Last Resort (Figure 5.11) isn't an "autosave" utility; it doesn't simply issue a Save command. Instead, it saves every keystroke you type into a separate text file. These files are arranged in chronological order and

FIGURE 5.10

The NowSave

utility CDEV

NowSave	
NowSave	3.0.1
Esterhazy SC+A	Now Software

Application	⏱	⌨	🗄	
✓ Word 4.0	5m	--	--	⬆
				⬇

Add Apps...	Remove
Configure...	Prefs...

placed in a folder named "Last Resort D," which is in the Preferences subfolder of the System Folder.

What's the use of such a file? Say you're putting the finishing touches on a memo, but before you can save it, a bomb box appears, or a power outage occurs. Your word processing document won't reflect the most recent changes, but the Last Resort file will. And since it saves your keystrokes in simple text format, the file can be opened by most word processing applications, enabling you to cut and paste the missing characters into your original document.

Last Resort should be viewed as just that—a last resort. Since it only saves text, it's not useful for graphics or sound files. Furthermore, since only the keystrokes themselves are saved, any special formatting (fonts, size, boldface, etc.) is lost. You'll also have to weed out the meaningless characters resulting from the pressing the backspace or delete keys—Last Resort saves *all* characters, including those that you later removed.

Viruses and Other Rogue Software

Before 1988, the realm of misleading, mischievous, and malicious programming was virtually unknown to Macintosh users: viruses and related programs

---

FIGURE 5.11

The Last Resort utility CDEV

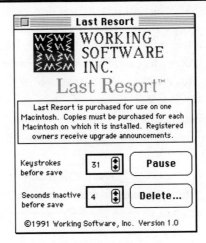

were an obscure subject in software engineering classes and an occasional topic for computer professionals. Although their presence had been reported on mainframes and other systems, rogue software seemed more a part of folklore than reality.

Then, almost overnight, their reality became all too apparent. A virus spawned in Canada began to appear on Macintoshes in several countries within a few weeks of its initial release. At the same time, at least one "Trojan horse" caused considerable grief among users in the US. The ensuing furor produced a lot of indignation, a little bit of panic, a few court cases, and the realization that Macintosh computing would no longer be the same. Relatively few people have been significantly affected by illicit Macintosh software, but even fewer can afford to ignore the issue it presents.

What Is a Virus?

Although it is often used to describe any code created with devious intent, the term "virus" refers a specific type of program that's been around (at least in concept) since the earliest days of computing: software that, like its biological equivalent, can spread from one host to another. A virus usually installs itself on a system without the user's knowledge. It then proceeds to quietly place copies of itself on any storage volume it comes into contact with—hard disks as well as floppies. When one of these volumes is later connected to another computer, the process begins anew.

A virus can also do more than reproduce itself—it can carry code designed to do a specific task, such as writing a message to the screen. After writing the message, the virus can then self- destruct, wiping out all evidence of its existence. Viruses do have their limitations, though—the code must be kept small in order to remain unobtrusive, and the program must be designed to anticipate and adapt itself to all possible operating system permutations.

Viruses were first presented as an intellectual exercise, a conceptual demonstration of the fact that computers, like humans, can be said to have "health" that exists as a function of an "ecology." The idea was an irresistible challenge to at least a few programmers, and system administrators soon incorporated testing for rogue software into their regular duties. But for decades, it seemed that viruses would remain limited to only mainframe and other large-scale systems, where the sheer bulk of processing tasks occasionally allowed them to slip through.

Why are viruses now afflicting microcomputers? There are a number of reasons. The personal computer boom has wrought a flood of new programmers, many of whom relish a challenge as much as their predecessors. Sophisticated programming languages have made it possible to pack more code into increasingly smaller packages. And since the success of a microcomputer relies in large part on how much third-party software is available for it, manufacturers have given programmers far more access to specialized information about circuitry and design than ever before.

But why has the Macintosh been especially hard hit? Part of the reason is the Toolbox architecture of Mac software, which enables small, illicit programs to complete a big job done simply by issuing commands to the ROM; on other PCs, the rogue program would need to include all the code necessary to do the job itself. Another factor is the Mac user interface, which makes some applications easy to use without documentation—which in turn makes it easier for users to use and pass along shareware, public domain software, and pirated software. Yet another reason is the proliferation of ties between Mac users; these can be social in nature (user groups), physical (local area networks), or electronic (modem-accessible bulletin board systems).

The Macintosh community responded swiftly and effectively to the first wave of viruses. A number of free or shareware utilities were created and distributed, by both individual programmers and Apple Computer. The custodians of bulletin boards started meticulously policing their contents. Commercial products began to incorporate tools for virus detection and removal.

A few years after their initial onslaught, it appears that the incidence of Macintosh viruses is on the wane. Perhaps the novelty of programming them is wearing off, or perhaps the "fun" of rogue software hacking has been spoiled by the effectiveness of anti-viral software—not to mention the stiff fines and sentences the courts have handed down to those convicted of such activities.

But the battle isn't over yet, and it's unlikely that it will be for the foreseeable future. Even the most effective virus-fighting resource can only find what it's been taught to look for; it may be helpless against programs that behave differently. Experts have cracked the secrets of the current crop, but viruses belonging to entirely new categories may eventually appear.

Should You Worry?

Viruses and their ilk are a cause for concern—but not worry, much less panic. Despite the large amount of alarmist attention placed on them, you're probably best off viewing them as just another factor to be addressed in your overall data protection strategy. With a little preventative effort, you can rest assured that your system is (and will remain) virus-free.

But do you really need to go to such an effort? Probably— even if you don't usually deal with networks, user groups, or bulletin boards.

You may not think of your Macintosh as belonging to a vast interconnected network, but only the most isolated users are completely immune from viral contagion. Just about every software source has been found to be infected at one time or another: electronic bulletin boards, shareware, even commercial programs fresh from the manufacturer. It's best to consider yourself at risk; even an apparently blank floppy could carry a virus.

What sort of threat to your data do viruses represent? So far most of the Macintosh viruses have been more or less benign, often doing nothing more than announcing their presence and promptly self-destructing. But even these programs represent an unanticipated presence on the system, and as such can inadvertently cause problems ranging from minor performance slowdowns to a hang up of the system. Furthermore, any virus is fully capable of taking command of the system or its online volumes; only restraint on the part of the programmer can keep it from causing lasting damage to your data.

Worms, Booby Traps, and Trojan Horses

There are three other types of rogue programs to watch out for, software designed to wreak havoc on the unsuspecting. Unlike viruses, they aren't self-replicating; they use other means of transmission. In Macintosh world, none of these types are as common as viruses, but their potential for destruction is just as great.

Worms are quite similar to viruses, and can in fact be written as a kind of virus. The main difference is methodology; while a virus reproduces itself one copy at a time, a worm produces a rapid population boom. Once activated, a worm can quickly occupy all available storage space and overwhelm the computer.

Booby traps rely on human curiosity to lure their victims by masquerading as an enticing piece of software. Typically these files have a name calculated to titillate (such as "Sex Survey") or convey confidentiality ("Corporate Espionage Report"). Once launched, a booby trap shows its true colors, often triumphantly declaring the nature and extent of the damage it has inflicted. Some booby traps are benign, but others have been known to cause irreversible harm.

By the time a booby trap goes off, it's often too late. But if you're suddenly faced with an unusual or ominous screen display—or other evidence that something's amiss—don't just wait to see what happens. Turn off the power as fast as you can, by flicking the power switch or even by pulling the cord out of the Mac or the wall socket. You can experiment with the suspect file further, but only when you're running from a floppy and all other volumes are safely offline.

Trojan horses are more subtle in their methods. Instead of merely pretending to be something else, they actually function as advertised. But at the same time, they also carry out other covert tasks. Trojan horses have taken the form of spreadsheets, word processing documents, and HyperCard stacks, and their unauthorized results have included everything from a simple message ("Gotcha!") to the erasure of an entire hard disk.

Because of their innocuous image, these programs can be especially insidious, quietly engineering changes that don't manifest themselves until days, weeks, of even months afterward. Like booby traps, Trojan horses are potentially more dangerous than viruses; they can contain more damaging commands since they're not confined to the size limitations required of an invisible file.

Fortunately, both booby traps and Trojan horses tend to be far less common than viruses and worms. They're disseminated only by intentional copying, and when one betrays its true nature, the news usually travels swiftly. The threat can usually be nipped in the bud by simply trashing the file. Some anti-virus utilities will check for boobie traps and Trojans as well, but the best way to guard against them is by testing new software before placing it on your hard disk (although you probably don't have to worry about brand new, profession-ally-produced software on an official master disk).

The "Scores" Viruses

The most common virus is the *Scores* variety, so called because it often places an invisible file of that name in the System Folder. The Scores virus behaves un-predictably: some Macs infected with it will display no ill effect, while others will undergo a severe degradation of performance. Problems commonly as-sociated with Scores are difficulties in using the Set Startup option, and in run-ning or printing from MacDraw. The virus has also been blamed for damaging MacDraw and Excel files, and for causing frequent system crashes.

The easiest way to check for the presence of a Scores virus is to examine the contents of your System Folder using the View by Icon format. Look for the Scrapbook or Note Pad resource files; their icons should look like miniature Macintoshes (Figure 5.12, left). If, instead, they look like documents (Fig-ure 5.12, right), it's likely that your system is infected. But the visual check is not a totally accurate indicator. If you still suspect the presence of the virus, there are two ways you can probe further.

The easiest way is to use a special utility such as Virus RX or Ferret that specifi-cally targets Scores viruses (see "Antiviral Utilities" below). The other method is to use ResEdit to examine the invisible files on your system. ResEdit is a

FIGURE 5.12

Scores viruses change resource files from custom icons (left) to default icons (right)

Finder   Finder

powerful program that should be used with caution; its use is described in Chapter 7.

If you're familiar with ResEdit, you can use it to open and examine the System Folder. You may see a number of invisible files, but you should be concerned only with ones named "Scores," "2 Virus ResEd," or "Desktop"—any one of these files is a symptom of Scores. Don't confuse a "Desktop" file nested in the System Folder with a file of the same name placed on the root level of your volume; the root-level "Desktop" file is supposed to be there, and should not be disturbed.

If a Scores virus is the diagnosis, the only treatment is radical surgery. Advanced users who are thoroughly familiar with the inner workings of the Macintosh may be able to use ResEdit or Norton Utilities' Disk Editor to eradicate all traces of the virus. Some commercial applications such as Virex or SAM do this automatically. Otherwise, your only recourse is to completely replace all of the applications on the infected volume.

To remove Scores, start by disposing of the complete contents of the System Folder; you can use the Font/DA Mover to extract installed fonts and desk accessories if necessary, but everything else should go. Then delete all applications (not your documents, just the applications), taking as much care as possible to ensure that they all are removed. Scores not only tries to reside in the System Folder, but in every application as well, and a single infected application could reinfect the entire volume.

Once the System and all applications have been eliminated, you can install fresh copies of the files on the volume and proceed as usual. But before you consider the crisis passed, check once again for a possible reoccurrence of Scores—the copy you used to restore an application may have been the original source of the infection!

nVIR Viruses

The second most common type of viruses belong to the *nVIR* genre; they're much less prevalent than Scores but more difficult to detect. Fortunately, they're not as disruptive or destructive.

Like Scores, nVIRs attach themselves to the resource files of applications, creating a unique resource with the "nVIR" ID. It also places its own INIT in the System Folder, which is then accessed whenever an infected application is launched. In most cases, this INIT does little more than cause the Macintosh to emit a beep during startup; if you have the MacinTalk speech synthesis application, you may hear the beep replaced with a calm voice saying, "Don't panic."

There *is* no need to panic. The nVIR virus is more a nuisance than a menace, and once again rehabilitation is a simple matter of removing and replacing the infected applications and System Folder. Some utilities such as Interferon (a shareware program) may be able to remove the virus without erasing your files (see below). Once eliminated, you'll need to check periodically for a reoccurrence of the virus. nVIR is exceptionally tenacious and can reappear even when you thought you had thoroughly removed it.

WDEF Viruses

The *WDEF* virus, named after the Macintosh Toolbox resource it infects (Window DEFinition), appeared in late 1989. It spread rapidly because it was the first virus that could replicate itself without any action being taken by the user. Any time an uninfected volume is mounted on an infected Macintosh, WDEF virus automatically copies itself to the volume.

Two strains of the WDEF virus have been detected to date. WDEF-A works silently, whereas WDEF-B emits a single beep whenever it infects a new volume. Both strains infect the invisible Desktop file, which the Finder uses to locate such information as directory contents and display formats. Although the WDEF virus doesn't appear to cause any intentional damage—its sole purpose seems to be to propagate itself—but there have been reports of WDEF causing crashes on the IIci, the original Macintosh Portable, and on any Macintosh which has 8 MB of RAM installed. Problems with displaying fonts and crashes while saving files under MultiFinder have also been attributed to the virus.

Recent antiviral utilities, such as Disinfectant and SAM, can detect the WDEF virus, but earlier utilities like Vaccine and GateKeeper often do not recognize it. Once detected, WDEF can be removed with a virus utility, or by simply rebuilding the desktop file (hold down the ⌘ and Option keys when starting up your hard drive, or when mounting another volume).

INIT-29 Virus

Dating back to 1988, the *INIT-29* virus distinguished itself as the first virus to attack documents as well as applications. As with WDEF, it seems to have been intended as a harmless virus, existing only for self-perpetuation. It can infect a volume whenever a file (application or document) is copied from an infected source.

The virus gets its name from its the fact that it installs itself in one of the Toolbox INIT resources, the one with an ID code of 29. Although the virus is usually benign, it's possible that an infected document could be adversely affected since the virus expunges the file's legitimate INIT number 29. SAM and recent versions of Virex and Disinfectant will detect and remove the INIT-29 virus.

ANTI Virus

Unlike other Macintosh viruses which operate by stealthily adding to the code of a file, the *ANTI* virus simply modifies existing portions of the code. This makes it especially difficult to detect and remove.

The ANTI virus, first discovered in France, is considered by some experts to have been written as part of a copy-protection plan. It replaces the initial portion of some applications with itself, so that the virus itself is accessed every time the application is launched. Once accessed, it infects a portion of the active RAM, and then infects other applications when they are launched. If left unchecked, the ANTI virus can infect every single application on your hard disk.

The virus doesn't appear to be intentionally destructive, but in order to operate, it makes certain assumptions about the structure of applications. If an application's code does not meet those assumptions, the application can either escape infection…or crash upon launching. Most commercial antiviral products can hunt down and eliminate ANTI.

ZUC Virus

Like ANTI, the *ZUC* virus does not simply add its code to applications, but instead modifies existing portions of the program. ZUC, which first emerged in Italy in early 1990, is especially virulent: it can infect applications even before they're launched, and it's designed to intentionally impair your working ability on the Macintosh.

Before March 2, 1990, ZUC was a "sleeper" virus, replicating itself with no outward symptoms of infection. But on that date, it sprang into action—much to the chagrin of Mac users. Since then, a ZUC-infested application usually displays the following behavior. Starting about 90 seconds after the application is launched, the cursor will behave erratically whenever the mouse button is depressed. The cursor may careen across the screen in random directions, rebounding every time it hits the edge of the screen. This quirk disappears when the mouse button is released. In addition, ZUC has been known to change the desktop pattern on some Macintoshes, and to cause sluggish performance and unusually high disk activity.

The ZUC virus works by raiding the Desktop file, but it doesn't infect the file itself. Instead, it determines the location of all applications on the volume. It then checks the applications against an internal "avoid" list (which includes some antiviral programs). If an application isn't on the list, it gets infected. Most commercial antiviral programs released after March 2, 1990 incorporate protection against the ZUC virus, but you should check before purchasing; since ZUC uses its "avoid" list to steer clear of them, earlier utilities may not work.

Dukakis Virus

The very name of the *Dukakis* virus dates itself. As you might imagine, it emerged in 1988, as the Presidential campaign of that year was drawing to a close. The Dukakis virus is noteworthy because it afflicts HyperCard exclusively; when you open an infected file (or stack, in HyperCard terminology), a message box appears declaring "Dukakis for President." Aside from its persistent (and now irrelevant) electioneering, the virus appears to do no harm.

The Dukakis virus is hard to detect with most antiviral utlities because it makes legitimate use of HyperTalk, the scripting language for HyperCard. HyperTalk makes it easy to write stacks that exchange information with other stacks, and even modify them when necessary. For that reason, you'll have to remove the virus yourself, by following these steps:

1. In the Home stack of your copy of HyperCard, set the User Level to 5 (Scripting). If you don't know how to do this, check your software documentation.

2. Open one of the infected stacks (your Home stack is a good place to start), then select Stack Info from the Objects menu. A dialog box will appear.

3. In the dialog box, click on the Script button. This brings up a display of the HyperTalk commands used to write this stack.

4. Click the "Find" button and search for "on openStack". Be sure to follow the unconventional spacing and capitalization.

5. This should lead you to the HyperTalk text containing the offending command. Select and delete the entire HyperTalk text, and then click OK.

6. Close the stack, and do not reopen it until all other stacks on your system are similarly cleaned up (if you reopen it before then, you'll only reinfect it).

7. Repeat the above steps on all other stacks. In many cases, it might be easier to replace than repair files; if you do copy over with fresh versions of stacks, don't launch them until *all* other stacks have been cleared of the virus. Otherwise the new copies will also be infected.

Antiviral Utilities

Almost as soon as viruses hit the Macintosh community, utilities were written to aid in detecting and combating them. Most of these programs were free or shareware, provided by prominent programmers more or less as a public service. Those programs have since been joined by commercial products, most notably Symantec Antivirus for the Macintosh (SAM) and Virex.

It's a good idea to make an investment in commercial antiviral software, even though shareware programs such as Virus Rx and Interferon are readily available from bulletin boards and Macintosh user groups. Shareware programs usually run only at the user's initiative, whereas most commercial programs operate passively, either during idle moments or when a new volume comes online. When properly configured, SAM, Virex, and other such programs can stand at constant vigil. They're also more likely to be continually upgraded, to fight more recent virus strains as they're discovered.

Working with SAM

SAM can run as a stand-alone application, but it also functions as a CDEV, with a number of user-configurable options. Instead of monitoring for virus *types,* it looks for suspicious software *activity,* particularly attempts to bypass, modify, or replace portions of the operating system. The window in Figure 5.13, which appears when the "Custom" option is selected, shows the general range of activity SAM monitors. The user can also indicate when scans for viruses should be made (on startup or shutdown, or when a floppy is inserted), and what areas should be scanned (the System Folder, the startup volume, or all mounted volumes).

Such coverage is certainly comprehensive, but it can lead to some confusion, since legitimate software can sometimes make "suspicious" modifications to the operating system. For instance, the addition of an INIT file to the System Folder can trigger a warning message from SAM, alerting you that an attempt has been made to "Add startup resource." Since the modification is valid, you'll want to click Allow.

For all its thoroughness, the SAM CDEV is essentially a warning system. It won't identify and remove a virus—it'll just let you know that unusual things are happening with the system software. It's up to you to determine if those actions are indeed illegitimate, and what steps (if any) you should take. If you do

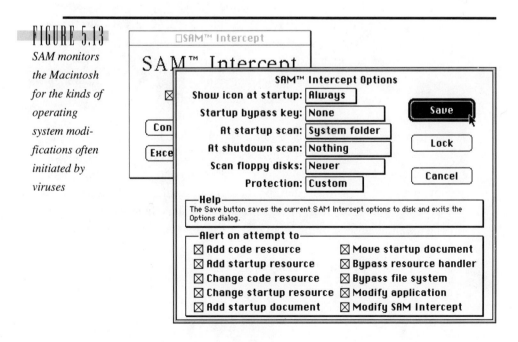

FIGURE 5.13

*SAM monitors
the Macintosh
for the kinds of
operating
system modifications often
initiated by
viruses*

decide to remove the virus, you can do so with the stand-alone application SAM Virus Clinic.

Online But Off Limits: Access Limitation

Thus far, we've covered the topics of protecting your data from accidental loss (with archiving and backups) and from other software (viruses and related programs). But there's another security factor that needs to be addressed: the human element.

For most people, a hard disk greatly enhances their work: it's the equivalent of a file cabinet in a compact, easily accessible package. But unlike a locked file cabinet, a hard disk can be easily accessed, tampered with, and even stolen. Work made easier by a mass storage unit can be made impossible by that unit's disappearance.

Your archive or backup storage may mean that your data isn't lost forever, but that's small consolation when replacing an expensive hard drive, or dealing with the prospect that sensitive information may have fallen into the wrong hands. Access limitation is a must for sensitive work, but it's also useful for anyone who just wants to keep some part of the system out of reach of certain people. Security technology is used by Macintoshes in the Pentagon—but it's also used by parents who want to let their children play on the computer, but don't want important files to be accidentally modified in the process.

There are three main approaches to access limitation: *password protection, data encryption,* and *physical security devices.* Password protection is the most straightforward and limited of the trio: it just refuses to mount a volume (or sometimes, to complete the startup process) without the proper password. Data encryption software uses a variety of mathematical methods to scramble the contents a file, unscrambling it only when the right commands are given. Physical security devices employ the brute force strategy, limiting hardware and/or software access by simply locking up the device.

Which Security Type Is the Best for You?

Of the three, which type of security meets your needs? Depending on the circumstances and the actual products available to you, your strategy may incorporate one, two, or all three of the methods.

Even though it makes no changes to the data it protects, password protection is generally considered an effective security technique. It's theoretically possible that an expert system cracker could, given ample time and equipment, copy some of those files to an unprotected disk; however, that would still be quite a feat. Most password-protected hard disks are so secure that if you forget the password, you may have no further recourse than to erase its entire contents with a magnetic field and start over.

Once installed, password protection is convenient, usually adding no more than a few seconds to the startup process. But it's not going to keep anyone from stealing the drive itself.

For those who need more flexibility in their security, data encryption offers a better solution. An encrypted file can be transferred and transmitted just like any other file—you can copy it to a floppy disk, post it on a network, or even download it from a bulletin board. But unless the person possessing a copy knows the keywords required to unscramble it, it'll amount to nothing more than a waste of storage space.

Encryption has a few drawbacks. It takes time during both the encoding and decoding processes. In addition, a secured file usually takes up more space than its normal counterpart. Some users may be a little disturbed by the fact that encrypted files can be duplicated freely, but there's no need to worry. Even with another copy of the encryption program, the most brilliant Mac hacker won't be able to overcome the scrambling scheme.

If the primary goal is to keep your hard disk in your possession, a properly installed physical security device can be a sound investment. Some devices, such as cabling systems, do little more than anchor your equipment to another, bulkier object, while others use metal bars and bands to make the system unusable when locked.

Such devices may foil the typical thief looking to make a quick getaway, but that doesn't mean they're foolproof. The locks tend to be no more complicated than what an experienced lock-picker would encounter elsewhere, and chains and cables need only to be cut. Given time and determination, a person could probably overcome such security—especially if they don't mind mutilating the Macintosh in order to extract its internal hard disk. Still, there's no safer alternative to prevent theft, save locking the system away in a safe.

WARNING

> Keep in mind that all access limitation products in the current Macintosh marketplace share one limitation: they might be able to keep others from reading or stealing your data, but they can't be counted on to keep your data from being destroyed. As with any magnetic media device, all it takes is a sufficiently strong magnetic field to blank out a hard disk. Extremes of heat will usually achieve the same effect by buckling the disk's platters or melting their coating. If the possibility of such a catastrophe concerns you, your best insurance is an up-to-date, safely stored backup.

Password Protection

When evaluating password-protection software, keep your eye on a number of features. A versatile program will accommodate multiple authorized users, as well as multiple passwords. It should also be compatible with all other user-customized aspects of the startup process, especially MultiFinder's Set Startup options. Another big advantage is a means of overriding the program (usually by means of a special floppy) in the event the volume is malfunctioning or the password has been lost.

All software-based methods of access limitation, no matter how sophisticated the programming, have a weakness that can't be eliminated: they rely on passwords or other user-defined codes. Even the fiercest protection strategy can be only as secure as the secret that controls it, just as an elaborate burglar alarm poses no problem to a thief who has its key.

When working with a password program, your biggest challenge will likely be the password itself—what to choose, when to change it, and where to record it in case it's forgotten. As you'll soon see, these tasks take us from the realm of technology to psychology.

Selecting a Password

You'll want a password that's easy to remember, but keep in mind that phrases which strike you as appropriate may strike others as obvious. If you're an avid golfer, for instance, stay away from passwords like "fore" or "birdie." There's nothing wrong with a password that holds a particular connotation for you, but the subject it evokes shouldn't be one that others would associate with you. Your co-workers may be thoroughly familiar with your interests and affinities, but it's unlikely that they know the name of the boy who sat at the desk directly in front of you in your seventh grade math class.

TIP

The ideal password is a word, term or phrase that is personally meaningful and therefore memorable, but so far removed from its original context as to place it beyond the reach of the educated guesser.

When choosing a password, stay away from the following types. These are among the most popular choices, and some "password-cracking" programs are instructed to try hundreds of terms that fit into these categories.

- **Common names, such as Bill or Margaret.** Many people use their middle name or their mother's maiden name.

- **Obscenities, especially of the four-letter variety.** Most password crackers will try them early on.

- **Science-fiction terms.** Among the more prevalent are "Spock," "HAL," and "I, Robot."

- **Common objects found in households and offices.** Steer clear of "file cabinet," "spider plant," and the like. Also, stave off the temptation to take refuge in the obvious, like "computer" or "Macintosh."

- **Common phrases.** Avoid especially those pertaining to greeting or getting down to work, such as "Good morning," "Wake up," "Hey, you," or "Get going."

Preserving the Password

No matter how strong your memory—or how memorable your password—there's too much at stake to trust your recollection. Once decided upon and duly entered, the password should be written down in a safe but unobtrusive place.

This can pose a problem. You might find it easier to remember a password than a set of directions to a secreted piece of paper, and besides, you're relying on the same memory to retain both pieces of information. That's why both password and hiding place are usually products of personality and force of habit, and why most would-be security crackers employ psychology as well as computer expertise.

Here's a trick that often works: hide the access code in a place that's not hard to find, but in a form or context that makes it all but impossible to identify as the password. One sterling example of this was devised by one user with a thoroughly undependable memory, who employed as passwords only seven-digit numbers. These numbers were even harder for him to recall than they'd be for most people, but this didn't concern him; when the password slipped his mind, he'd simply turn to the address book on his desk, just inches from his Mac. There, entered under the name of a mythical "Mr. Strubinski," he'd duly recorded the seven-digit password in the form of a phone number.

If you think your memory isn't up to even this simple plan, find someone you can trust to keep the password both safe and confidential and enlist their help. If you give the password record to, say, your spouse for safekeeping, all you'll need to remember is that you've done so. Even if you forget *that*, you're covered: your confidante will in all likelihood learn of your plight and remind you of your precaution.

Changing Your Password

Some people manage the task of password retention by painstakingly remembering a password, then sticking with it indefinitely. But circumstances do arise in which a new password is appropriate, and some users would do well to change passwords as a matter of routine. Don't become a creature of habit, and don't hesitate to replace your password whenever it seems like the right thing to do. Although there's no need to for paranoia, anything that leads you to suspect a security breach is probably cause for a new code.

If your workplace is so situated that others can watch the keystrokes you make (even from a distance), you may want to change your password as a precaution against the possibility of someone discerning the access code from your finger movements.

You may occasionally need to give temporary access to someone else, in which case you should change your password as soon as the person has completed the task. Sometimes you'll have no choice but to disclose your current password (such as when you're calling in sick), but in other instances you may not need to part with it permanently; just change it to a temporary password and then change it back when the sharing is done.

The security problems implicit in passwords are evident enough on a single-user system. It's much thornier when multiple users and past users enter the picture. In such cases, passwords should probably be changed whenever someone who knows the current one will no longer be using the system, even if the person is completely trustworthy and changing passwords would be inconvenient for other users.

It's not a matter of trust, it's a matter of human nature: your password remains very important to you and others who rely on the system it protects. But to a person who'll no longer need the access it provides, the password is now just a useless piece of information, and as such will likely be handled both consciously and unconsciously with considerably less care. The departing person may have no real stake in maintaining confidentiality. The secret will be maintained not out of practicality, but out of a more abstract sense of ethics or expectations.

In this light, a policy of frequent password changes should not be seen as a sign of mistrust, but as a courtesy to those who are departing: the password becomes a piece of trivia that they won't have to worry about inadvertently divulging. And you won't have to worry about temptation striking in times to come.

Data Encryption

Most encryption programs employ a method similar to that used by compression utilities, and some applications offer both features in one package. The contents of a file's data and resource forks are broken down, analyzed, and substituted with a representational code; reconstituting the file is the reverse of the process.

Yet while compressors perform this task in the same manner every time, encryption software creates a new set of rules for each file. Unlike simple codes based on the substitution of one letter for another, most encryptor codes substitute one multidigit number for another, which creates allows for a vast number of possibilities and increases the code's complexity.

Just how complex can this encryption be? Well, many programs offer DES (Data Encryption Standard)—the same method used by the government to protect top secret data. Until recently, DES was considered to be the ultimate, "unbreakable" coding system. A team of specialists did succeed in breaking it, but the task required weeks of calculations on one of the most powerful super-computers in the world. Thus, your encrypted data is probably safe.

If you're interested in data encryption, you may want to look for a package that offers different encoding standards to meet your different needs—the more elaborate the method, the more time and storage space involved. For example, Sentinel offers three: SuperCrypt, BlockCrypt, and the formidable DES. Super-Crypt is fast, space-efficient, and simple only in comparison to DES; both it and the more complex BlockCrypt provide sufficient security for most Macin-tosh users.

Like password protectors, encryption programs require that you establish and maintain passwords or user authorization lists. This entails the effective use of psychology as well as software, but the flexibility of encryption also adds new twists. You may need to keep track of multiple passwords for multiple files (although you could apply one password to them all), and if you send en-crypted files to someone else, you'll need to safely convey the password to them as well.

Hardware Security Devices

Macintoshes are compact, relatively lightweight, and easy to unplug and discon-nect. Even a top-of-the-line Quadra isn't much bigger than the average TV and VCR. These features may make the Mac easy to use, but they also make it easy to steal. Any computer theft represents a significant monetary loss, but that loss is compounded when your hard disk is among the missing items. Valuable, if not irreplaceable data, may be gone for good. And as if that's not frustrating enough, it's likely that the very data that is priceless to you will be useless to the thief, and will likely end up deleted from the disk.

It's a grim scenario, but an avoidable one. Small as it may be, the Macintosh can actually be secured more easily and thoroughly than many other computers, thanks to its insightful design. As the original Mac was being developed, Apple realized that big value in a small box could appeal to thieves, so security slots were incorporated into the casing. Although they look like simple notches from the outside, these have internal spines that distribute weight across a large surface area; when a cable or chain is passed through them, it can't be pulled out with anything short of a power winch, which would tear out a large part of the case.

There are a variety of anchoring packages available. Some use hard-to-pick locks, some use metal rods instead of cables, and others use super-strong adhesives to supplant the slots. The adhesives are useful when you cannot or don't want to drill holes through your furniture.

WHEN

SOMETHING

GOES

WRONG

Maybe you'll be lucky and never have a major hard disk problem—but the odds are against it. Even the best-engineered, best-maintained hard drive is susceptible to mishaps, software bugs, and wear and tear. Preventative measures go a long way toward protecting your data, but they're only part of the picture. You'll need to know how to identify and rectify a problem when it does occur.

In this section, we'll discuss the skills and tools necessary for doing just that. Chapter 6 shows you how to diagnose both software- and hardware-based malfunctions, and how to contain such problems. Chapter 7 takes you through the steps of recovering, repairing, and replacing your hard disk's contents.

DIAGNOSING AND CONTAINING A PROBLEM

FEATURING:

→ Responding to Problems

→ Crashes, Bombs, Freezes, and Hangs

→ Diagnostic Utilities

→ Diagnosing and Repairing Problems

To a Macintosh user, few things cause more frustration (not to mention fear) than a hard disk that isn't working properly—or worse yet, not working at all. If you're currently suffering through either of these scenarios, this chapter should help you isolate the problem. But no matter how certain you are of your diagnosis, take care to read its entire contents before moving on to the recovery methods outlined in Chapter 7.

Even if you're not currently in the midst of a hard disk crisis, it will be worth your while to read this chapter. You'll be able to learn about these tools and techniques under less stressful circumstances, and be much calmer and have more confidence when disaster *does* strike.

Don't Panic—Ponder

Before getting into the gory details, a note of encouragement is in order: when proper precautions have been taken, *the data on all but the most severely malfunctioning hard disk can be recovered*. The Macintosh system is very forgiving—it makes it extremely difficult to accidentally damage or delete information. In fact, hard disks are safer than floppy disks, because the storage media is more durable and the platters are unlikely to be *completely* erased, even by an intentional erasure. Recovery may take time, and your hard disk itself may be a lost cause, but your data is likely to be retrieved. So don't panic, okay?

IP

View the situation as an exercise in deductive reasoning. Tracking down and remedying a problem can be an achievement that will make you feel more in control of the technology. Even if your quest is unsuccessful, consider it a lesson in being conscientious about data preservation in the future.

Approaching the Problem

This chapter will provide you with step-by-step procedures for troubleshooting a number of problems. These procedures are ordered by major symptom under three main categories. "Software-Centered problems" encompasses malfunctions that appear to be mostly or entirely due to software. The term is intentionally ambiguous; although these problems are manifested in software, they may originate in, or otherwise involve, hardware. "Hardware-Centered problems" covers those problems that originate in hardware. "Nonspecific problems" discusses those problems not clearly attributable to hardware or software, and problems that may implicate both.

These procedures aren't exhaustive, but they should track symptoms at least to the point of determining that expert help is needed. Read through the entire procedure before performing its steps, and don't proceed if you're unclear on any of the instructions. You may also want to read the other procedures in that category; many have common procedures, and you may better understand a step in one explanation than in another.

Looking at the Big Picture

Although hard disks are our primary subject, effective troubleshooting requires looking at all aspects of the Macintosh: computer, peripherals, wires and circuitry, programs and other data, as well as the standards and assumptions by which they all operate.

Why do we need such a comprehensive approach? Because your computer system is truly a *system*, an interdependent, interactive environment capable of functioning—and malfunctioning— in a highly complex manner. Hardware problems can trigger software problems (or vice versa), and such secondary effects may beget still more repercussions. Some problems are caused by neither hardware or software alone, but arise instead from their interactions.

That holds true for most computer systems, but the line between hardware and software (or cause and effect) is even more blurred on the Macintosh. The Macintosh operating system is a firmware/software hybrid, and even basic operations require the coordination of a number of separate elements. Moreover, the manner of this coordination is far from fixed. While it may seem that an application is "in charge" of a document, just as the System file is "in charge" of an application, a document may make demands of an application, which may in turn give orders to the operating system.

Under such circumstances, even seemingly clear-cut problems may stem from a multitude of possible causes, have a number of consequences, and require more than one manner of treatment. Thus the best approach to finding and defining problems is to take nothing for granted, to start troubleshooting from general causes and to proceed to specific causes by means of experimentation and exclusion.

Effective troubleshooting takes more than the ability to identify problems. It also requires an understanding of the factors behind those problems—the conditions in which they arise and the elements they may affect. With a proper understanding of your computer and software, you'll be able to ferret out many more problems than this chapter could possibly address. You may also be able to spot and eliminate potential trouble before it occurs, or recognize one problem as a symptom of another.

TIP

Your attitude and approach may make the difference between success and failure. If at all possible, try to set aside the time to do the job right. Proceed step by step, and don't start fixing a problem until you're confident in your diagnosis; improper cures can often cause further problems. Don't be afraid to investigate the obvious. Is everything plugged in? Is the wall socket supplying current? Does the disk have a valid System file? Is a missing file really missing, or just misplaced? You'd be surprised how many "major" problems have a simple solution.

What Can Go Wrong?

Every element that makes up a working Macintosh system can be grouped in three categories, each of which presents its own set of problems:

- *Mechanical components* (such as disk spindles, read/write heads, keyboards, monitors, indicator lights, and the like) wear out with use or the passage of time. Some of these, such as the power supply or the flyback transformer, may have no moving parts but nonetheless have a finite useful life. Some imminent malfunctions may be signaled by symptoms, such as eccentric operation or unusual noises. Other parts fail without warning, turning your Macintosh into an unusable box.

With few exceptions, the repair of most mechanical problems is beyond the skills of the average Mac user. Expert technical know-how and authorized replacement parts are probably required, which makes these problems more expensive than others to fix. Fortunately, it is rare that data is lost completely due to these kinds of malfunctions, and with the help of a specialist, the contents of even a ready-for-the-junk-heap hard disk can be recovered.

- *Electronic components* won't wear out, but they can be damaged and disconnected. These include hard disk controllers, the Mac's CPU, the RAM, the ROM, and the rest of the system's circuitry, plus all the wires that connect them. Although an informed user can diagnose many electronic problems, in most cases repair can only be done by experts. Since most components are solid-state and extremely small, these components are more likely to be replaced than repaired.

- *Software* is the most common cause of malfunctions, primarily because even the simplest program must perform a number of intricate interactions with the operating system, the Finder, and other software. Fortunately, software problems are the ones that best lend themselves to user solutions. Unfortunately, they're also the type of problems most likely to involve data distortion or loss.

When Help Is Needed

In general, you should turn to the expertise of others *after* you've done as much to pinpoint the problem as possible, and *before* you resign yourself to any seemingly permanent results of the problem. Keep your preliminary diagnosis in mind when shopping for help; if it's clearly a software problem, the expense of an Apple-authorized technician may not be necessary, but even the most brilliant and experienced Mac enthusiast may find a hardware dilemma beyond his or her reach. Some situations require special tools and special training, while others need only insight and persistence.

Whatever you do, don't make matters worse by declining to seek help out of pride or fear of ridicule. Whatever happened, *it's not your fault*; it was either an accident or a product flaw. Even if the problem arose as a direct result of some step you took, there's an engineer or programmer who should have made that action impossible.

Don't hesitate to take advantage of the fact that most manufacturers of Macintosh software and peripherals stand behind what they sell, and may be the best qualified and prepared to help. Find out if the troublesome component in question is still covered by a warranty, or if the manufacturer provides a "customer service" or "technical support" phone number. Most companies use these departments not only to please individual customers, but also to detect bugs that may have eluded discovery during in-house testing. Software companies in particular pay special attention to support services, viewing you as a "field tester" as well as a customer.

TIP

Experts can tell you what needs to be done, but only you can decide if the data to be rescued is worth the time, effort, and cost involved. Some documents are vital, unique, and irreplaceable, while the loss of others represents only a minor inconvenience and repetition of effort. While making your decision, take stock of the resources you might use to reconstruct the missing information: your archive or backup, miscellaneous floppies, the storage volumes of a co-worker, or even printouts or a non-computer source. The documents aren't important—what matters is the data they contain.

The Terminology of Malfunctions

Before we look at tools and troubleshooting, let's define some of the terminology of malfunction. In general, Macintosh problems are most likely to manifest themselves as *crashes*, *bombs*, *freezes*, and *hangs*.

Crashes are the most serious signs of malfunction. The term encompasses any condition in which the computer is misbehaving so profoundly that it's essentially no longer a computer. A crashed Mac might display only a blank or garbled screen, or it may not work at all. Crashes may be caused by either a hardware or a software problem, or a combination of both.

If your screen suddenly shows the haywire behavior characteristic of a crash, turn off the power to the Mac at once, even if that means pulling its plug. (Any unsaved data in an open document has probably been lost anyway.) Crashes of this sort are the likely result of a software error or the failure a crucial component. Such crashes should not be confused with hard disk *head crashes*, which occur when a read/write head touches a disk platter and damages its surface.

Bombs are those occasions when a variation of the "bomb box" appears on the screen. Although these problems may be just as catastrophic as crashes, they're also a sign that things remain at least somewhat in control. The bomb dialog boxes, which are part of the firmware of the Macintosh operating system, appear whenever the machine cannot interpret instructions it's receiving from the System file or from an application. The box usually presents you with no option other than to select the OK button; this automatically reboots the computer, and any unsaved data is lost. In some cases, you'll be presented with another button, usually labeled "Resume." It's worth trying this button first, but its effectiveness depends on the application that was running when the system error occurred. Things may return to normal, but even then it's a good idea to check for data loss.

Not all bomb boxes are alike. Some have a multi-digit number in the lower right-hand corner. This code number, generated by the firmware, is intended to describe the circumstances that caused the system error. Although it's not infallible, this code can be an important diagnostic tool. The meanings of the more prominent of these codes are listed in Appendix C, although they're really more meaningful to programmers than troubleshooting users. Some applications also use the codes in other, specialized dialog boxes; in this case, they're usually preceded by a minus sign.

Since System 6.0.7, many error ID codes have been discontinued in favor of specific messages, such as "floating point error" or "coprocessor not installed." In some cases, this information may prove more useful than an error code. In others, it can be too vague or general to be enlightening.

Freezes happen when all of a sudden nothing happens—when everything on the screen, including the mouse pointer, is frozen in place. When this happens, your first step should be to check the connection of your mouse and keyboard; that's the usual culprit. If that doesn't work, locate another mouse or keyboard, one that you know is operational, and hook it up. If that fails to unfreeze things, it's time to flip the power switch or pull the plug.

Hangs are caused when the screen refuses to change, but the mouse pointer can still move freely. This usually signals that either the System file doesn't know how to carry out a command, or the application has started a task that can't be completed. The proper response to this condition is dictated by the form of the mouse pointer. If the pointer is the standard arrow or text-insertion beam (Figure 6.1), reboot the computer. If the pointer is in its "wait" form (a watch, a beach ball, or an hourglass), then give the computer fifteen minutes or so to complete the task before shutting down. Those indicators mean that the Macintosh is reading to or writing from memory, and a variety of circumstances can slow these processes down to a crawl.

These four types of conditions are by far the most common signs of crisis on the Macintosh, and each is an unambiguous indication that something has gone

FIGURE 6.1
Common
cursor forms

awry. Although each condition has its own cause and significance, some diagnostic procedures work equally well in response to more than one type. It's often convenient to refer to the four types collectively as interchangeable indicators of a single problem. Therefore, this book uses the term *malfunction* only for circumstances involving bombing, crashing, freezing, or hanging.

Software Tools

Software developers have created programs to deal with the various malfunctions you might run up against. I will discuss these utilities at various places throughout this book. In this section, I will introduce a few of the most common and useful software utilities: DiskMaker, the Norton Utilities' Disk Doctor, and Apple Computer's Installer.

Examining the SCSI Bus with DiskMaker

If a SCSI volume does not show up on the desktop, but otherwise appears to be operational, the problem may not be in the device, but in the SCSI bus itself. A cable connection might be loose, a wire may have shorted out, a port may have become disconnected from SCSI circuitry, or a conflict may exist between SCSI addresses.

You can test for all these possibilities by using a special utility that looks at the SCSI bus itself. One such utility, DiskMaker, includes a control panel device that displays the current status of the SCSI bus (Figure 6.2). It lists all seven SCSI ID numbers, either displaying the device's miniature icon or indicating "no dev" if no device is found to correspond with a number.

FIGURE 6.2

*Scanning the
SCSI bus with
DiskMaker*

To examine your SCSI bus, click on the Scan Bus button in the lower left corner. After a few moments, the devices currently on the SCSI will be listed. Click on a drive's icon, and DiskMaker will display the drive's desktop icon, its manufacturer, model name, and maximum capacity. All connected volumes should appear, even if it isn't currently mounted on the Macintosh's desktop. If a volume doesn't appear—and you believe it to be properly connected, terminated, plugged in, and powered on—hold down the ⌘ key and click on the Reset button. The bus will be rescanned.

DiskMaker has a number of uses:

- You can use it to determine the exact make and model of a hard disk without resorting to opening the computer or external drive case. (Remember, the disk mechanisms of external drives are often manufactured by a company other than the name appearing on the drive case.)

- You can use it to determine if a device's software SCSI ID is the same as its physical ID.

- If you're adding a device to the bus, you can use it to see which ID numbers are available.

- If a volume does not appear on the desktop but does appear in Disk-Maker, you may be able to mount it with the Mount command.

- If repeated scans of the SCSI bus refuse to recognize a volume (and that volume only), you can conclude that the problem is isolated to the volume itself.

Using Norton Disk Doctor

If you have installed Norton Utilities on your system, you'll want to use Norton Disk Doctor before proceeding to more elaborate measures. Disk Doctor is the application's general-purpose diagnostic and repair utility. While it can't solve all problems, it's definitely worth using as your first recourse when trouble strikes.

When launched from the Norton Utilities main menu, Disk Doctor performs a series of tests on the selected volume, as shown in Figure 6.3. These tests can detect the majority of problem areas on the Macintosh volumes. Even severely damaged floppies and hard drives can be examined with this automated process.

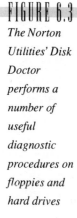

FIGURE 6.3

The Norton Utilities' Disk Doctor performs a number of useful diagnostic procedures on floppies and hard drives

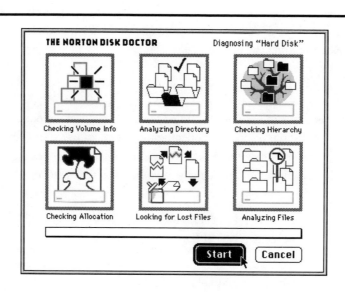

Disk Doctor begins by examining the general volume info, confirming that the boot blocks and related files are accurate and in working order. It then performs a similar verification of the directory level, and moves on the check the extents and B-tree catalog to determine that files and folders are placed in a functioning hierarchy. Next, it analyzes the block allocations, making sure that files are being read from and written to in a logical fashion. It then attempts to reconstitute any files that seem damaged, and inspects all files for irregularities that could lead to potential mishaps. If any are found, Disk Doctor reports on it promptly. Whenever possible, it will ask for your permission to attempt to fix the problem. The results of each diagnostic session can be saved into a file, and even printed out if necessary.

TIP

Because it can spot possible problems before they happen, it's a good idea to run Disk Doctor regularly, even on volumes that seem trouble-free.

System Transplants with Installer

As you'll soon see, one common remedy for disk trouble is the replacement of an unusable or unreliable System file with a fresh one. You may not relish the prospect of such a task, since your System probably contains customized features such as fonts and desk accessories, but fortunately, there's a way to perform a System transplant without losing that personalization. Since 1987, Apple has included a utility called Installer on all System disks. Not only does Installer automate the process of System installation and replacement, it can do so without disturbing your file customization. It will also optimize the new System file to best suit your model of Macintosh. Installer works on any mass storage device or floppy, but only when the volume's current System is not presently in use as the startup file.

When launched, Installer presents a single dialog box (Figure 6.4). Start by clicking to select the entry that corresponds to your Mac. If you have a 512K or earlier model Macintosh, you'll note that your model is not listed. That's because Apple recommends you stick with an earlier System version. Although trying the Plus option may work, it won't produce any change in performance, it's probably best to heed Apple's advice. Contact your Apple dealer for information on the best System software for your Mac.

Next, specify the target volume and wait while Installer calculates whether the volume has enough space for the new System file. If so, you're then apprised of how much storage space will be used and how much will remain. Give it the go-ahead by clicking the Install button. You'll be informed when the job is done.

Just how does Installer tailor the system to your Macintosh? It eliminates the System features you won't need, includes ones you will, and modifies some dialog boxes so that the Mac images used in dialog boxes and the like will more closely resemble your machine. For example, Installer will include display formats and color CDEVs in a System file for a Mac II or Quadra, but will omit them in a Classic or PowerBook System file since they would only waste storage space.

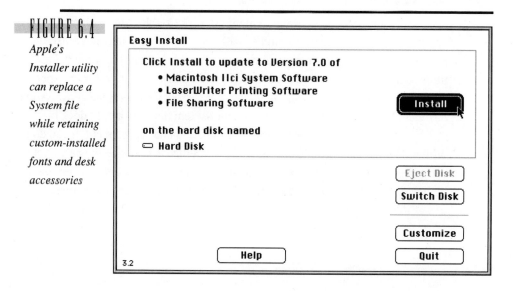

FIGURE 6.4

Apple's Installer utility can replace a System file while retaining custom-installed fonts and desk accessories

Easy Install

Click Install to update to Version 7.0 of
• Macintosh IIci System Software
• LaserWriter Printing Software
• File Sharing Software

on the hard disk named
▭ Hard Disk

Install

Eject Disk

Switch Disk

Customize

Help   Quit

3.2

Using Diagnostic Procedures

You'll find that most of the information in the following procedures applies to floppies and other storage devices as well as hard disks, but for the sake of clarity and conciseness, it's assumed that you have at least one SCSI hard disk connected to your Macintosh, and that you are using it as your startup volume.

Internal hard disk users may find fewer answers in the following sections to their problems than those with external units. This isn't because the principles outlined here don't apply, but because they may prove impossible to apply. A non-working internal hard disk often means a non-working Macintosh, and vice versa. Most internal hard disks have special problem detection resources either built in or bundled with the drive, so check your user manual or contact the manufacturer's technical support staff for information on troubleshooting these drives.

One final note: it's possible that you might find yourself at the end of a procedure with still no answer in sight. Although the following sections include the most useful means of tackling the most likely causes of difficulties, there's been no effort to anticipate and address every possible problem. For the average user, such an effort would prove overwhelming, intimidating, and of little benefit. If a diagnosis remains elusive, don't give up the situation as a lost cause. Look at other troubleshooting information, both in this book and elsewhere. And keep in mind that sometimes, answers don't come because the wrong question is being asked: make sure that you fully understand the nature of the problem, and have correctly identified all the symptoms.

Software-Centered Problems

In addressing the problems that seem rooted in software, we've broken down the pertinent procedures into three categories. "Problems upon Startup" covers the conditions that show up during the startup process, the period in which the computer is turned on, booted up, and all mounted volumes are brought online. "Problems upon Application Launch" looks at the malfunctions that can occur when the user launches documents, applications, and related files. "Problems upon In-Application Command" tackles the mishaps that can occur while working within an application.

Problems upon Startup

The startup sequence (explained in Chapter 2) is one of your Macintosh's busiest times: the boot blocks have to be read and obeyed, as does the PRAM (see below). Among other things, the System file must be loaded, INIT file commands must be carried out, the Finder needs to be launched, the desktop has to be rebuilt, and the directories of all online volumes must be confirmed and at the ready. The more work that goes on, the greater the chance that something can go wrong, and since the Mac is just getting down to work, there's not much of a context with which to determine the cause of a problem. The positive side of startup problems is that they almost never involve your personal data; most startup errors simply announce a System or a hardware malfunction.

You can't be certain that a startup has been successful until you've actually used the Mac for a while without incident. However, the first sign that things are proceeding as planned is the "happy Mac" icon (Figure 6.5). This indicates that the Mac has recognized a volume, located its System file, and started the loading of the same file.

Introducing the PRAM

There are numerous problems that can plague the startup process, but one factor may be suspected in most, if not all, startup applications: the Parameter RAM, or PRAM (Figure 6.6).

FIGURE 6.5

The "happy Mac" icon signals that the startup process is underway

FIGURE 6.6

*The General
Control's panel
displays some
of the functions
controlled by
Parameter
RAM*

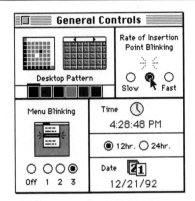

The PRAM is the Mac's third type of memory, neither permanent like ROM nor temporary like RAM. It's a 256 KB storehouse for data the Mac uses for consistency from one session to another, such as the clock/calendar's time and alarm settings, the configuration of non-SCSI ports, and all the custom options available in the Control Panel. Unlike regular RAM, its contents don't disappear when the machine is turned off, thanks to a battery located in a compartment in the back of the machine (on the Mac Plus or earlier models) or deeper within the workings (on Mac IIs, SEs or Quadras). Like RAM and ROM, however, it can be corrupted or damaged.

If a startup problem can't be attributed to any other factor, you can purge the PRAM and see what happens. (You'll have to reset the clock and all your Control Panel preferences, but that's probably a small price to pay. If your Mac's battery compartment is in the back, purging the information is a simple matter; just open the door, remove the battery for at least three to five minutes, then replace it and close up.

In the case of other Macs, zapping the PRAM requires a slightly more complicated purging procedure, since the battery is soldered directly to a circuit board and can't be removed by the user. To purge PRAM on these models, press the Option, Shift, and Command keys simultaneously while selecting the Control Panel from the Apple menu. This will trigger a dialog box (Figure 6.7), but only if you're running System 6 or earlier. Under System 7, this is not an option.

You can, however, reboot from a System 6 floppy, then flush the RAM.

This procedure takes a few moments. Even if you choose not to continue, the dialog box may remain on the screen for a half-minute or so.

No Screen Display

Problem: After the power is turned on, the Macintosh screen does not display the "disk requested" icon (Figure 6.8). The screen either remains dark or displays only snow or other garbled images.

Diagnosis: If you have an external monitor, first check your connecting cables and the monitor's power supply. If they seem to be in order, test the monitor itself by either connecting it to a functioning Macintosh, or by connecting a working monitor to your Macintosh.

If you succeed in isolating the trouble to the monitor, follow servicing procedures for your particular model. But unless the manufacturer specifically directs you to do so, *do not open up your monitor's casing*. The monitor's cathode ray

*Flushing the
Parameter
RAM summons
a dialog box*

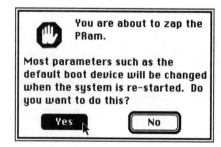

*This icon
appears when
the startup
volume isn't
recognized*

tube (CRT) assembly includes parts under high pressure, and parts capable of storing high voltage, *even if unplugged.* By poking around in there, you'll probably do more harm than good—to your Mac and to yourself.

If your monitor works fine on another Mac, or if you have a compact or portable Mac with an internal screen, see the section "Complete Function Loss" later in this chapter.

Startup File Not Recognized

Problem: Even though a volume with a valid startup file has been placed online, the "disk requested" icon either remains displayed or is replaced by the "disk rejected" icon (Figure 6.9).

Diagnosis: Does the question mark in the middle of the icon continue to flash on and off? If not, consult a technician; a ROM problem is likely. If it does, shut down, take any SCSI volumes offline by switching them off or disconnecting them, then try to reboot from a floppy you know to be a valid startup disk.

If that does the trick, it's likely that the startup file on your SCSI volume has been rendered unrecognizable. Replace it, and then reboot three or four times from the replacement before resuming business as usual. If a System transplant doesn't eliminate the problem, replace any INITs that may be in the System Folder.

If booting from the floppy results in no change, or if "disk requested" is replaced with the "disk rejected" icon, you'll need expert servicing. The problem may be in the ROM, the RAM, the CPU, or connective circuitry.

FIGURE 6.9
This icon appears when the startup file isn't recognized

Startup Aborted

Problem: The "disk requested" icon, the "happy Mac" icon, or the "Welcome to Macintosh" message box is replaced by the "sad Mac" image (Figure 6.10).

Diagnosis: This icon indicates that a System file has been located, but the Macintosh is unable to read all or part of it. First, consult the icon's error code to determine if the problem is in the hardware or the software (see "Trouble-shooting with the 'Sad Mac'" below). If it's a hardware problem, call in the pros. If it's a software problem, shut down and take all SCSI volumes offline, then try to reboot from a startup floppy placed in the internal disk drive.

If this works, it's likely that the System file was somehow corrupted; shut down again, put your SCSI volumes back online, and then reboot, making sure that the startup floppy is still in the internal drive. If the volume with the suspect floppy subsequently appears on the desktop, replace its System file and see if it now functions as a startup source. If not, reboot from the floppy once more, replace any INITs in the System Folder and use the Installer program, then try again. If the volume does not mount, you may have a corrupted directory; see Chapter 7 for information on recovery from these problems.

Troubleshooting with the "Sad Mac"   The "sad Mac" icon is more than an irreverent image designed to put a whimsical twist to a sobering situation. It's the result of the Mac failing the diagnostic tests built into its ROM. Unlike the

---

FIGURE 6.10
The "sad Mac" icon signals that system startup cannot be completed, due to faulty or missing bootup data

error codes of the "bomb box," the "sad Mac" can yield information about the nature of the problem that's useful to the general user.

Beneath the icon is a code which can hold a number of meanings. Let's look at the important information it provides (Figure 6.11).

The first two characters indicate whether the problem is in the hardware or the software. 0F indicates a software failure; any other characters point to hardware. 01 declares a ROM problem, while 02 to 05 mean the RAM is at fault.

The remaining characters are used to further define the problem. If the first two characters are 0F, the final characters pinpoint the type of software problem. If the first two characters indicate a RAM problem, the others will specify the memory chip that isn't working properly.

From a user's standpoint, the most important use of the "sad Mac" codes is to determine if the problem is in the software or the hardware. If it's the former, a System replacement is in order; if the latter, you'll require repair services from an expert.

Alternating Icons

Problem: The "disk requested" icon continuously alternates with the "happy Mac" icon, and startup proceeds no further.

FIGURE 6.11

The numbers and letters beneath the "sad Mac" identify the nature of the problem

Diagnosis: Because a seeming file glitch can sometimes be an error in reading the file instead, the Mac is sometimes instructed to try again. Odds are that your System file has problems, but the computer doesn't know when to give up and display the "sad Mac." Follow the instructions under "Startup Aborted" scenario to identify the root of the problem.

Redundant Icons on Desktop

Problem: Numerous (usually five to seven) copies of the same volume icon appear on the desktop after startup (Figure 6.12)

Diagnosis: First, resist the temptation to click on any of these icons (unfortunately, your hard disk has not miraculously multiplied), then shut the Mac down as soon as possible. This visually dramatic quirk is caused by an online device with the SCSI address 7. As noted in Chapter 2, that number is the SCSI ID of the Macintosh itself, and the computer is understandably confused. Reset

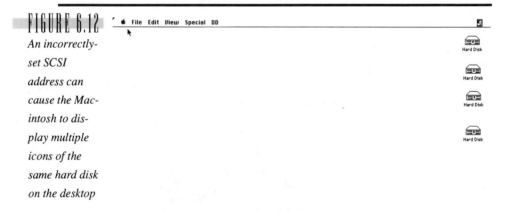

FIGURE 6.12
An incorrectly-set SCSI address can cause the Macintosh to display multiple icons of the same hard disk on the desktop

the device's address to a number between 0 and 6, then restart and check for possible data loss.

Volume Icon Missing

Problem: A normal desktop is displayed, but the icon of an online hard disk or other SCSI volume is nowhere to be found.

Diagnosis: It's likely that (1) the SCSI bus is faulty or disconnected, (2) the volume hardware just isn't working, or (3) the volume has a damaged directory, and thus cannot be mounted by the Mac. Investigate the problem in that order.

First, shut down the Mac and check its cabling; make sure that the terminators are in place, the connectors firmly seated, and while you're at it, check the power cords as well. Then reboot and see if the icon finally appears. Don't do this while the Mac is up and running, since the computer confirms the presence of volumes on the SCSI bus only during startup; bringing a SCSI device online at any other time can, in fact, cause crashes and hangs.

If the device icon is still missing, look for signs of life from the hard disk itself. Is the fan working? Restart the Mac; can you hear the usual sounds of the read/write heads moving from their parked positions? If it has an indicator light, does it light up at all during startup? If there's any indication that something's amiss with the unit's hardware, turn to the section "Other Hardware Problems" in this chapter.

If the unit is operating normally but the icon still refuses to appear, a repair utility may be able to mount the volume and replace a damaged directory or FAT. The use of these programs is covered in Chapter 7. Until you have restored these files, don't use your Macintosh unless the hard disk has been safely disconnected.

Icon Missing from Directory

Problem: The contents of a folder are normally displayed, but the icons of one or more files are missing.

Diagnosis: Start by making sure that the files are really missing. Perhaps they were deleted from the volume, moved to another folder, or renamed. Use Find File or another mass volume search utility to see if the file is located elsewhere on the hard disk or on another volume; if it's possible that your system has been used by someone else, inquire (discreetly, if need be) if changes have been made to your folders. If the lost file is a document, browse through other documents of the same type to determine that it hasn't been renamed; advanced search utilities like GOfer can do this for you. If its an application, peruse folders under the View by Icon format and look for its distinctive icon.

If you are certain that the file has indeed disappeared, all is not lost: it's possible that the volume directory has somehow lost track of it, or that it has been converted into an *invisible file*. What's an invisible file? It's a file that is meant to be read by the Mac but not by the user (such as the Desktop file). As such, it does not have an icon. Invisible files can be located, opened, and modified with utilities such as ResEdit, which is covered in Chapter 7.

ARNING

> Until you've retrieved the file, refrain from working with any
> other file on the hard disk, or adding a new file to the disk.
> This is to keep the Macintosh from changing any area on the
> hard disk, and possibly writing over the file.

Changed Volume Icon

Problem: The icon of a hard disk or other online storage volume is displayed, but its appearance has been modified or replaced by another icon (Figure 6.13).

Diagnosis: Do *not* open the volume. Shut down immediately and reboot under another System file. If the icon returns to normal, replace the System file used previously. If the problem persists, then the volume is unable to identify itself correctly; use one of the utilities described in the next chapter to attempt repairs. In a worse-case situation, you may need to reinitialize the volume (which obliterates its contents). But even if you don't have a current backup, all is not lost. Some utilities, such as Norton Utilities' Disk Editor, allow you to copy the contents of a hard disk without actually mounting the volume.

Changed Application Icon

Problem: An application can be located, but when seen in the View by Icon or View by Small Icon display format, its icon has been modified, or replaced by the default "generic" icon, as in Figure 6.14.

Diagnosis: If the default icon is displayed, don't proceed until you're confident that the application does, in fact, have a distinctive icon. Although the vast majority do have their own icons, some (especially amateur and public domain programs) don't and display the default icon instead.

If something really is wrong, do not launch the application. Instead, shut down and reboot the computer with a fresh System file. If this works, replace the first System file. If it doesn't, replace the application with a fresh copy.

If for some reason you don't have a fresh copy at hand, you may want to risk launching the application anyway; it's possible that only the code governing the

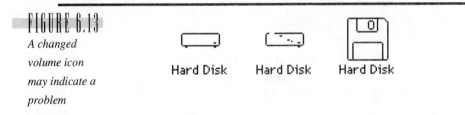

FIGURE 6.13
*A changed
volume icon
may indicate a
problem*

FIGURE 6.14
*Appearance of
the default icon
may indicate
trouble*

icon has been corrupted. But before you do so, take a few precautions. If you're running System 6, make sure you're running Finder rather than MultiFinder, since the latter has a greater potential for corrupting other applications. Make duplicates of any documents you wish to use, and plan on working with them only. Finally, launch the application, but don't just forge ahead, even if everything seems normal. Before getting down to business, make sure that the application can open, create, save, and reopen documents without problem.

If the application malfunctions upon launch, chances are that the icon display code isn't the only corrupted part of the document's resource fork. You might be able to pinpoint the problem with the help of one of the utilities described in Chapter 7, but the inner workings of applications are usually too complex and convoluted for anyone but programmers and software engineers to understand. You're probably better off obtaining a clean copy of the application.

Changed Document Icon

Problem: The distinctive icon of a document has been modified or replaced by the default "generic" icon, as shown in Figure 6.15.

Diagnosis: If the default icon appears, the document's *creator ID* may have been deleted or damaged. This part of the resource fork tells the Finder which application the document belongs to, and describes the icon that should appear on the screen. A misdrawn icon usually indicates heavier damage to the resource fork than the default icon.

In either case, the next step is to test the document's viability. First, open or create another document of the same type to make sure that parent application is not corrupted. Then return to the Finder and make a duplicate of the document

FIGURE 6.15
*Distinctive icon
(left); default
icon (right)*

in question. Finally, while running only under Finder with no other open documents, use the Open command from within the application to locate the document's home folder.

Are the document and its duplicate listed in the scrolling contents field? If so, try to open the duplicate. If the Mac bombs or otherwise misbehaves instead of opening the document, then at least one of the file forks has been corrupted beyond the computer's comprehension. Turn to Chapter 7 to retrieve the information in the file.

If the duplicate of the document does open, inspect it for omissions or additions. If any of the text is worth saving, copy it to a brand new document. If the formatting has been scrambled, you may want to use the Cut and Paste commands instead of the Scrapbook, which copies both the text and formatting. If the file's contents appear so garbled as to be unusable, it's still possible that only the file's resource fork has been damaged, and that the data fork is intact; see Chapter 7 on how to determine whether this is the case.

Did the document not show up in the scrolling field of the Open dialog box? That means that the program cannot recognize (and therefore, cannot open) the file. Some applications have commands such as Import or Open Other that can interpret various document formats; if such a command is available, it's worth giving it a try.

If none of these procedures work, quit the application, return to the Finder, and try to launch the duplicate of the document by clicking on it directly. There's an outside chance that the parent application will be launched and the document opened, but the odds are more in favor of the appearance of a dialog box similar to that shown in Figure 6.16. If the file still fails to open, it's time for the techniques of Chapter 7.

Don't let the dialog box discourage you. All it indicates is that the document's creator ID is unreadable; the Mac can't launch the application because it doesn't know which application to launch. You'll find the tools for rectifying that condition in the next chapter.

Non-Startup Volume Not Recognized

Symptom: The startup process appears successful, but an online volume other than the startup disk is not mounted by the Macintosh. Instead, the dialog box shown in Figure 6.17 appears, asking if the disk should be initialized.

Diagnosis: Probably no Macintosh message is more disheartening than this one, but in just about every circumstance, the situation is not as dire as it may seem. There's a lot you can do before instructing the Mac to initialize the disk, and the odds are good that most if not all of your data is far from lost.

The dialog box doesn't mean that the volume is blank—just that the Mac can't figure out how to read it. Most of the Macintosh user interface is designed to minimize problems—to make it as difficult as possible for even the neophyte to make an unintentional move that has permanent consequences. But the

FIGURE 6.16

This usually means the application needed to open a document is missing

> The document "Moana's Mac Backup" could not be opened, because the application program that created it could not be found.
>
> OK

FIGURE 6.17

This appears when the Mac cannot read a volume's formatting

> This disk is unreadable:
> Do you want to initialize it?
>
> Eject   Initialize

initialization dialog box is one aspect of the interface can be downright misleading, and even an unnecessary source of grief.

The box seems innocuous enough. It appears when a brand-new floppy or a floppy previously formatted for a different kind of computer is inserted in the Macintosh. But if it appears when you insert a floppy that you know has already been formatted for a Macintosh, *do not initialize the disk except as a last resort*. The initialization dialog box is problematic because it gives you only two courses of action: eject the disk or initialize it. Initializing the disk obliterates any information already on the disk. Initialization of the disk is not inevitable, although this message may imply as much.

In most cases, there's a good chance that much if not most of the data on the floppy is still intact—it's just that the disk directory has been damaged. In the next chapter, we'll detail the procedures for regaining access to the data on disk.

If you insert a high-density disk, you won't be given an option; it will be automatically formatted as a 1.44 MB disk. If, however, the disk is not high-density, you'll be asked if you want to format it as a single-sided or double-sided disk. One last item of advice: if you do wish to initialize a disk, choose the "Two-sided" option only if the floppy is manufacturer-designated double-sided (800 KB) disk. Single-sided 400 KB disks can be intialized on both sides, but resist the temptation to do so; the second surface of a single-sided disk is coated but not tested, and can fail at any time. In fact, some single-sided are actually double-sided disks that didn't pass inspection on one side. If your data is worth saving, it's worth saving on a reliable floppy.

Problems upon Launch and Command

Two other events tax the Macintosh's resources: the launching of an application, and the carrying out of commands made from within that application.

Launches are problematic because the compiler needs to perform so many duties. The application must be located and loaded into RAM, its instructions followed, its resource files consulted, its fonts accessed, its windows drawn, a new or existing document must be displayed, and so on. All this needs to be done smoothly and consistently, in as few seconds as possible.

Commands within applications are often as exacting and elaborate as the launch sequence. For instance, when you select the Open command, the application calls on the user interface portions of the Toolbox to draw the standard File dialog box, and relies on the System to list file and folder names in the correct order. Since four separate software elements are operating at more or less the same time (the application, the document, the System, and the Toolbox), an incompatibility between any of them can trigger a malfunction.

Why are so many problems caused during launches and commands? The are a number of reasons, but perhaps the most important is that these are the times when the hardware/software package created by Apple Computer comes into contact with software created by someone else. And since thousands of people have written thousands of applications, this is the time when human error is most likely to show.

Since its earliest days, the Macintosh has had a reputation among some programmers for being idiosyncratic and problem-prone. The truth of the matter is that all Macintosh models are extremely reliable, but they're also extremely difficult to program. Even a modest application must conform to the user interface, access the right elements of the ROM Toolbox at the right times, and be versatile enough to reshape its operations to accommodate any of a number of variable factors, such as CPU types, RAM availability, or the presence of Multi-Finder. These constraints are more than mere conformity; they're the standards that allow the Macintosh to place most of its resources at the program's disposal. In effect, your Macintosh does not run an application so much as the application runs your Macintosh, at least until control is returned to the Finder. That's why Macintosh programmers must follow a mind-boggling set of rules.

Of course, the more things there are that need to be programmed right, the more things there are that can go wrong.

What follows are a few of the more prevalent malfunctions encountered during the launch process and application commands. Since many of the troubleshooting techniques for startup-related problems are also useful here, you'll often be referred to procedures discussed before. As before, the goal is to recognize the problem; full-fledged repairs are covered in the next chapter.

Launch-Triggered Malfunction

Problem: The Macintosh bombs, crashes, hangs, or freezes when the user attempts to launch an application.

Diagnosis: Were you running the application under MultiFinder? Some applications were written when only the Finder's RAM management rules applied, and therefore are not compatible with MultiFinder. Start up under the Finder and try again.

Is the application capable of running on your computer? The SE and Macintosh II models were designed to run software created for the Mac Plus, 512K, and 128K, but only if the software had been written in accordance with Apple's programming protocols. Unfortunately, many software authors didn't strictly follow those protocols; thus some applications make assumptions about hardware that don't hold true for the SE or Macintosh II. Many such programs have since been rewritten for full compatibility; if your application is still supported by the manufacturer, find out if an upgraded version is available.

Of course, the opposite may also hold true: the application is intended only for Macintoshes more advanced than yours. Most software is written to be compatible with as many models as possible, but some applications rely so heavily on the superior computing power of the high-end models that running them on a Mac Plus or earlier model would be impractical, if not impossible. That's why it's a good idea to determine a product's limitations and system requirements before making a purchase. And before you make a choice between jettisoning the application and buying a more powerful Mac, find out if the program could run on your current system with the help of a hardware upgrade or enhancement; some extra RAM may be all you need.

Is the application compatible with the entire contents of the System Folder? Some applications need a particular version of the System, the Finder, or a printer driver. Others are allergic to INITs and CDEVs. Check the manual or user guide, and while you're at it, double-check for any other special requirements which may have been overlooked.

Still no solution? Replace the application with a fresh copy. If it's a program that incorporates numerous options and customizations that you'd rather not lose, you might want to copy the suspect version onto a floppy rather than just tossing it in the Trash. In any case, take the precaution of first removing the application on the hard disk entirely, and only then copy the new version to disk. Don't use the update method that triggers the "Replace current version?" dialog box (Figure 6.18), since that may make the change by directly overwriting the sectors currently occupied by the file, and we haven't ruled out the possibility that the fault lies in physical damage to those sectors.

This dialog box signals that a file with the same name and creator ID is already present at the target location

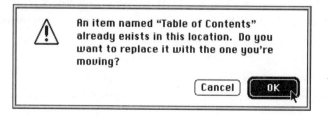

Does the new application work fine? If you hung on to the previous version in hopes of retaining its customization, bid it farewell and get started on duplicating those features in the new version. The problem may have been in the software alone, but what if it physical platter damage was involved? Your hard disk should automatically identify and avoid the affected areas in the future; both Norton Disk Doctor and Symantec Utilities for Macintosh identify and isolate such areas.

If the new copy also triggers the malfunction, your System file is suspect. Install a new System file and try again; if that does the trick, go ahead and reinstall the original version of the application onto the disk, if that's your preference, but be sure to first try it out.

Application Cannot Be Launched

Problem: Although the Macintosh does not hang, bomb, crash, or freeze, an attempt to launch an application is met with the dialog box shown in Figure 6.16 announcing the Mac's inability to open the application. In rare cases, the command is ignored entirely.

Diagnosis: If you're in MultiFinder, reboot under Finder and give it another try. If a document created by the application is at hand, try launching the application by opening a new duplicate of the document. Finally, try to launch a few other applications residing on the disk.

Do the other applications launch without incident? If so, then the Mac considers this application to be so damaged that it does not even attempt to launch it. Follow the removal and replacement instructions of the previous procedure.

If more than one application is unlaunchable, it's likely that the Finder or Multifinder is faulty, and a new System file is needed. This may solve the problem but not repair the damage it caused, so if the applications remain unlaunchable, they should be replaced as well.

Still no results? There may be an incompatibility between the software and the contents of your System Folder. Check your user manual or any related documentation for System-related requirements or limitations.

Insuffient Memory for Launch

Problem: The Macintosh refuses to launch an application, displaying instead a dialog box (Figure 6.19) declaring that available memory is inadequate for the task. In most cases, the dialog box goes on to ask if the user wants to proceed anyway.

Diagnosis: The memory in question is RAM, and it's possible that the application simply requires more than your Mac is capable of supplying. Minimum RAM requirements are usually noted in the application's documentation and in its Get Info box. (If you're unfamiliar with the Get Info box, see Chapter 3.) If working with such software is worth the investment, you may want to look into memory upgrades.

Is the application supposed to run on your configuration of Macintosh? It may be that other programs are currently gobbling a disproportionately large amount of RAM, or that the Mac has been looking for more memory than the application actually needs. If you're running under MultiFinder, this means you should free up RAM (or to quit one or more open applications), or shut down and reboot under Finder. But even if these steps work, don't conclude that you'll always need to launch the application in this manner; use the techniques under

This appears when the launching of an appli-cation requires more RAM than is available

 There is not enough memory to open "Adobe Illustrator® 3.0" (2,000K needed, 545K available). Closing windows or quitting application programs can make more memory available.

"Managing Memory Allocation" below to see if the memory allocation can be adjusted instead.

If the problem persists under Finder (or if MultiFinder wasn't a factor in the first place), read "Managing Memory Allocation" to learn about the issue of memory allocation. Then open the Get Info box and make sure the application's allotment is no bigger than necessary, adjusting it if needed. But for the moment, avoid setting it any lower than the recommended minimum.

Still can't launch the application? It's time to take a look at the big picture. You can do this by selecting About this Macintosh from the Apple menu. (In System 6, this command is called "About the Finder.") Unless you're using an outmoded System file, the resulting display should be a variation of the one in Figure 6.20.

This box gives you an up-to-the-second snapshot of your RAM—the amount your Macintosh is equipped with; the amount currently being used by the System, the Finder, (and other applications when you're running under Multi-Finder; and the amount remaining in reserve. If the Largest Unused Block figure is less than the application's recommended minimum, your only recourse is to seek a simpler, less memory-hungry situation in which to launch the application.

FIGURE 6.20

The About this Macintosh box provides an overview of your Mac's memory

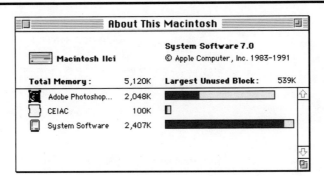

The most effective way to free up more memory is by cutting frills from the System Folder. If you have a monitor capable of displaying color or gray scales, deactivating those options may make a big difference. Other possibilities are custom backgrounds, special sound files (for warning beeps and the like), INITs and CDEVs, fonts, and DAs. Remember the criteria is appetite, not size: you're looking for software that effects the Mac's general operations, and as such is likely to be kept in RAM. In extreme situations, the best solution is to keep a bare-bones System Folder on a floppy to boot up from before launching the application.

Managing Memory Allocations You'll notice that an application's Get Info box differs from those of the Finder and documents. It has two extra informational categories directly below the text box, as shown in Figure 6.21. Suggested Memory Size displays the minimum memory recommended by the application's programmers, while the boxed figure following Application Memory Size records the amount of RAM the Macintosh will in fact use when launching this application.

FIGURE 6.21

In the Get Info box, extra entries beneath the text box record both the recommended amount of RAM (top) and the amount the Mac will actually allocate (bottom)

Adobe Illustrator® 3.0 Info

Adobe Illustrator® 3.0
Adobe Illustrator® 3.0

Kind: application program
Size: 953K on disk (975,349 bytes used)

Where: Hard Disk:

Created: Wed, May 1, 1991, 10:50 PM
Modified: Mon, Dec 21, 1992, 5:21 PM
Version: 3.0 © 1987-1990 Adobe Systems
Incorporated. All Rights Reserved.
Comments:

☐ **Locked**

Memory
Suggested size: 2,000 K
Current size: 3050 K

These two figures usually start out as identical, but the second figure can be increased or decreased by the user. Why does the Mac make such a distinction? Because the minimum RAM recommendation is based on normal performance expectations, and the demands you place on the application may be far from normal.

If you have the memory to handle it, increasing the memory allocation can speed up an application's performance considerably, especially when dealing with large, complex, or multiple documents. More RAM means less time spent reading from the disk. You'll want to consider this option for your word processor if you're writing a book, or for your desktop publishing program if you're working with scanned photographs.

Decreasing the allocation may be called for when RAM is at a premium, and when the application is unlikely to be pushed to its limits. Such reductions can be risky since memory inadequacies tend to announce themselves with malfunctions, but most applications can run with a memory allocation that is smaller than the official minimum. The threshold varies, however, and the only way to find it is through trial and error.

To change the memory allocation in either direction, just delete and replace the current figure (the box it's in is actually a text field). Remember that your specifications are retained as an integral part of the file, and as such will be passed along with any duplicates you may make.

Malfunction During Document Opening

Problem: Launching an application by clicking on one of its documents results in system malfunction.

Diagnosis: Is the malfunction triggered by the document or the application? If you can't open other documents or launch the program directly, go back to the procedure outlined in "Launch-Triggered Malfunction." If the problem seems isolated to the document, see if you can open it from within the application using the techniques outlined in the "Changed Document Icon" procedure.

If that doesn't work, you may need to unlock the file's contents with one of the utilities described in Chapter 7.

Application Not Found

Problem: Launching an application by clicking on one of its documents results in a dialog box, shown in Figure 6.16, indicating that the parent application cannot be located.

Diagnosis: Well, is the application in fact present? Use a volume searcher like Find File to make sure. And don't just check the startup volume—look at any other volumes on which the application might reside. If the application doesn't turn up, make a fresh copy of it from your backup.

If it is present, try opening the document from within the application using the method described in the "Changed Document Icon" procedure.

Document Has Been Changed

Problem: A document opens as usual, but its contents are garbled, reformatted, missing, or otherwise modified.

Diagnosis: System changes can cause some documents (especially text and page layout files) to change dramatically. If text created in one font is now displayed in another, make sure that the original font has been installed in your current System file, and that the document's application can access it automatically (some programs require separate font installations). If line spacing and page breaks seem to have been affected, check the Chooser desk accessory (Figure 6.22) when the document window is open and active. The Macintosh reconfigures page setups for different printers, and a document created when the LaserWriter driver is chosen will be different than one created under Image-Writer. Selecting the proper printer driver will correct page setups, even when you have no intention of printing the document.

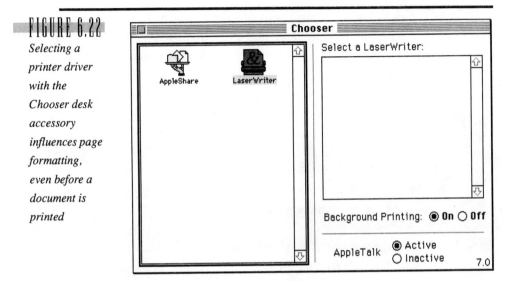

FIGURE 6.22
*Selecting a
printer driver
with the
Chooser desk
accessory
influences page
formatting,
even before a
document is
printed*

Still no luck? The document itself may be fine and the changes may be due to
the Mac's incorrect reading of the file's resource forks. Close the file immediately, making sure to choose No when the Save changes? dialog box appears.

When you've returned to the desktop, make a duplicate of the document. Open
the duplicate; if the unwanted changes were temporary, things should be normal. If the problem persists, the changes made are permanent. If you have a
backup copy, use it instead. If your primary goal is to save the document's text,
you may be able to do so; refer to Chapter 7 to find our how.

Malfunction Upon Command

Problem: The Macintosh bombs, crashes, freezes, or hangs when a command is
given.

Diagnosis: If the Mac is frozen or has hung up, it may have unexpectedly run
out of RAM in the midst of carrying out the command. Wait a few minutes to
make sure that the CPU isn't just taking its time, then shut down and try again.

Take steps to free up memory before launching the application: if you were running under MultiFinder, restart with Finder. If you had multiple documents open within the application, try accessing only one at a time.

If the malfunction is a bomb or crash, than an incompatibility needs to be tracked down and eliminated. Follow the steps listed under "Launch-Triggered Malfunction" above.

Document Will Not Print

Problem: When the user attempts to print a document, the Macintosh responds as expected, but the document does not print.

Diagnosis: Is your printer correctly connected to the Macintosh? Keep in mind that both the printer port and the modem port are serial connections, and either can be connected to a Macintosh-compatible printer. After checking the connection, open the Chooser and make sure the right printer driver has been selected.

Is the appropriate printer driver not available in the Chooser? Make sure that the driver is present in the uppermost level of the System Folder.

Hardware-Centered Problems

Thus far, we've been tackling problems in much the same way a detective would unravel a mystery: using deductive reasoning, zeroing in on the answer by methodically looking for clues, then following the trail of telltale signs until it leads us to the culprit.

But some Macintosh and hard disk problems don't lend themselves to this approach quite as easily as others. Sometimes there's only one symptom: something just doesn't work. Perhaps your entire system is inoperative and unresponsive. Or perhaps there are some vital signs, such as a flickering screen or a whirring fan. Maybe the Macintosh itself patiently displays its Disk Requested icon and remains oblivious to the hard disk that serves as its startup volume.

The symptom may appear at different times and in different magnitudes, but its character is essentially the same.

In such cases the powers of deduction are still useful, but the diagnostic process is much shorter and less enlightening. Problems caused by accidental disconnection (or misconnection) are easily diagnosed and remedied by the average user, but beyond that there's usually little to do other than identify and isolate the nonfunctioning unit and then seek qualified help.

If it's your hard disk that's out of order, bear in mind that only the most severe physical mishaps pose a threat to data, and even when data is damaged, the loss is usually far from total.

If the casualty is your computer itself, take heart in the fact that all Macintoshes have been designed with remarkably few parts, all of which are readily available and easily replaceable, and many of which are relatively inexpensive. And just because your Mac isn't working doesn't mean that your work needs to come to a standstill; nearly almost all serviceable hard disks can be transferred, temporarily or otherwise, to another system.

Transferring Your Hard Disk When your Macintosh is ailing but your hard disk is healthy, downtime doesn't have to be unproductive time: you can connect your hard disk to another Mac and resume business as usual.

Transferring an internal hard disk may be problematic; some disks can be removed only by experts, and reinstalled only in a similar Macintosh model. But any external SCSI device can be attached to any Mac with the appropriate port, even if the unit is formatted for a model different from the temporary computer.

Whether internal or external, a hard disk initialized on a member of the Mac II or Quadra families may not perform as swiftly when attached to a less powerful model due to the disk's quick interleave ratio. The inverse, however, does not hold true: when a Mac encounters a hard disk with a slower interleave than it's capable of, it simply conforms to that ratio. The drive may be capable of speedier performance, but only reformatting will tell for sure.

N O T E

> When hooking up your disk to another Macintosh, take care to address all SCSI bus issues. Are there any potential SCSI address conflicts? Is a device already attached, and can it be safely daisy-chained with yours? If a daisychain already exists, where in the physical sequence should you add your unit? Remember that the Mac searches the bus for startup files in descending order of ID number from 6 to 0, so your intended startup volume should have the highest address of the daisy-chain. And when working on a multi-volume system, try to avoid later confusion by making sure none of your files accidentally stray onto another volume.

Noises

Keep an ear out for unusual noises—they're often the first sign that things aren't operating as usual. Although not every strange sound signals an imminent crisis, a change in the normal repertoire of clicks, hums, and whirs should be assessed as a sign of potential trouble. Here's a rundown of the basics of sonic diagnosis.

Noises During General Operation

Problem: The hard disk sounds consistently louder than before, emitting new noises whenever turned on.

Diagnosis: Something's wearing out—perhaps it's just the fan, but it could also be the drive's motor, or the shaft-and-bearings assembly on which the platters rotate.

You'll want to get the drive serviced right away. The cause of the noise can be determined only by opening the unit. If it is the fan that's acting up, it can be easily replaced. If the noise comes from the main mechanism, that's a sign that it's severely worn; most are engineered to work silently for the bulk of their useful life.

Noises During Reading and Writing

Problem: The strange noise is heard only when the Macintosh is reading and writing to the hard disk. Many external hard disks have an indicator light that flashes when read/write operations are underway.

Diagnosis: There's been a loss of function in the read/write heads mechanisms, the parts that move the heads over the platters to the desired tracks and sectors.

This condition calls for immediate servicing, since the read/write heads are hovering a fraction of an inch above the platter surface. Any further deterioration and the heads could crash down on the platters, obliterating your files and rendering the entire drive beyond repair.

Lack of Normal Noises

Problem: A sound usually made by the Mac or hard disk is absent.

Diagnosis: If the units themselves continue to operate, the new silence is probably caused by the failure of a fan. You can keep using your system long enough to save your data and shut down, but don't push your luck any further than that. Get the unit serviced before getting back to work.

Some users have been known to intentionally disconnect fans, but in doing so they almost certainly reduce the life of their equipment. The computer itself may be able to operate for days or weeks with no visible mishap, but the hard disk is another matter entirely: a lot of moving parts are packed into a tight package, and the combination of proximity and motion creates a lot of heat. Fans are so important in hard disks that some manufacturers have designed fail-safes into the unit, ensuring that when the fan doesn't work, neither will the drive.

Modular Macs: Tones Upon Startup

Problem: Your modular Macintosh does not function when switched on; instead, it emits a brief series of musical tones.

Diagnosis: This is a special feature unique to the modular Mac. It signals a failure somewhere in the RAM resources—the ROM has run a check of available memory prior to beginning the startup process, and it has discovered that something is amiss.

In the modular Mac, RAM is stored on Single Inline Memory Modules (SIMMs), a series of microchip units that snap into an array of eight slots. This modular approach makes for easy upgrades: SIMMs can be removed and replaced quickly. But since they're not soldered in place, they can also come loose.

The RAM failure tones can indicate that one or more SIMMs is burnt-out or broken, but can also indicate that a SIMM isn't correctly connected, or that any of the eight slots is vacant. Apple recommends that you leave memory problems to authorized service sources, but you may want to check first for a simple solution. Opening your modular Mac doesn't void its warranty, so a quick inspection for loose SIMMs may be in order, provided that you or a friend know what to look for.

Performance Problems

Some problems don't announce themselves in a cataclysmic fashion. Instead they arrive gradually, often so subtly that they're not recognized as a problem until months, if not years, go by. When a Mac's performance begins to deteriorate, your first reaction may be to take it in stride; it's natural for things to slow down as they get older, so why complain?

Well, unlike cars and old gray mares, your system should always function at the same performance level. Mechanical parts may wear out and need to be replaced, but on the Macintosh even the most tired component shouldn't slow down such normal functions as launching applications and opening files. When such a symptom shows up, don't just live with it—solve it.

Slow Startup

Symptom: The Macintosh's startup process takes considerably longer than it used to.

Diagnosis: Most likely, the Mac is taking more time because it's been given more things to do. INITs, CDEVs, custom screens, and other specialized software all add to the startup sequence, and especially elaborate ones can take several seconds to load. Check your System Folder; if you're loaded with startup related files, either remove a few or accept the delay as the price you pay.

If a stuffed System Folder doesn't seem to be the problem, it's possible that some part of the data used in the startup process has developed a glitch, one so minor that the Mac deals with it without notifying the user. Take another inventory of your INITs, and other files. Has anything that should have been accessed been skipped instead? If so, replace it; if not, install a fresh System file.

Still no luck? Check the connectors and addresses of all SCSI devices—something might be sending confusing signals down the SCSI bus, which is read by the Mac during startup. If the slow boot up process is followed by overall slow performance, open the About the Finder box to find out if your total amount of RAM has diminished. If it has, you have a hardware problem.

Slow Access Time

Problem: Basic Finder operations, such as the opening of folders and the launching of applications, seem slower than they used to be.

Diagnosis: Is the problem confined to your hard disk? Comparisons with other volumes may help you determine this, although most floppy disks will run slower than even an extremely sluggish hard drive. If the hard disk has been in use for a while, the problem could be file fragmentation, which is easily remedied. Fragmentation and its treatment are explained in Chapter 8.

Does the Finder dawdle on other volumes as well? Maybe it doesn't have sufficient RAM. If you're running System 7, or under MultiFinder with System 6, open the About the Finder or About this Macintosh box and see if something else is using up the memory. If you're running the Finder only, check that same box to confirm that the overall amount of RAM is the same as it should be.

Keep in mind that sluggish operations on networked Macs can also result from heavy network activity and do not necessarily indicate hardware problems.

Slow Document Handling

Problem: While working within a document, commands affecting large portions of the file (scrolling, cutting and pasting, font or text substitution) take an unusually long time to carry out.

Diagnosis: The application may have less RAM resources than it used to, or simply less than it needs to swiftly perform the current task. If you're using Multi-Finder, the About the Finder box in System 6 or About this Macintosh box in System 7 may show cramped memory conditions, in which case you'll need to quit other applications (and even MultiFinder itself) in order to free up the RAM.

If there is no RAM crunch or if you were running under Finder in the first place, perhaps the application's memory allocation has been set unnecessarily low. Check this figure in the application's Get Info box, resetting it if necessary. Of course, the most thorough solution would be to increase the amount of available RAM by adding more SIMM chips.

On drives with little free disk space, file fragmentation can slow document handling. See Chapter 8 for information on defragmenting files.

RECOVERING YOUR DATA

FEATURING:

- → The Types of Data Loss
- → Using Disk First Aid
- → SUM II and Norton Disk Editor
- → Data Recovery Services

In the previous chapter, we looked at the general principles of troubleshooting and treatment. But sometimes a problem can't be completely fixed; instead, it has to be coped with, and its permanent effects have to be minimized. That's the concern of this chapter.

It's often possible to restore damaged files to their previous, uncorrupted state. But since our prime concern is not the *files* themselves but the *data* they contain, this chapter offers a variety of possible solutions—everything from restoring an accidentally-erased hard disk to extracting strings of text from unopenable documents.

If you're reading this chapter in search of a solution to a current crisis, don't proceed any further unless you've already followed the diagnostic instructions in Chapter 6. Many of the procedures and resources detailed here are of a more drastic nature than those in the previous chapter, and you probably won't want to try them until after you have pursued all simpler options. Still, if the simple methods fail, the information contained in this chapter may save your data.

The Four Types of Data Loss

Unfortunately, the Macintosh offers about as many ways to lose data as it does to preserve it. Whether stored on a hard disk, a floppy, or other media, Macintosh files are vulnerable to heat, strong magnetic fields, and just plain human error. In general, incidents of data loss fall into the four categories of directory deletion, directory damage, file overwrites, and hardware crashes.

Directory Deletion

A file is considered "deleted" whenever it has been expunged from your Macintosh folder system, whether intentionally or not. This is usually accomplished by dragging a file icon to the trash and selecting Empty Trash from the Special menu.

WARNING

> **Under System 6 or earlier, the Macintosh will delete a file placed in the Trash if it needs the extra storage space occupied by the file. So files can be deleted from the Trash even when the Empty Trash command has not been given. With System 7, files remain undeleted until you give the command.**

But putting a file in the Trash is not the only way it can disappear. If you're running System 6 or earlier, the Macintosh doesn't always wait for the Empty Trash command to throw out a file you have put there. Even if you place a file in the can without selecting Empty Trash, the Macintosh may delete the file automatically when it needs the storage space occupied by the trashed file. Likewise, the contents of the Trash are purged whenever you launch a new application or shut down the Macintosh. Under System 7, none of this applies; once dragged to the Trash, the file remains there until you select the Empty Trash command. The Trash will remain full even through successive startups and shutdowns.

If you have inadvertently trashed a file, your first step should be to open the trash by double-clicking on the Trash Can icon in the lower right-hand corner of the desktop. The Trash Can is similar to other file folders—it just has a unique icon. If the Trash Can is bulging, it still contains the files you threw out. If you decide you don't want to throw a file away, you can drag it out and deposit in a folder. On the other hand, if the Trash Can is not bulging, either no files have been thrown away during the current work session or the files placed in the Trash have been deleted.

Some applications give you the option of deleting files without placing them in the Trash. This option, when it exists, is usually accessible from the File menu. When you delete a file directly from the File menu, you do not have a chance to reverse your decision. As soon as you select OK, the file is deleted.

As we've already noted, a file that is "deleted" from a hard disk is not actually expunged from the drive's magnetic-media platters. Instead, the file's entry is removed from the volume's directory. The actual data in the platter's tracks and sectors remains until the space it occupies is needed to store a new file. When the space is reused, the data is finally overwritten by new data, and therefore is lost to the ages.

Directory Damage

Directory damage is the second most common way data is lost. In this case, the information needed to locate, display, and manipulate a file is mangled or misplaced, and the file simply disappears from the Mac's directory. The file itself is not really lost—it continues to occupy tracks and sectors on the volume's storage medium. However, because the computer cannot access it appropriately, neither can you.

Directory damage can be repaired with utilities such as Norton Utilities' Disk Doctor (see Chapter 5) or Volume Restore (see below). The key to minimizing loss is to act swiftly and take steps to restore a file as soon as you note its absence. When you notice that directory damage has occurred, don't save another file to the same disk. If you do, there's the possibility that you won't be able to recover your missing data.

File Overwritten

Overwriting means that a file has been deleted from a directory, and that one or more of the tracks and sectors it used to occupy is occupied by another file. Overwriting occurs when the information needed to locate a file is lost, and you save a new file to the hard disk. This is why you should try to recover a missing file at once: if you save a new file, it may occupy space that holds data from your missing file.

A completely overwritten file cannot be reconstituted by any utility. All of the information stored on the overwritten sectors has disappeared. But in some cases, if the entire file has not been overwritten, the data in the remaining sectors can be saved without formatting (this is especially useful with text-only documents). For the most part, however, an overwritten file is permanently lost. Even if you do recover part of the data, it may not include the critical information that an application needs to open and use the file.

Hardware Crashes

The final and most profound type of data loss is caused by a physical problem. Data is lost when the magnetic storage media of a hard disk are stressed or corrupted, or when intricate mechanical parts collide. A head crash or disk crash occurs when a Macintosh is dropped from a table or subjected to similar strains, and the drive's read/write heads come into contact with the platter's surface.

Head crashes and disk crashes have significant consequences. Usually the data in the affected sectors is obliterated. Moreover, the sectors themselves usually become unusable. Fortunately, most hard disk drivers will identify damaged sectors and automatically avoid using them.

Working with Disk First Aid

Disk First Aid, Apple Computer's recovery utility, has been included in the System software package since version 5. Although it's not as effective or flexible as some third-party programs, it's worth using if you have got it on hand. At the very least, it's a good step to take before resigning yourself to reinitializing a volume and losing all of the data on it.

Disk First Aid is limited in that it can repair only volume-level problems, not file-level ones. Although it is useful when you cannot mount a volume or when a directory has been damaged, it won't help you recover a corrupted application or a deleted document. Use Disk First Aid when you attempt to mount or open a volume and a Reinitialize dialog box appears. It may provide the solution when your system won't boot from the hard disk.

Using Disk First Aid is a simple matter of launching the application and designating a volume for testing (Figure 7.1). The default choice is the floppy disk in either the internal or external drives, but if there isn't one, Disk First Aid selects the current startup volume. To choose another drive, click the Drive button until its name appears in the dialog box. You can select and test a volume even if the Macintosh cannot mount it on the desktop. If the disk drive with the unmountable disk is connected and operational, your problem lies with the disk, not the drive, and Disk First Aid will tell you so by announcing "Disk With Bad Name." This usually means that Disk First Aid cannot read the disk.

Make sure that the volume you're testing was not used as the startup and is not write-protected. Disk First Aid can examine a startup or write-protected volume and verify any damage, but it can't make repairs to it. If you need to run Disk First Aid on your hard disk, copy it to a bootable floppy and start the system with the floppy.

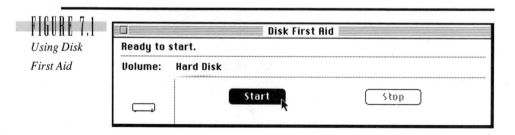

FIGURE 7.1
Using Disk First Aid

To use Disk First Aid:

1. Click on the Start button (Figure 7.2). This puts Disk First Aid through its paces.

2. The Ready to Start message is replaced by the Verifying volume message. It takes Disk First Aid a couple of minutes to check a hard disk. The program does not display the wristwatch or other wait cursor while testing is underway. You can abort, pause, or resume testing at any time by clicking the appropriate button.

3. When Disk First Aid has finished its check, a diagnostic message appears.

The primary diagnostic messages are:

- **Finished. No repair necessary.** Be careful with this message. While it sometimes means that the volume is normal, often it means that the volume needs repairs beyond what Disk First Aid can offer.

- **This is not an HFS disk.** This message can be misleading. Disk First Aid doesn't work with volumes formatted under the earlier MFS standard. The message might mean that you have an MFS volume, but it could also mean you have an HFS volume whose formatting has been garbled or corrupted.

- **Verification completed, but cannot repair.** Although this ambiguous message doesn't seem to do so, it is really recommending that you repair the disk. It appears when you test the startup volume. When you

FIGURE 7.2

*Testing a
volume with
Disk First Aid*

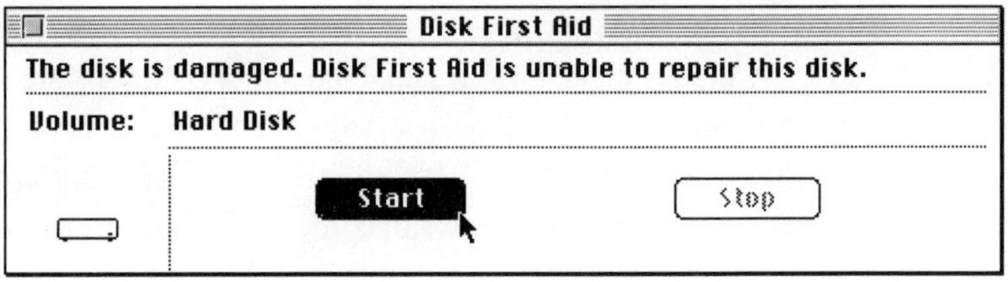

Disk First Aid

The disk is damaged. Disk First Aid is unable to repair this disk.

Volume: **Hard Disk**

Start   Stop

see this message, reboot from a floppy or other volume that contains Disk First Aid, relaunch Disk First Aid, and go through the steps again. You should then get the **Disk is in need of repair** message.

- **Disk is in need of repair** This message appears in its own dialog box and indicates that Disk First Aid thinks that it has identified and can fix the problem. You have nothing to lose by clicking the Repair button—there's no danger of losing any data on the volume. At worst, Disk First Aid will do nothing; at best, it will mend your disk. In a minute or less, Disk First Aid will say whether the repair was successful or not. If it declares the repair a success, don't assume that all your troubles are over. Quit the application and see how the volume functions from the Finder. Open some files to be sure that all of their contents appear correctly. If Disk First Aid was unsuccessful, it's time to try another utility.

- **Disk is damaged. Disk First Aid cannot perform repairs.** This means that the application recognizes the problem as one too complex for its powers. When this message appears, go directly to a more advanced application, such as the Norton Utilities' Disk Doctor.

Working with SUM II

One package of potent data recovery utilities is Symantec Utilities for the Macintosh II (SUM II). Similar to the Norton Utilities but with a more technical flavor, it's a very effective tool not only for retrieving lost data, but also for restoring a crashed disk to proper working order.

SUM II is not a single utility but rather a group of programs controlled by the Disk Clinic application (Figure 7.3). Each program can be used individually, but Disk Clinic is the hub from which the other programs are initiated. SUM II offers a number of nice utilities for defragmenting your hard disk, exploring its contents, and even making quick copies of files. But in this chapter, we'll concern ourselves with Disk Clinic's data recovery capabilities.

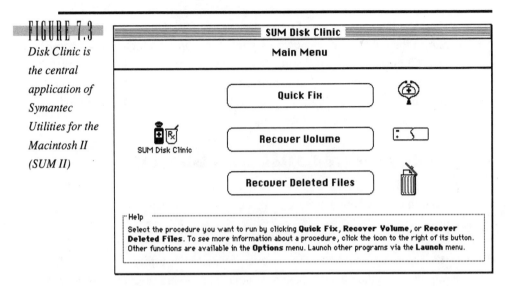

FIGURE 7.3

Disk Clinic is the central application of Symantec Utilities for the Macintosh II (SUM II)

A glance at the main Disk Clinic menu shows the three choices that Disk Clinic offers.

- Quick Fix is the court of first resort. It's the utility SUM II uses to repair minor damage to volumes, without resorting to such elaborate measures as reinitialization or reformatting. When a problem arises, you'll probably want to try Quick Fix without proceeding further.

- Recover Volume can retrieve files from volumes that have crashed, or even from volumes that have been reinitialized by mistake. Its speed and effectiveness are dependent on whether or not SUM's Shield INIT was installed on the volume beforehand, with the Volume Restore Record option selected. The installation of Shield was covered in Chapter 5.

- Recover Deleted Files functions similarly to Norton Utilities' Un-Erase feature, rescuing files that have been trashed. For maximum effectiveness, you need to have installed Shield and selected the Deleted File Record option.

You can click on any one of these choices and Disk Clinic will automatically launch the utility you've chosen. If you're not sure of which one to choose, Disk Clinic can help you decide. Select "Symptoms and Solutions" under the Options menu, and you'll find yourself in a helpful diagnostic tutorial guiding you through possible options (Figure 7.4). Take the time to read and follow these instructions before proceeding.

Recovering Deleted Files with Disk Clinic

With the Recover Deleted Files command, you can resurrect many of the files missing from a floppy or hard disk, including those that you intentionally deleted.

It's important to note that the Recover Deleted Files utility can recover files missing from the directory, but not damaged files still present in useless form on the disk. If the tracks and sectors of a deleted file have not been overwritten, Recover Deleted Files will try to retrieve the file data, which it can do with an extremely high rate of success.

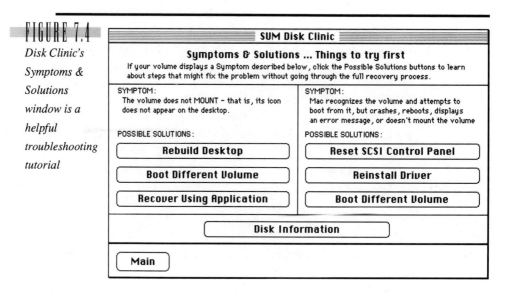

FIGURE 7.4

Disk Clinic's
Symptoms &
Solutions
window is a
helpful
troubleshooting
tutorial

File Restoration with Shield Installed

After you launch Recover Deleted Files, Disk Clinic asks whether you have installed SUM II's Shield feature on the target volume (Figure 7.5). Shield makes retrieving your files much easier by saving relevant file information to that Recover doesn't need to search the disk. If Shield is installed, click on the Recover Volume button in the Disk Clinic main window, and then click on the "Deleted File Record IS installed" button in the ensuing dialog box.

Next, select the volume and click Continue to reach the main window of Recover (Figure 7.6). In the center of the window is a scroll box that lists all deleted files that can still be identified. You can use the pull-down List and By menus to arrange the files by whatever criteria you'd like.

Note the two different type styles in the UnDelete Window. Unlike Norton Utilities' UnErase (described in Chapter 5), you're not given an estimate of your chances for recovering any given file. Instead, files in roman type are those that can be recovered while files in italic type have already been at least partially overwritten and can't be recovered. Another important column is

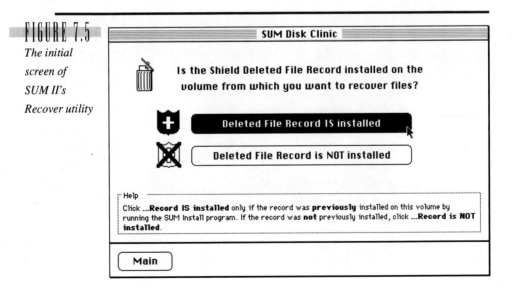

FIGURE 7.5

The initial screen of SUM II's Recover utility

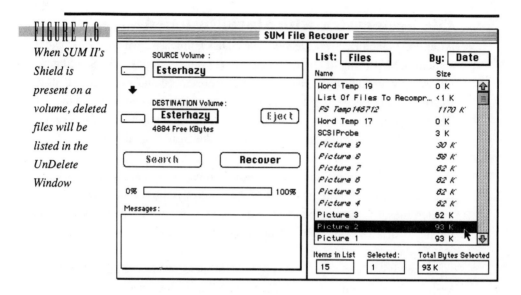

FIGURE 7.6
When SUM II's Shield is present on a volume, deleted files will be listed in the UnDelete Window

Size—a 0 in this column may indicate that a file is recoverable but devoid of data.

To restore a recoverable file listed in roman type, select one or more files and select Recover. After a minute or two, depending on the size of the file or files you want to recover, the utility will inform you that the restoration process is complete.

Restored files are placed in an automatically generated folder on the volume's root level. The first is named "A.SUM Recovered Files." All subsequent files placed in the folder will have the same designation but the next available alphabetical prefix, which in this case would be "B.SUM Recovered Files." You'll note that you're not given the opportunity to restore those files directly to another volume; they're automatically restored to the same volume on which they were found.

File Restoration Without Shield Installed

If it so happens that you didn't install Shield on the volume whose deleted files you wish to restore, SUM II may still be able to save the day. The search takes longer than it would if you had installed Shield. Moreover, SUM II will only list files that can still be retrieved, not files that have been overwritten.

When Shield is not present on the target volume, Recover Deleted Files offers the option of selecting a destination volume for recovered files. I strongly suggest that this volume not be the one from which the recovery effort was made. When you retrieve and store on the same volume and file corruption is present, you'll only make things worse. You're better off saving the data on a floppy disk. Files recovered from a volume are placed in a root-level folder labeled "A.Recover."

Recovering Entire Volumes with SUM II

SUM II also offers a method for recovering entire volumes which have become unusable—volumes that Disk First Aid cannot repair. If Shield is installed on your System Folder, you can use SUM II's Recover Crashed Disk button to reclaim the data on the volume. You can use this feature even if Shield was not installed—SUM II will scan the disk and try to recover as many files as possible (Figure 7.7).

Volume Recovery with Shield Installed

If Shield was installed on the system before the hard disk crashed, you need to answer only a few questions before using SUM II to recover your deleted volume. This is because, when Shield is installed, the utility knows where to look for all the information it needs to recover the disk. If Shield was installed, click on the Recover Volume button in the main Disk Clinic window, and then click on the button reading "Volume Restore Record IS installed" in the dialog box that follows.

SUM II then asks you to select the device you are trying to recover. SUM II can recover crashed floppy disks, hard disks, or partitions; it can recover partitions

FIGURE 7.7

SUM II can
recover crashed
hard disks
whether or not
Shield was
installed

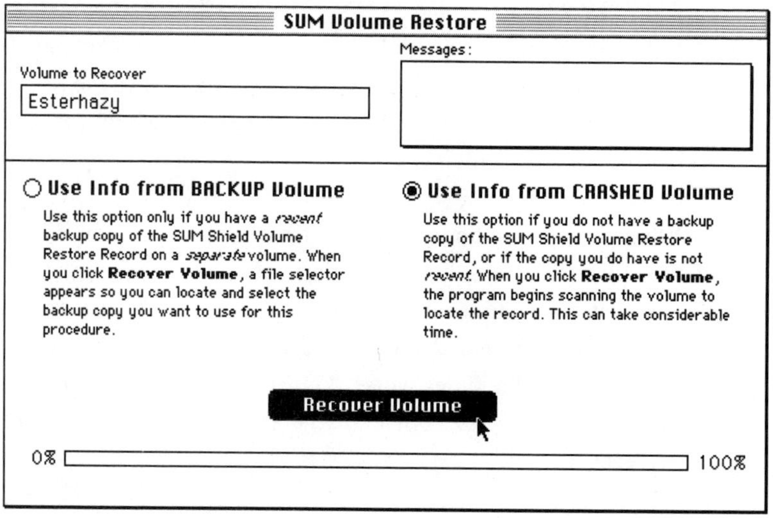

```
┌──────────────── SUM Uolume Restore ────────────────┐
│                                      Messages:       │
│   Volume to Recover              ┌─────────────────┐ │
│   ┌─────────────────────────┐    │                 │ │
│   │ Esterhazy               │    │                 │ │
│   └─────────────────────────┘    └─────────────────┘ │
│                                                       │
│   ○ Use Info from BACKUP Uolume  ◉ Use Info from CRASHED Uolume │
│     Use this option only if you have a recent    Use this option if you do not have a backup │
│     backup copy of the SUM Shield Volume         copy of the SUM Shield Volume Restore │
│     Restore Record on a separate volume. When    Record, or if the copy you do have is not │
│     you click Recover Volume, a file selector    recent. When you click Recover Volume, │
│     appears so you can locate and select the     the program begins scanning the volume to │
│     backup copy you want to use for this         locate the record. This can take considerable │
│     procedure.                                   time. │
│                                                       │
│              ┌───────────────────────┐               │
│              │    Recover Uolume     │               │
│              └───────────────────────┘               │
│                                                       │
│   0% ┌─────────────────────────────────────┐ 100%    │
│      └─────────────────────────────────────┘         │
└───────────────────────────────────────────────────────┘
```

made with its own partition driver and partitions made with drivers from hard disk manufacturers. Specify the volume, and then click Continue.

Now that SUM II has all of the information it needs, the Volume Restore Window will appear (Figure 7.8). From here you tell Shield where to locate the volume restore file—the file with the information SUM II needs to restore the volume. It can be located either on the crashed hard disk or on a different disk (specifying its location is part of the Shield installation process). Click on the Restore button and SUM II will go to work; if the volume restore file you chose was on the crashed disk itself, the process may take several minutes. If the process succeeds, you'll be requested to quit SUM II and reboot your Macintosh. The repaired hard disk should reappear on the desktop and function properly, although you might want to run a general diagnostic check with Norton Utilities' Disk Doctor (see Chapter 6) before proceeding.

Volume Recovery Without Shield Installed

Even if you didn't install Shield on the volume, Disk Clinic's Recover Volume command can scan a disk and attempt to copy files to a healthy volume. This

FIGURE 7.8
SUM II's
Volume Restore
window

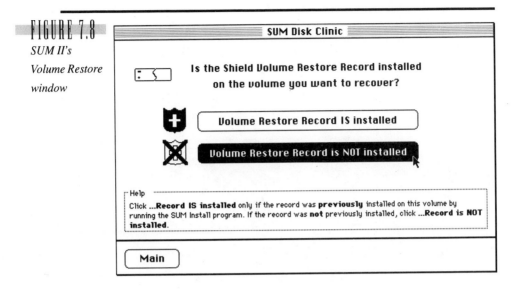

takes more time than with Shield, since you need to give SUM II more information before proceeding, and the operation won't be as thorough as it would have been with Shield installed. Still, you may be able to save vital files from a crashed volume.

The big difference between SUM II alone and SUM II with Shield installed is the type of retrieval method used. With Shield installed, SUM II has a specific place to look for all the information that it needs to recover from the disk. But without Shield, SUM II must compile that information on its own, and in order to do so, it has to know something about the nature of the problem. The program asks you to indicate your the type of problem with your disk (Figure 7.9).

● The Crashed Volume category covers the gamut of large-scale malfunction: volumes that refuse to mount, volumes that mount intermittently, and volumes that your computer doesn't recognize as formatted for the Macintosh. If your problem doesn't fall clearly into the other two categories, this is the option you should choose.

FIGURE 7.9

When recovering files on crashed disks without Shield installed, SUM II needs to know the nature of the problem

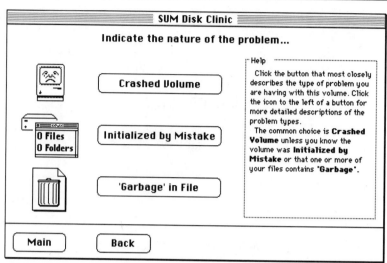

SUM Disk Clinic

Indicate the nature of the problem...

Crashed Volume

0 Files
0 Folders

Initialized by Mistake

'Garbage' in File

Help

Click the button that most closely describes the type of problem you are having with this volume. Click the icon to the left of a button for more detailed descriptions of the problem types.
The common choice is **Crashed Volume** unless you know the volume was **Initialized by Mistake** or that one or more of your files contains **'Garbage'**.

Main   Back

- Initialized by Mistake is the problem category to use when a hard disk appears on the desktop, but seems devoid of files and folders. SUM II will scan the entire volume and try to restore the files that occupy the physical disk but do not appear in the disk directory. This is one of the few SUM II commands that can work only on a hard disk, not on a floppy disk.

- The condition of 'Garbage' in File occurs when a volume seems to operate normally, but many of the files, when opened, contain garbled, extraneous, or otherwise unrecognizable data. Unfortunately, SUM II is not able to actually repair such files. Instead, it will offer general advice about recovering the data, such as opening a text file with a word processor other than the one that created it.

Recovering Crashed Volumes with Norton Utilities

Norton Utilities' Format Recover command works quite similarly to SUM II's Recover Crashed Disk command (both packages are produced by the same manufacturer, Symantec). Format Recover looks first for the volume recovery file (in this case labelled FileSaver rather than Shield), and if such a file cannot be found, it attempts to rebuild the volume from the information on hand. We covered the installation of the FileSaver INIT in Chapter 5; if you're working with Norton rather than SUM II, it's a good idea to make FileSaver active on all your volumes. Norton Utilities provides a special "Emergency" floppy disk, which can be used to startup your Macintosh when you hard drive is down. This disk includes most of the diagnostic features of the software, including Disk Doctor, Disk Editor and Format Recover. You should make a backup copy of this floppy, and use it as the startup source.

When a volume refuses to mount on your desktop, or does mount but appears to be empty, your first step should be to run a basic diagnostic with the Norton Disk Doctor (covered in Chapter 5). Often times Disk Doctor can identify and eliminate minor problems with the boot blocks or directory files, which can give the appearance of a major problem. However, if Disk Doctor doesn't help, proceed by following these steps:

1. Return to the main window of Norton Utilities. Select "Format Recover."

2. In the ensuing dialog box, specify if FileSaver was or was not installed on the volume in question.

3. Select the volume you want Norton Utilities to open. If the volume appears but not under its correct name (a title like "Disk with Bad Name" may be given), proceed. If the volume does not show up on the SCSI bus no matter how many times you hit the Drive button, Format Recover can't help you. Recheck the cabling, power and termination setup, then try again.

4. If FileSaver was present on the volume—and Volume Restore is able to locate it—you'll then be presented with the date of the File-Saver file, and asked if you want to use it to restore the volume. Remember, the restoration will be only as recent as that date. If you're sure that a more recent FileSaver file exists on the volume, you can click on the "Keep looking" button. Otherwise, hit the

"Restore" button. In a few minutes you'll be notified that the restoration is complete. Your volume should then reappear on the desktop under its proper name.

5. If FileSaver was not present—or if the file was corrupted or otherwise unusable—you can instruct Format Recover to keep looking, or to proceed with a recontruction. An unprotected volume is unlikely to be as throroughly reconstituted as one with a valid FileSaver file, but you should be able to at least get the volume once again mounted on the desktop.

6. Once restoration is complete, launch Norton Utilities' UnErase feature (discussed in Chapter 6), a retrieve any files you need.

Recovering Text Documents

If you have a word-processed file that you cannot open with the application you used to create it, you may still be able to recover the file by converting it to text-only format. Although you will lose any formatting information you included in the original document, and some garbage characters may appear in the document, all of the text should remain in the file. Cleaning and reformatting a file is usually a lot easier and faster than retyping the entire document, but a short document with a lot of formatting might not be worth recovering in this fashion.

You can convert a document to text-only by entering a program that allows you to edit the application type of a document (such as Norton Disk Editor, described below, or DiskTop), and changing the four-character code that defines the file type. Once you have converted the file to text-only, you should be able to open it with almost any word processor.

Working with Norton Disk Editor

One utility capable of making such a modification to a file is Disk Editor, another portion of Norton Utilities for the Macintosh.

Disk Editor maintains a low profile in the Norton Utilities. You'll note it's not listed in the main menu that is displayed whenever the Utilities are launched.

This is probably because Disk Editor is a powerful application, one that could easily damage files if used incorrectly. It's a very good idea to make a duplicate of the file you will be working on before proceeding since you could easily make the file even more unreadable. However, sometimes the Macintosh cannot copy a damaged file; if this is the case, you may want to open up the file itself, but proceed cautiously.

ARNING

Whenever possible, only use Disk Editor on duplicate copies of files. Otherwise, you might make the problem worse than it already is, or even make it impossible to retrieve the data you want.

Since Disk Editor isn't on the main menu, you launch it by selecting Norton Disk Editor on the Utilities menu. You'll be asked which volume you want to Explore, and after you make your selection, you'll enter the Disk Editor's main window (Figure 7.10).

You can navigate in this window to select the file in question, double-clicking on any folders if necessary. Note that each file's creator ID code is listed. Once you've located the file, click on the Edit Info button. The information displayed should be similar to that in Figure 7.11.

As you can see, the window lists a number of elements pertaining to the file: name, creation and modification dates, and whether the file is on the desktop or invisible. You can modify any or all of these attributes, but let's limit ourselves to the file type. In the Type text field, enter the word *TEXT* . This tells Disk Editor that you want to change the file's type to text-only. Make sure that you're changing the four-character Type code, and not the similar Creator code. Select OK, then quit the Norton Utilities. Save your changes when prompted by the program.

FIGURE 7.10

*The main
window of Disk
Editor*

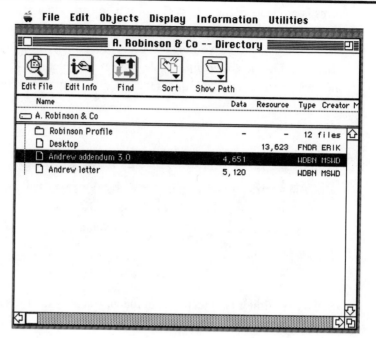

Now your file can be opened from almost any word processor or text editor; launch the program, and then see if the file is recognized in the Open dialog box. If so, all you need to do is open it, remove any extra characters that were inserted, and recreate the document's formatting.

It's also possible to completely "graft" a file to an application, that is, to modify it so that it is "adopted" by the application as if it had been its creator. This is done by substituting a type code other than "TEXT" and adding the correct creator code. For instance, if you designated "WDBN" for type and "MSWD" for creator, the Macintosh's Finder would then treat the file as if it had been created by Microsoft Word. However, that method isn't recommended, since sometimes the application can't successfully open the "grafted" file. It's a safer bet to make the file a text-only file, open it from inside your word processor, and then use the Save As command to create an entirely new file.

*Opening the
Edit Info
window*

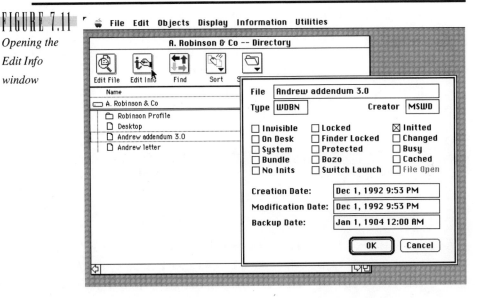

Be careful in case any passages you deleted from the text
have reappeared in the document. Some word processors,
such as Microsoft Word, do not really erase deleted text but
rather mark it as deleted so the program knows not to display
or print it. After converting the file to text-only, some of this
deleted text may reappear.

Using ResEdit to Examine Resource Files

ResEdit is a powerful utility developed by Apple for examining and modifying
the resource fork of an application. Every file on the Macintosh has two distinct
components: the data fork and the resource fork. A file may have an empty data
or resource fork, but the fork still exists even when empty. Resource forks contain the information that an application needs to operate, such as icons, pictures,

text, dialog boxes, menus, and computer codes. Data forks hold the data that you create with an application. This is not always the case, however. It is possible to store applications in the data fork and documents in the resource fork. Sometimes a file is stored on both the data and resource forks. An empty file might be stored on both an empty data and empty resource fork.

OTE

Data forks and resource forks are examined in detail in Chapter 3.

Using ResEdit to modify the resource fork of an application or document can be dangerous—you might make the application nonfunctional. Only use ResEdit to examine duplicate copies of applications. Before you launch ResEdit, select the document that you want to examine from the Finder, then select Duplicate from the File menu. Now, when you pick a file from ResEdit, be sure to pick the duplicate of the application that you want to examine.

ARNING

Only use ResEdit to examine duplicate copies of applications. You don't want to damage the originals.

ResEdit also provides an easy way to locate hidden files that are in the directory but do not show up from the Finder. In its file list, ResEdit includes hidden files along with the others. For example, when you look at the root level of the hard disk you should see the Desktop file. Desktop is a hidden file that the Finder uses to assign documents to the appropriate applications.

When you launch ResEdit you are presented with a window listing all the files at the root level of all mounted disks (Figure 7.12). To move into a folder, just double-click on the one you want. This will open a new window listing all

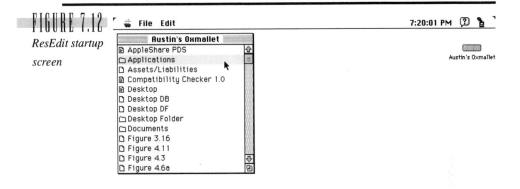

FIGURE 7.12

ResEdit startup screen

the files in the folder (Figure 7.13). To move towards the root, click the close box on each window until you are at the desired level. Once you have the file you wish to open in a window, double-click on it. ResEdit will show another window listing all of the resources in the file (Figure 7.14). To examine a resource, click on its name. Either the resource or a list of resources will appear. If a list of resources appears, click on one of them and the resource itself should be displayed.

Although it's a powerful program, ResEdit has only limited usefulness for data retrieval. But here are a few suggestions of how it can help you diagnose a problem:

- Most document files have no resource fork. If a malfunctioning document appears in ResEdit with a resource fork, while a document created with the same application has none, the contents of that fork may be causing the problem. You might try deleting all resources in that fork by selecting the Clear command.

FIGURE 7.13

ResEdit with a folder open

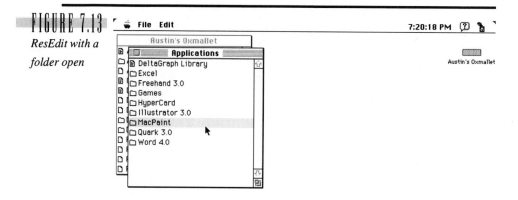

FIGURE 7.14

ResEdit displaying resources in MacPaint

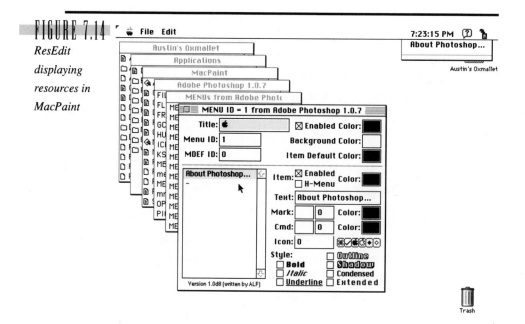

- Some document files saved in special formats do have a resource fork, which usually contains one or two resource types. For instance, a Photoshop document saved as a TIFF file will have one resource labelled 8BIM (the number of resources under the type may vary); the same document saved as an EPS file will have both 8BIM and PICT resources. You can use ResEdit to confirm that the file was saved in the correct format—once again, compare its contents with the contents of similar, properly working files.

- All files, even invisible ones, will appear in ResEdit's windows. You can check for duplicate or unecessary files, then delete them (once, when I was baffled by a hard disk's quirky performance, I browsed with ResEdit and found a second Desktop file in a sub-directory). To delete a file with ResEdit, highlight its name then select the Clear command.

- If you're running with MultiFinder active, you can encounter an error message and not know which of the currently active applications triggered it. With ResEdit, you can examine the ALRT resources of each. These display mini-screenshots of the error messages belonging to the individual application.

When All Else Fails...

Even if you've exhausted your resources in trying to retrieve data from a crashed hard disk—and you don't have a complete backup of your data—all is not lost. Your last resort is to turn to a firm that specializes in data recovery, in hopes that they'll be able to succeed where you haven't.

The number of data recovery services has grown in recent years, for two main reasons: more people are coming to rely on hard disks, and more hard disks have been in use long enough for reliability to become an issue. These firms are expensive: $100 an hour is a not-uncommon charge, and even a relatively straight forward data extraction can take from three to eight hours. That fee might seem like a lot, but it can be cheap compared to the costs of recreating valuable data. A reputable recovery service is more than a computer repair-person with a workbench; most employ specialized tools and technicians, and make an active effort to keep up to date with manufacturer specifications. Several services even maintain their own "clean rooms," similar to the conditions under which hard disks are built.

You can find data recovery services in your phone directory, or in ads in Macintosh magazines. If you do decide to seek one out, it's a good idea to ask the following questions:

- *Are they experienced with Macintosh hard drives?* Drives formatted with MS-DOS present a different set of recovery problems, so make sure that the service has a solid track record in repairing Mac disks.

- *What kind of success have they had with drives of your specific model type?* If they quote a success rate, ask if that applies to drives from which they've recovered 100 percent of the data, or just drives with which they have achieved partial success.

- *Do they have the technical information and diagnostic tools needed to work with your kind of drive?* Most competent services maintain ties with hard drive manufacturers, and are able to communicate with them when they need specialized information.

- *Will they keep your files confidential?* If security is of the utmost importance, ask if they'll sign a non-disclosure agreement before proceeding. If they do succeed in recovering your data, will they send you a copy of your files and then destroy their copy as soon as you've received it? If they destroy their copy earlier (or send you the only copy), you run the risk of it being lost or damaged in the mail.

MAXIMIZING

HARD

DISK

PERFORMANCE

It's now time to look at the more advanced aspects of using Macintosh hard disk technology. In this section, we'll cover many of the ways you can enhance and expand your hard disk system, from reorganizing its contents to using it in networks and other multiple-device configurations. With this information, you'll be able to keep your hard disk efficient and effective.

Even a well-organized hard disk can become sluggish in time, as a once logical directory layout becomes cluttered and confused. Chapter 8 will give you advice for streamlining your file structure, including information on reformatting your hard disk and eliminating file fragmentation. Chapter 9 examines a number of advanced-level organizational tools, as well as such hard disk "fringe benefits" as macro keys, printer spoolers, and utilities for the Finder. Chapter 10 looks at incorporating new hard disks or other devices into your SCSI setup to keep up with your system growth. And since not all Macintosh hard disks are conventionally connected to a computer, Chapter 11 addresses networking issues such as networked hard disks and file sharing.

FILE MANAGEMENT

FEATURING:

→ **Evaluating Hard Disk Organization and Performance**

→ **Reorganizing the Folder Structure**

→ **File Defragmentation**

→ **Reinitializing the Hard Disk**

→ **Partitions and Partitioning**

→ **Choosing the Proper Interleave Factor**

O rganization is merely the first step in getting the most out of your hard disk; the next step is maintenance. You'll find that maintaining your hard disk's performance is an ongoing process, requiring frequent evaluation and adaptation.

Time changes things, and your hard disk is no exception. A directory structure that once perfectly suited your needs can become antiquated and awkward, adhered to only by force of habit. Files and folders that were once in logical locations can soon languish in out-of-the-way places. And all hard disks eventually slow down as the hours of usage take their toll.

Fortunately, all of these symptoms are easy to identify and remedy. With the proper tools and techniques, you can keep your hard disk tuned up and in shape for ycars to come.

Evaluating Organization and Performance

There are two main aspects to file management, and they affect all operations. The first is *clarity and convenience.* Is your organizational setup easy to use and understand? Or do you find yourself misplacing files, or plowing through an excessive number of subfolders?

The second aspect is *capacity and capability.* Is the hard disk operating slower than usual, taking more and more time to carry out basic operations? Does it contain a large number of little-used files?

Since these factors develop gradually, many users don't identify these problems so much as adapt to them. You should make a habit of evaluating organization and performance, keeping a running critique "in the back of your mind" while working with the Macintosh. One way to monitor performance is to period-ically run the "Check Disk" portion of the Norton Utilities' Speed Disk utility; it'll give you an exact percentage of the extent of fragmentation on the disk, and recommend when defragmentation is necessary (see "Using Speed Disk" below).

When to Reorganize?

In most cases, file management is a matter of refinement, not renovation. In general, your hard disk's organization should change when your needs change, a process which can be slow or sudden depending on your circumstances. Modifications can be as subtle as placing a much-used application directly on the desktop while moving another to a folder, or as radical as completely refor-matting the disk and starting anew. Changes should result out of a *need,* not a *crisis:* update your setup when it becomes more hindrance than help, rather than waiting for it to become a complete handicap.

A good time to address file management issues is when you perform your backup or archiving chores, since inspection can be incorporated with preser-vation. If you use a cataloging utility, such as those discussed in Chapter 4, you can search for little-used files by scanning the "date last modified" field. Some search utilities can compile a similar list.

**Make it a habit to review your hard disk organization
whenever you backup your hard disk or archive your files.
Move frequently used files to the root level or desktop, group
related files together, and remove inactive files if necessary.**

Here are a few rules of thumb that may be useful:

- *Relocate a file you frequently use if it's nested three or more folders
down the directory hierarchy.* If it's a high-priority file (such as a
report), place it directly on the desktop. If the file is needed for a
current on-going project, place it (along with any other necessary
files for the project) in a new folder on the hard disk's root level. If
you expect to be working with an application regularly, give it its
own folder on the root level—or, if you have System 7, place an
alias of the application directly into the Apple menu. For example,
you may currently have Photoshop in your Graphics folder which is
nested in your Applications folder. However, if you find that you
use Photoshop regularly, you should create a root-level folder of
its own.

System 7 can make documents or applications even more accessible
by allowing you to put them in the Apple Menu Items folder nested
in the System Folder. When so placed, they can be accessed under
the Apple menu in the same fashion as desk accessories (Figure 8.1).

Unless you want to give your files a new, permanent home, file shuffling can lead to confusion since a file can have two addresses: its
temporary location and its long-term home. If you're running System 6, the best way to keep track of where a file belongs is to record
the home path name in the comment field of the file's Get Info box.
Under System 7, an alternative is to create an "alias" of a file, and
place it in a convenient location. We'll talk more about aliases in
Chapter 9.

FIGURE 8.1

Applications and files placed in the Apple Menu Items folder can be accessed on the Apple menu, much like Desk Accessories

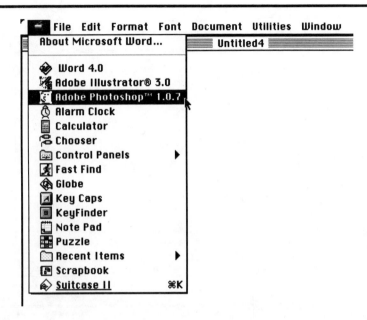

- *Create a new folder only when there's no easier way to group related files together.* It's easy to create and populate new folders, but be wary of over-organizing your disk to the point that files are tidy but tedious to locate. Each new folder adds another set of mouse clicks and keystrokes to the task of finding a file.

As a general rule, there's no need to create a new folder when you have only one or two files to place in it. If a group of files must be identifiable as a unit, use the features of the folder window's view format to distinguish them (Figure 8.2). If the files are displayed with icons or small icons, the files can be arranged in a row or in a cluster. If the folder uses View by Name format, they can be grouped together by giving them all a common prefix; for example, you can use a non-alphabetical prefix such as ! or * to group the files at the top of the folder window and File dialog boxes. If you have a color monitor, you can use the View by Color (View by Label in System 7) format to identify related files at a glance.

FIGURE 8.2

Folder

alternatives:

clustered icons

(above),

specially-prefixed

file names

(below)

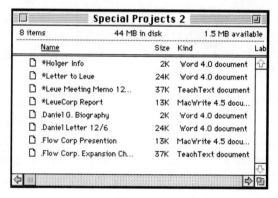

- *Remove files from the hard disk when you need the space they occupy, or when you're confident you won't need the files to be on hand.* You may want to move inactive files off your hard disk and onto your archive floppy disks; but if they contain reference data and your disk is not unduly crowded, why not keep them around? They may come in handy someday. Since most backup software ignores files that have remained unchanged since the last backup, these files don't add any time to your regular backup chores. If you keep these files on disk, you may want to change their names to

better reflect their current status (i.e., "Inventory" should become
"Inventory/1992").

When should you consider your hard disk "full"? Theoretically you could continue to squeeze in files to the absolute capacity of your drive, but in general,
you should clean house when your disk approaches 80 percent of maximum
capacity. Keep in mind that overall performance speed is really a function of
the number of files on disk, not storage space occupied, and a drive containing
a few files of massive size will run faster than one with a multitude of small
files.

TIP

**For maximum performance, keep your disk at 80 percent of
total capacity or below.**

File Fragmentation

Probably the biggest correctable factor affecting hard disk performance is *file
fragmentation.* Fragmentation is a by-product of normal disk usage. It occurs
when data being copied to the disk cannot be placed in contiguous sectors on
the disk. Instead, the file's data is stored in sectors scattered around the surface
of the platter. A fragmented file takes longer to access because the read/write
heads must move around the disk to access the file information, as illustrated
in Figure 8.3.

Why aren't all files read into consecutive sectors? They usually are when a hard
disk is newly formatted, but after a while, the most convenient locations for
new files are the sectors vacated by deleted files. The remaining files are not
automatically reorganized to make room for more contiguous space. Since the
available contiguous sectors rarely match the exact storage needs of a new file,
the file must be split among a number of sectors in different areas on the drive.
As files continue to be added and removed, the platter surface becomes a hap-
hazard patchwork of files in scattered segments.

FIGURE 8.3

Files occupying consecutive sectors (above) can be accessed swiftly, whereas fragmented ones (below) slow down operations

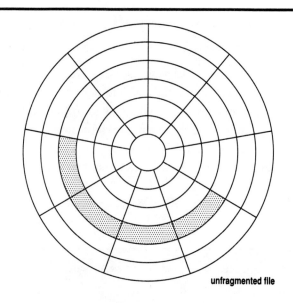

unfragmented file

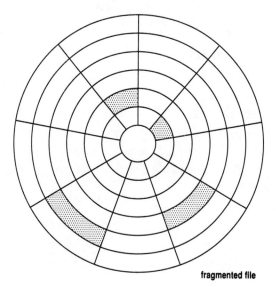

fragmented file

Detecting and Treating Fragmentation

File fragmentation is usually first manifested in slower performance, but it's possible to identify and eliminate it long before it has an impact on your work. A number of diagnostic utilities can detect fragmentation, and provide other useful information about the state of your hard disk's performance.

Using Speed Disk

Speed Disk (Figure 8.4) is part of Symantec's Norton Utilities for the Macintosh package, and is accessible either directly or via the Norton Utilities application itself. The utility uses a two-step process to repair fragmentation: first, it analyzes the extent of fragmentation, and then it recopies files to contiguous sectors. The analysis procedure reviews the locations of current files, calculates available noncontiguous space, and produces an overview of track and sector efficiency.

Optimization with Speed Disk requires no file replacement, but it does take a while: allocate about three minutes for every megabyte of space occupied on your hard disk. It'll rearrange as many files as possible, copying and regrouping them to free up contiguous tracks and sectors.

FIGURE 8.4

Analyzing file
fragmentation
with Speed Disk

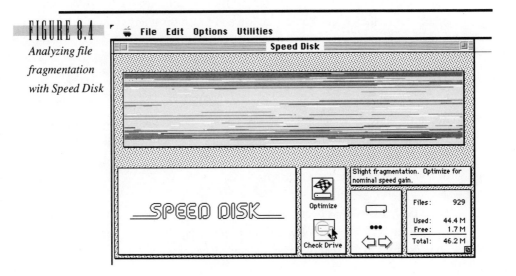

Although you can keep a copy of Speed Disk on your hard drive to check on fragmentation, in order to start the defragmentation process, you'll have to re-start from the Application disk provided as part of the Norton Utilities package. If at all possible, try to use a backup copy of this disk rather than the original.

TIP

> If Speed Disk or a similar utility reports that more than 2 percent of the total number of files are fragmented, it's probably time to defragment the disk. Up to 10 percent of your files can be fragmented before the drive's performance becomes noticeably slower, but it's best to play it safe— especially since the files that fragment first are the System and desktop files.

Speed Disk will keep you apprised of its progress, and identify files that cannot not be unfragmented. If you can't complete the entire task, hit the Stop button at any time (it may take a few moments to finish what it's doing). Stopping Speed Disk will leave the unfragmented files in their new locations, and the other files as they were. You can return and finish up at any time without affecting your operations.

Defragmenting with Reinitilization

There's another way to defragment your hard disk, one that's more drastic but doesn't require a special utility. If you've made a complete backup of your files, you could reinitialize the hard disk by selecting Erase Disk from the Finder's Special menu. You'll have to boot off of a floppy disk first, since the Macintosh will not erase a startup volume.

Once the hard disk has been purged and reconfigured, you can replace your files, using your backup software's restoration capabilities. Most programs will copy the files in consecutive fashion, and since the tracks and sectors are now blank the fragmentation will be eliminated. Most users will likely find a defragmenting utility preferable to this method—restoring from a backup requires a lot of time and shuffling of floppy disks, and you're gambling on the soundness of the floppy copies.

Partitioning Your Hard Disk

We've already noted that hard disks can be partitioned, or formatted so that it functions as more than one volume. Partitioned volumes are handled by the Macintosh as separate entities (*logical volumes*), each with its own directory and icon, and each capable of being mounted and unmounted at will. What are the benefits of giving your hard disk a split identity? Although they're not for everyone, partitions can be useful organizational tools.

When two or more people need to share a single Macintosh system, assigning each user to a partition may make matters easier for everyone. That way, compromises and confusion can be eliminated: each user can arrange their files according to their individual needs and preferences, and any changes made by one user will not affect the others.

Partitions can also be helpful when multiple groups of data not only need to be accessible quickly, but also kept as segregated as possible. For example, a scientist working simultaneously on several experiments may have similar sets of statistical files for each of them. These files could be assigned separate folders on a single volume, but an accidental misfiling could prove disastrous. It's safer and faster to store each group on its own partitioned volume. If only one volume is mounted at any one time, the prospect of a misfile is minimal.

System Folders can be configured and augmented in numerous ways—fonts, DAs, INITs—and any single set of customizations may not be equally useful for all kinds of work. Each partitioned volume can have its own System Folder, and each can be used as the startup volume when its features are needed. A volume for page layout projects could be installed with numerous fonts and a LaserWriter driver, whereas one dedicated to spreadsheets may not need such options.

The potential of partitioning goes beyond organization alone. Used in conjunction with password protection (see Chapter 5), a partition can create a software "safe," a storehouse that keeps important files off-limits while leaving the rest unrestricted. If you're fortunate enough to have a hard disk with more than twice the capacity you currently need, one partition could serve as backup storage for the other; however, since they'll both be vulnerable to the same hardware problems, you'll still need a conventional backup. I recommend a conventional backup instead.

WARNING

> **Do not back up the contents of a drive to a partition on the same hard disk without also making a backup to floppy disks or another physical drive. Otherwise, you may not be able to recover your backups if the Macintosh cannot access the hard drive.**

There are many partitioning utilities commercially available. Some, such as DiskMaker, are part of a general utility package, while others are stand-alone applications, such as HDD Formatter, shown in Figure 8.5. But before you partition your drive, consider the drawbacks. The process expunges the drive's current contents, and a hard disk partitioned into five volumes will store less than it would with a single partition, since the extra formatting files take up disk space. But the biggest limitation is flexibility; once created, the size of partitions can't be modified without reformatting the entire disk. Different sets of files grow at different rates, and it can be frustrating when one volume is filled to capacity while another has room to spare.

Making Format Modifications

While organizational concerns can be attended to casually and gradually, performance changes require more radical methods. Most format modifications shouldn't be undertaken lightly—they take time, and can involve the complete

FIGURE 8.5
The HDD Formatter utility creates logical volumes

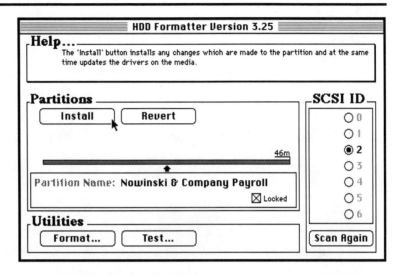

replacement of the hard disk's contents. You probably won't want to carry them out until they're clearly necessary, and even if file replacement isn't called for, you shouldn't proceed without a complete backup of the drive. Here are the major circumstances that call for modifying the formatting of your disk:

- *When the drive is transferred to a different Macintosh model, it should be reformatted to match the new Mac's capabilities.* If you are transferring the disk to a more powerful Macintosh, the reformatting will produce a notable improvement in performance. If the new Macintosh is less powerful than the previous one for which the drive was originally formatted, the drive will run no faster or slower, but the new format will reduce possible mishaps. When moving a hard disk from one Macintosh to another, don't forget to check the drive's SCSI address and change it if a conflict arises.

Many people use a hard disk in conjunction with one or more Macs, shuttling the unit back and forth between systems at home, in the office, and in the field. When such a situation involves different Macintosh models, configure the hard disk for the most powerful model; the operational speed will be automatically adjusted when working with the slower CPUs.

OTE

> If a disk that has been formatted with a higher interleave ratio
> than the Macintosh it's connected to can handle, the Mac will
> still be able to access the disk, but operations will proceed at a
> rate much slower than the Mac's capacity. If you plan to keep
> the drive connected to the new Mac for any length of time,
> you should reformat it to change its interleave factor to match
> the CPU's capability.

- *When the unit was previously configured for a computer other than the Macintosh, you must reformat the drive, even if the drive appears to behave normally.* Macintoshes aren't the only computers that can utilize SCSI devices. While a hard disk from another system may be recognized as a legitimate volume by the Macintosh, don't just delete its contents. Be sure to carry out a complete reinitialization of the drive, and even then, proceed only if you're sure that the drive is completely Mac-compatible. Apple's SCSI standards deviate slightly from the norm, just enough to cause confusion during normal drive operations, and more severe problems somewhere down the line.

- *When the hard disk was previously configured for the Macintosh, but for purposes other than conventional mass storage under the Hierarchical File System, reinitialize it before proceeding.* This applies to units that have been used as file servers on a network, those broken up into unwanted partitions, and any Macintosh hard disk previously used for specialized purposes, such as storing MS-DOS or A/UX files and directories, or acting as a downloadable font storehouse for a laser printer.

- *When the current driver is not the appropriate one for the drive, the drive should either have a new driver installed, or be reinitialized.* The driver is the software that controls the hard disk, and most drives are supplied with one specially designed for the product.

How do you determine driver types? Check your user's manual or other documentation; it should mention the recommended driver choice. Another way is to look at the volume's icon; many models have distinctive icon designs. If your model doesn't appear on the desktop with the correct icon, try to find the appropriate formatting software and make the necessary changes.

NOTE

Sometimes a driver from one manufacturer is used to format a hard disk from another. While a drive formatted with another driver might function well, it may not perform as well as possible. Be sure to use the driver designed for your model of hard disk when formatting your hard disk. If you do not have the appropriate driver for your disk, you can get one by contacting the manufacturer of your hard disk.

Using HD SC Setup

In Chapter 7, we discussed using Apple's HD SC Setup utility, included as part of the System Disk software, as a troubleshooting tool. It's also useful for general performance evaluation purposes, and it should be part of your regular utility arsenal.

You can use HD SC Setup to detect potential problems before they erupt. Select the Test button and the utility will examine the unit for hardware-based problems and inconsistencies, testing the driver, the platters, the read/write heads, and the SCSI cabling. It will not analyze or affect the data on the disk itself. If a problem is found, the dialog box will display an assessment of its nature and extent. You may need to reinitialize the drive, but before you do, be sure to give HD First Aid a try (also discussed in Chapter 7).

EXTRAS, OPTIONS, AND ALTERNATIVES

FEATURING:

- → **Virtual Memory**
- → **Macro Utilities**
- → **Command Key Shortcuts**
- → **PrintMonitor and Other Print Spoolers**
- → **Finder Alternatives**
- → **System 7 Aliases**
- → **Custom Icons**

Besides being a convenient, central location for your files, a hard disk gives you features that would be impractical, if not impossible, to implement with a floppy-disk-only system. In this chapter, I'll take a look at some of these features. You'll learn how to use your hard disk to augment your Macintosh's RAM, and how to streamline elaborate commands into just a few keystrokes. Then we'll explore background printing with PrintMonitor spooling software, and examine a few tools designed to supplement the Finder. Finally, I'll survey a few hard disk-relevant features unique to System 7.

Augmenting RAM with Your Hard Disk

In earlier chapters, we went to great lengths to distinguish hard disk "memory" (i.e., storage space), from Macintosh "memory" (RAM). But System 7 blurs that distinction by using hard disk space to do the work of RAM. It's called virtual memory, and it can be used on all members of the Macintosh II and Quadra families, as well as the SE/30, Classic II, and the PowerBook 140 and 170.

Virtual memory works by designating an otherwise unused area of your hard disk as a "buffer zone," to work in conjunction with RAM. When conventional RAM is full, the Macintosh uses this buffer zone as a temporary storage space, reading and writing from it up to several thousands of times per minute. When enabled, this pseudo-RAM is treated just like conventional RAM: it'll be shown in the About the Finder and About this Macintosh windows, and you can use it to increase the memory allocations of individual applications.

The amount of virtual memory available to you depends on the amount of free space on your hard disk; the Memory control panel (Figure 9.1) calculates and displays that figure. You can adjust the amount of virtual memory, but the changes won't be enacted until you restart the machine.

Considering that virtual memory offers the equivalent of "free" RAM, you might be tempted to set it to the maximum and leave it on at all times. But this RAM has its price: the hard disk space assigned to it can't be used by your files. Also, virtual memory is significantly slower than conventional RAM, and you'll notice considerable sluggishness in your Mac's operation, especially if you're working with sound or motion applications. In general, it's best to turn up the virtual memory only when you have a temporary need to handle a large file, such as a detailed graphic or a large database.

FIGURE 9.1

Adjusting virtual memory with the Memory control panel

Memory		

Disk Cache
Always On   Cache Size   256K

Select Hard Disk:

Virtual Memory   ⬒ Hard Disk ▼
● On   Available on disk: 16M
○ Off   Total memory : 5M
                        After restart   13M

32-Bit Addressing
○ On
● Off

Use Defaults

v7.0

Using Macro Utilities

If you're like most Macintosh users, you probably find yourself performing certain sequences of tasks over and over again—multistep procedures such as opening an application and several documents, or selecting multiple options for printing a file. With a macro utility, these steps can be consolidated into a single command.

In Chapter 4, we mentioned System 6's Set Startup feature, which can open selected files and desk accessories automatically during the startup process. Macro programs perform a similar function; however, they can be run at any time, and the work they do isn't limited to locating files and launching them. A single macro could create a new document, format it according to business correspondence standards, import a letterhead design, and type in the date and salutation. Another could save a document, make multiple copies, print out some copies, and send others to specific destinations by network or modem.

Creating, storing and using macros can be a complicated process: there's a whole new set of command sequences to remember, and even simple macros don't always work flawlessly in all conditions. But if some aspects of your work are repetitive and systematic, macros can really increase your efficiency.

Using MacroMaker

MacroMaker is Apple Computer's macro utility, an INIT included in the System 6 software package but discontinued in System 7. Although it contains fewer features than other macro programs, its "cassette tape" metaphor makes it easy to understand and use (Figure 9.2). The program looks and functions like a cassette tape player, and keystroke macros are recorded, filed, and loaded as "cassettes." These macros can incorporate mouse actions as well as keystrokes, but can only be used with the application that is active at the time of the macro's creation.

When placed in the startup System Folder, MacroMaker announces its active status by adding a cassette tape icon (which is actually a menu item) to the right side of the menu bar (Figure 9.3). To create a macro, select Open MacroMaker

Apple's
MacroMaker
uses a cassette
tape metaphor
to create and
store macros

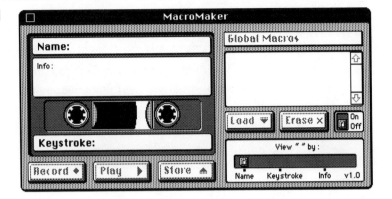

FIGURE 9.3

Opening
MacroMaker;
note the current
macros listed
as menu choices

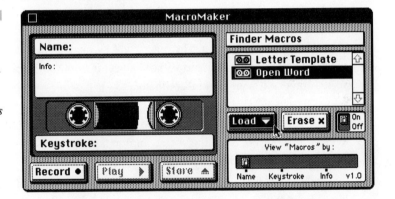

from the tape icon menu, and then designate a name for the current "tape." Add a description of the macro if you wish, then place the cursor in the Keystroke field and press the keystroke combination you want to use to activate the macro. The combination is displayed in the field, with special symbols for non-character keys. There are no character limitations, but only one alphanumeric character can be used in the keystroke.

ARNING

> Be sure to use alphanumeric characters in conjunction with
> the Option, Control, or ⌘ keys; do not assign only a single
> letter or number as a macro keystroke. Otherwise, the macro
> will run each time you press that key.

Click on the Record button. MacroMaker disappears, but its menu icon blinks on and off to indicate that macro recording is in progress. Perform the various commands you want included in the macro. When you are done, select the Stop Recording command from under the MacroMaker icon. (Don't worry. Your selection of the command won't be included in your macro.) If you are not satisfied with the macro you recorded, click the close box and try again. When you're ready to save the macro, click Store. The macro will be loaded automatically whenever the application is running, and you can select it from the MacroMaker menu as well as invoke it with the key command.

MacroMaker isn't perfect. It can erase macros but not edit or modify them, and even simple ones performing such common tasks as text entries or save/close/print requests cannot be copied from one application to another. Furthermore, since it can't be instructed to wait until certain conditions exist, it won't work with programs that require pauses between commands.

The program's greatest limitation, however, is the fact that it is indeed little more than a cassette recorder for commands. MacroMaker doesn't recognize the actual steps incorporated into a macro; it simply mimes the motions. This differs from other macro utilities, which don't actually record actions so much as replicate the end result, enabling the utility to adapt to contexts different from the one in which the macro was originally created. MacroMaker is, in essence, a "player piano" for the Macintosh. If you record a sequence that includes opening a folder, and then later move the icon even an inch or so from its original position, the macro won't find it. If another folder happens to be in its place, it will be opened instead. If the space is now occupied by an application or document, MacroMaker's attempts to treat it like a folder may cause the Macintosh to crash or bomb.

TIP

> When using a macro utility like MacroMaker that records
> sequences of keystrokes and mouse movements, create
> keystroke-only macros (which are not position-specific)
> whenever possible, and take pains to keep things in their
> original locations when mouse movements must be used.
> Otherwise, your macro may not work and may even cause
> your computer to crash or hang.

Using QuicKeys

QuicKeys (Figure 9.4) is a system extension billed as a "keyboard enhancer," which is an accurate description since it produces not only multistep macros but also new keyboard configurations. If you favor a keyboard layout other than the traditional QWERTY order, QuicKeys rearranges key functions to suit. If you regularly use special foreign language or mathematic characters, you can use QuicKeys to invoke them.

QuicKeys is superior to MacroMaker in a number of respects. Macros made with QuicKeys can be made to apply to any application, including the Finder. Macros can be recorded in two ways—as a precise sequence of actions to be duplicated in "real time," as with MacroMaker, or as a set of executable commands. With the latter, the macro records the *command* rather than just a simple *sequence* of keystrokes and mouse movements. This method is definitely preferable: a "real time" macro will only work if the folders and icons remain in the same positions as when the macro was recorded, but command macros don't have this restriction. As such, a command macro for opening a specific file will open that file even if the file's icon has moved since the macro was created (but not if the file has been moved out of the folder entirely).

FIGURE 9.4

The QuicKeys keyboard enhancer desk accessory

TIP

QuicKeys macros can also be instructed to pause between steps, and one macro can be incorporated into another's functions. Furthermore, unlike MacroMaker, QuicKeys is fully compatible with System 7.

Macros and Hard Disks

The streamlining ability of macros makes them helpful in just about every aspect of using the Macintosh—but they come in especially handy for a number of hard disk tasks. Here are a few suggestions for creating your own shortcuts:

- Automate your backup process with a macro that launches your backup software and specifies the parameters of the backup. You may not need a macro program for this, since some applications offer automatic backups. If you create a macro to backup at the end of your workday, don't just launch it and blithely walk away; monitor it to make sure it's functioning before you leave, or you might end up with a botched backup.

- If you need to access other volumes via your network, write macros that mount those volumes on your desktop.

- If you have multiple networked printers to choose from, write macros that open the Chooser and select individual printers. You can use the same macro to subsequently open the Print dialog box.

- Under System 7, the Trash is not emptied until the Empty Trash command is selected from the Special menu. Write a macro that performs the same function.

- If you want to assign a custom label to a number of files, use a macro the selects the label from the Label menu.

Other Special Key Commands

Even if you don't have a macro utility, you can take advantage of the macro-like keystroke combinations that have been built in to the Macintosh system software. You don't have to master and use them all, but it doesn't hurt to be familiar with them.

Two-Part Commands

The Macintosh operating system is chock-full of "shortcut" keystrokes. Most are simply the equivalent of a mouse operation, but some perform actions that can't be done any other way. When using any two-part command, you don't have to enter both steps simultaneously—just make sure that the special function key (the ⌘, Shift, or Option key) is pressed first. These keys are also referred to as modifier keys.

Most alternatives to choosing and clicking with the mouse utilize the ⌘ key, the one to the left of the space bar (it's sometimes called the Command or Apple key). The ⌘-key equivalents for any application's menu commands will be displayed next to the menu items themselves (Figure 9.5).

FIGURE 9.5

Most

applications

display ⌘-key

equivalents

next to the

commands

themselves

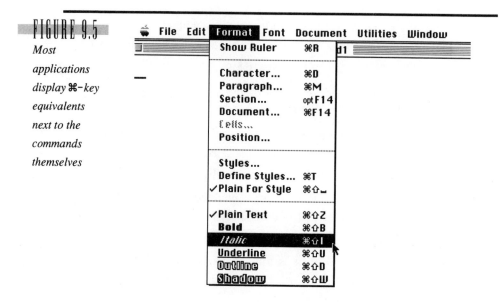

You can use these keystrokes at any time: it doesn't matter where the cursor happens to be, or if any text is selected. Table 9.1 lists a few of the most common ⌘-key commands.

The majority of Macintosh applications use these keyboard equivalents, but some applications do not. In SuperPaint, for instance, ⌘-W simply changes the window display size. In WriteNow, ⌘-T opens the print dialog box, not ⌘-P.

More ⌘-key combinations are listed on the inside covers of this book.

Option-Key Commands

While the ⌘ key usually performs the keyboard equivalent of a mouse function, the Option key invokes a number of unique two-step functions. Here are a few of the most useful.

Option-Drag Normally, dragging an icon to another folder will simply move the file to that destination. However, if you press the Option key while dragging the icon, the file will be copied (not *moved*) to the new location.

TABLE 9.1 *Common ⌘-key commands*

Keystroke	Function
⌘-N	Opens a new document from within an application
⌘-O	Begins the process of opening a existing document, presenting a dialog box with which to locate the file
⌘-W	Closes the currently active document; in the Finder, it closes the current folder window
⌘-S	Saves the changes made to the document
⌘-X	Removes a selected area of text or graphics, saving it on the Clipboard for placement elsewhere
⌘-C	Copies a selected area to the Clipboard, without removing it from its context
⌘-V	Places the Clipboard's contents (generated by ⌘-X or ⌘-C) at the cursor's insertion point; this command can be used repeatedly to make multiple copies
⌘-P	Opens the Print dialog box
⌘-Q	Closes the active application and any open documents belonging to it

Option-Key Characters The Macintosh also uses the Option key to extend keyboard functions. The System software assigns each key a second character, which can be entered by pressing Option first. These characters include general-purpose graphics, specialized symbols, and non-English-language characters.

Option characters vary according to the current font. The best way to keep track of them is with Key Caps (Figure 9.6), a desk accessory installed on all standard System files.

Key Caps creates an on-screen representation of the keyboard, which changes according to key selections. Open Key Caps and press Option; note that most keys now display a new character assigned to them. While Key Caps DA is open, any keystrokes will be listed in the text window above the keyboard map.

FIGURE 9.6

*The Key Caps
desk accessory
displays
Option-key
character
alternatives*

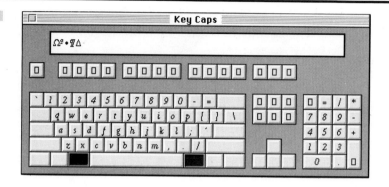

You can use this feature to practice Option-key alternatives before using them
in text documents.

Another class of special characters are accessed via dead keys. These two-step
commands, all of which use the Option key, do not produce results of their
own; instead, they modify the keystroke that follows. They are font-specific
like other special characters and are usually used for writing characters in other
languages or mathematical equations.

You can determine dead keys by experimenting while the Key Caps DA is
open. While some modify any subsequent keystroke, others function only when
followed by an appropriate character. Some of the more common dead keys are:

- Option-u places a German umlaut (ü) over vowels only.

- Option-e, Option-` and Option-i produce the French acute (´),
  grave (`), and circumflex (^) accent marks.

- Option-n inserts a Spanish tilde mark (~) over the letters a, n, and o.

Other Option-key combinations are listed on the inside covers of this book.

Keystroke-Mouse Combinations

Other two-part shortcuts involve one keystroke and one mouse click. A few of these are listed below.

Shift-Select Pressing the Shift key while pointing and clicking with the mouse lets you select more than one item in a folder window. If you accidentally select an unwanted file or folder, click on it again to exclude it. While pressing the key, you can scroll through the folder without deselecting your current choices, and you can choose items anywhere in the window (Figure 9.7).

Once you've made your selection, clicking on any one selected file will cause all selected items to respond as a group; any command applied to one file will apply to them all. To cancel the grouping, click on an unselected icon.

Option-Empty Trash Selecting the Empty Trash command while holding down the Option key will override the message asking you to confirm the deletion of the files in the Trash. This shortcut will also delete any locked files which were trashed; usually, the Trash refuses to delete locked files.

FIGURE 9.7

Selecting multiple items with the Shift command

Special Projects 2				
8 items	42.9 MB in disk		2.5 MB available	
Name	Size	Kind	Label	Last Modified
American sales territory	37K	TeachText document	—	Thu, Apr
CEO Biography	2K	Word 4.0 document	—	Mon, Jan
Certificate	24K	Word 4.0 document	—	Sun, Dec
Daniel Letter 12/6	24K	Word 4.0 document	—	Sun, Dec
Form Reply	2K	Word 4.0 document	—	Mon, Jan
Fred Love Bio	37K	TeachText document	—	Thu, Apr
Leonard Presentation	13K	MacWrite 4.5 docu...	—	Tue, Oct
Report 12/17	13K	MacWrite 4.5 docu...	—	Tue, Oct

Window Management Combinations

System 7 includes some window management shortcuts.

- Pressing the Option key while clicking on the active window's close box will close all windows down to the desktop level.

- Pressing the Option key while double-clicking on a file's icon will close the file's folder window while opening the file.

- Pressing the Option key while clicking on a window's "zoom" box will resize the window to the maximum size of the screen you're currently using. This applies primarily to Finder windows, although some recent applications also recognize this shortcut. Remember, since windows remember their size, you'll want to use this command sparingly when viewing files that will later be viewed on a Macintosh with a smaller monitor.

Three-Key Combinations

A few three-key combinations have specialized purposes that will work no matter which application is running. You can press two of the keys (⌘ and Shift) at the same time, then push the third key at the same time or shortly thereafter.

⌘-Shift-1

This combination ejects the floppy disk in the first internal disk drive. The floppy's icon will remain on the desktop, however, and the Macintosh may ask you to reinsert it during the shutdown process. If you want the floppy to be excluded completely from the current work session, drag it into the Trash instead. It'll be ejected (but not erased), and its icon will disappear.

⌘-Shift-2

This combination performs the same ejection function for the external drive, or the second internal drive on Macintoshes equipped with more than one.

⌘-**Shift-3**

Under System 6 and earlier, this combination takes a snapshot of the current screen on the Macintosh, and saves the image as a PICT file, which can be read by applications such as MacPaint and Photoshop. This file is automatically stored on the root level of the startup volume; the first one is named "Screen0," the second "Screen1," the third "Screen2," and so on, up to "Screen9." After that, the images will not be saved unless the earlier screen shots are renamed.

Under System 7, the screen-capture process has been improved somewhat: the image is saved as a TeachText file (which can then be cut and pasted into most graphic and word processing files), and is named "Picture 1," "Picture 2," and so forth. Aside from the capacity of your hard disk, there is no limit to the number of screen shots you can take. In addition, System 7 lets you know the capture has been successful with an audio signal, reminiscent of the click of a camera shutter.

TIP

This command is useful for illustrating the steps and procedures of working on the Macintosh, but it can't always take an accurate picture of the Macintosh screen. If another command is running (such as a menu item selection or a watch cursor indicating a delay), the computer will wait until the first command is completed before taking the screen shot. If you need a screen shot of a command under operation, use an image-capture utility such as Capture or Camera.

⌘-**Shift-4**

This key combination also takes a picture of the screen, but instead of saving it as a document, it generates a printout on an ImageWriter or other dot-matrix printer. If you want to print the screen picture on a laser printer, use the ⌘-Shift-3 command, and then print out the resulting file.

"Empty" Keystrokes

If you have an Apple Extended keyboard (or a similar non-Apple model), you'll notice an entire row of keys labeled F1 through F15. These are the *function keys*, sometimes known as "f-keys". In contrast to their name, they're not all that functional for most Macintosh users: they're intended for those who work in alternative operating systems, such as MS-DOS or A/UX. If you are using the Macintosh System software, you'll find that most of these keys don't do anything when pressed. Many newer applications at least support the basic functions of F1 (Undo), F2 (Cut), F3 (Copy) and F4 (Paste), which are listed below the keys.

TIP

You're free to assign macros to any of the function keys. However, double-check to see if an application has already assigned a function to them. Some applications, such as Microsoft Word, make extensive use of the function keys, and assigning a macro to a function key could create conflicts.

Working with Printer Spoolers

One of the biggest fringe benefits of having a hard disk is the ability to use printer spoolers. If you've ever stood by idly for minutes (or even hours) at a time while your Macintosh printed a file, you'll appreciate the advantage they provide.

With a printer spooler, you can continue working while printing is in progress. You can send a multitude of files to the printer, and rearrange the order in which they're printed. You can even order the Macintosh to print out a lengthy document at a certain time, such as overnight or during your lunch hour. How can spoolers do all this? By taking advantage of the fact that printers work more slowly than computers.

When a print command is given, the Macintosh begins by compiling a set of instructions for duplicating every page of the document. If a LaserWriter or similar printer is used, the instructions are in PostScript, a language which interprets text and images in terms of lines. If the printer is an ImageWriter or other dot-matrix model, the instructions are in bitmaps, which break the file's contents down into sequences of dots.

Once completed, these page descriptions are conveyed to the output device. However, it takes the printer much longer to act on these instructions than it took the computer to compile them, and rather than being transmitted to the printer all at once, the instructions are sent bit by bit, in quantities the printer can handle. If you do not have a print spooler, your computer (and your work) must wait until the printer translates the descriptions into physical actions.

A spooler does the waiting on behalf of the Macintosh. It intercepts the print command, and saves the document description as a document in its own right. The spooler then passes on the description to the printer at a pace the printer can handle. The Macintosh itself must still pass the information to the printer, but the spooler waits for the times when you're not using it, such as the seconds between your keystrokes or the moments when the screen doesn't need to be updated. Once the job is done, the spooler deletes the saved document description and then deactivates itself.

Such capabilities do have their costs: even with the best spoolers, printing takes longer than it would normally, and operations on the Macintosh can become quite sluggish. Incompatibilities between the spooler and other applications can affect the printout and any other work in progress, and some spoolers offer less feature flexibility than conventional printing. Still, spoolers provide greater control over the printing process, and greater access to the Macintosh itself.

Using PrintMonitor

PrintMonitor (Figure 9.8) is Apple's spooler utility, which has been included as part of the system software package since Version 5.0. It works with PostScript-compatible laser printers only, and only when the printer is connected via Local-Talk (formerly called AppleTalk). It's especially useful when printers are shared

FIGURE 9.8

*The queue
window of
PrintMonitor,
Apple's spooler
for PostScript
laser printers*

```
┌────────────────────────────────────────────┐
│ ▣▣▣▣▣▣▣      PrintMonitor      ▣▣▣▣▣▣▣       │
│                    Printing                  │
│ ┌──────────────────────────────────────────┐│
│ │ 🖨 HD Chap 9 @ Blinky                      ││
│                    Waiting                    │
│ ┌────────────────────────────────────────┐ ⬆│
│ │                                          │  │
│ │                                          │  │
│ │                                          │ ⬇│
│ └────────────────────────────────────────┘  │
│                                              │
│  ┌─────────────────┐   ┌──────────────────┐ │
│  │ Cancel Printing │   │ Set Print Time...│ │
│  └─────────────────┘   └──────────────────┘ │
│  Printing Status: HD Chap 9                  │
│  Pages To Print: 24                          │
│  status: preparing data                      │
│                                              │
└──────────────────────────────────────────────┘
```

via a network, since it can control the traffic flow from several Macs into one printer, or distribute a batch of print jobs from a single Macintosh to multiple printers. Each file to be printed is logged in a queue window, which tallies them in order of precedence. The first files placed in the queue are normally the first out of the printer, but priorities can be changed by shuffling or canceling print commands.

TIP

PrintMonitor can be set to print at specific times; if you have a large document but don't want to dominate the printer during regular business hours, you can leave your equipment on and have PrintMonitor process it overnight.

Finder Augmentation

For most people, the Finder is the program that makes the Macintosh a Macintosh. It's the application that runs more than any other—the one that supplies the familiar elements of the Mac's user interface. The desktop, the folder display formats, and the sizes of windows are all controlled by the Finder.

Yet sometimes conventional Finder operations aren't the fastest way to get things done. Sometimes experienced Macintosh users prefer to bypass the features that make the computer easy for beginners to understand (graphic icons, file-cabinet-like directories) in favor of increased performance. That's why there are a number of utilities available that either augment or bypass the Finder for the sake of speed and convenience.

Using DiskTop

DiskTop (Figure 9.9) is the Swiss Army knife of the Macintosh world, a multi-purpose utility compacted into desk accessory form. It's one of the more versatile Finder alternatives available, and it also functions as a volume searcher, a high-speed copier, and a resource modification tool. It can be used to rename, relocate, create, and delete items; launch applications; convert graphic documents from one format to another; and even create custom menus.

FIGURE 9.9

DiskTop is a Finder alternative and multipurpose utility in desk accessory form

DiskTop
Copy Move
HFS 44278K Used 95%
Hard Disk
Delete Rename
2338K Free 5% 30 items
Drive(s)
Find Sizes	system folder	Eject Unmount

Name	Kind	Size	Modified
Apple Menu Items	15 files/folders	---	12/20/92
Apple Menu Items (disabl...	0 files/folders	---	11/23/91
Clipboard	System document	40K	12/20/92
Control Panels	27 files/folders	---	12/20/92
Desktop Pictures	0 files/folders	---	1/2/92
DiskDoubler™ App	application	209K	12/22/91
E-Machines Help	E-Machines document	271K	6/26/91
E-Machines Preferences	E-Machines document	2K	11/20/91
Extensions	14 files/folders	---	12/20/92
Extras	1 files/folders	---	12/20/92
Finder	System document	355K	12/6/92

J. Russell Roberts   #48889

DiskTop provides a window that looks and functions much like the traditional desktop, with the icons of all mounted volumes in the upper right corner and the Trash icon below. But extra information is also provided: whether each volume is HFS or MFS, how many bytes are occupied, and how many remain. You can add, rename or delete files and folders from within DiskTop, and even modify directory information such as creator code, file type, and modification date. And since Disk-Top is a desk accessory, you can use it while applications are active.

Using OnCue

OnCue provides only a single, straightforward Finder shortcut, but it's one that makes the utility well worth its price for System 6 and earlier users (System 7 has a similar feature built in). OnCue places a pull-down menu in a corner of your screen (Figure 9.10), which you can configure to contain the names of applications and documents you frequently use. To open the file or launch the program, simply select it from the OnCue menu.

The advantage of using OnCue is that you don't have to sacrifice convenience for organization. A file can be placed in its proper location—even if that means burying it within nested folders—and yet accessed with ease.

FIGURE 9.10

With OnCue, frequently used applications and documents can be launched from a convenient menu

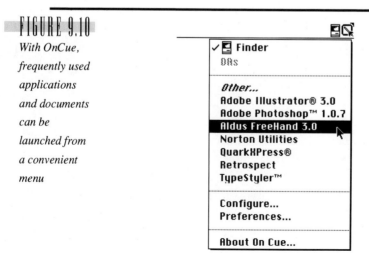

IP

> If you're running System 7, you can achieve the effect as
> OnCue by creating aliases of files, and placing those aliases in
> the Apple Menu Items folder in the System Folder (see below).

More System 7 Extras

I've already extolled the virtue of a number of special features in System 7, such as virtual memory, new display options, and advanced search capabilities. But that's just scratching the surface; System 7 offers you a wealth of power and possibilities. If your Macintosh is capable of running the software, I recommend taking the time to explore System 7. A good place to start is Marvin Bryan's *Introduction to Macintosh System 7* (SYBEX, 1991).

What follows are brief descriptions of some hard-disk-related options unique to System 7.

Using Aliases

One excellent innovation of System 7 is its ability to create an alias of any file. To the user, an alias looks and acts just like a normal file: it has an icon, it can be moved, copied and renamed, and it can be opened by double-clicking. But the alias isn't the duplicate of the original file, but rather a sort of "pointer" to the original. When you double-click on an alias, System 7 locates the original file and opens it up instead. To create an alias, highlight the original file and select Make Alias from the Finder's File menu (Figure 9.11). The resulting file will have "alias" added to its name, but you can rename it if you'd like. There's no limit to the number of aliases you can make of any file; a typical alias takes up only 1-2 KB of disk space, no matter the size of the original file. Any file that shows up in the Finder can have an alias—you can even make an alias of an alias, if you'd like. Aliases are distinguished from original files by the fact that their names are displayed in italics.

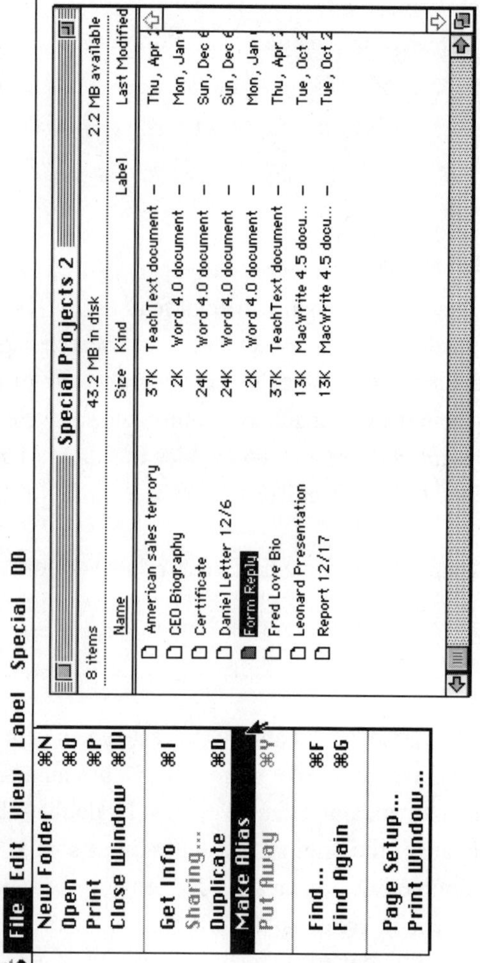

FIGURE 9.11

Creating an alias of a file

File Edit View Label Special DD

New Folder ⌘N
Open ⌘O
Print ⌘P
Close Window ⌘W

Get Info ⌘I
Sharing...
Duplicate ⌘D
Make Alias
Put Away ⌘Y

Find... ⌘F
Find Again ⌘G

Page Setup...
Print Window...

Special Projects 2

8 items   43.2 MB in disk   2.2 MB available

Name	Size	Kind	Label	Last Modified
American sales terrorry	37K	TeachText document	—	Thu, Apr 2
CEO Biography	2K	Word 4.0 document	—	Mon, Jan
Certificate	24K	Word 4.0 document	—	Sun, Dec 6
Daniel Letter 12/6	24K	Word 4.0 document	—	Sun, Dec 6
Form Reply	2K	Word 4.0 document	—	Mon, Jan
Fred Love Bio	37K	TeachText document	—	Thu, Apr 2
Leonard Presentation	13K	MacWrite 4.5 docu...	—	Tue, Oct 2
Report 12/17	13K	MacWrite 4.5 docu...	—	Tue, Oct 2

The advantage of aliases is that they effectively enable a file to be in several places at once. If several people need to contribute to a report, for instance, an alias of the report file can be placed in each individual's work folder. If you need to temporarily call attention to a file without moving it, you can park an alias of it on your desktop.

Aliases can engender some confusion, however. Sometimes it's hard to keep track of which file is pointing to which. When in doubt, inspect the file's Get Info box (Figure 9.12). Not only will it indicate whether the file is an alias, but clicking on the Find Original button will lead you to the source file—the Finder will locate the original and highlight it in its opened folder.

Designating Apple Menu Items

Before System 7, the Apple menu was the exclusive province of Desk Accessories, which had to be installed using either Font/DA Mover or Suitcase. But now the convenience of the Apple menu location can be extended to any file or application. Within the System Folder is another folder entitled Apple Menu

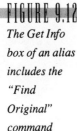

FIGURE 9.12

The Get Info box of an alias includes the "Find Original" command

Form Reply alias Info

Form Reply alias

Kind: alias
Size: 1K on disk (595 bytes used)

Where: Hard Disk : Special Projects : Special Projects 2 :

Created: Sun, Dec 20, 1992, 6:33 PM
Modified: Sun, Dec 20, 1992, 6:33 PM
Original: Hard Disk : Desktop Folder : Special Projects : Special Projects 2 : Form Reply

Comments:

☐ **Locked**   **Find Original**

Items. Anything placed in that folder will appear on the Apple menu (Figure 9.13).

TIP

To prevent the System Folder from getting too bulky, which can slow down performance, and to keep your applications separated and organized, place only aliases of the original files in the Apple Menu Items folder.

Keep in mind that items on the Apple menu are displayed in alphabetical order: if you want a file to appear at the top of the menu, you can either rename its alias or preface it with spaces, numbers or special characters (*, #, ., etc.).

FIGURE 9.13

Placing a file in the Apple Menu Items folder will make the file accessible at all times, much like a desk accessory

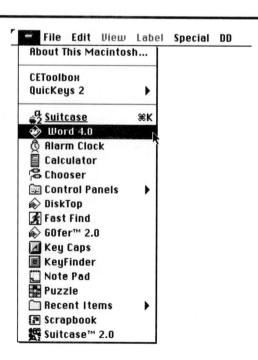

Creating Custom Icons

Macintosh users have always been able to customize the pattern of the desktop, but System 7 allows a more useful form of customization. Just about any file or folder icon can be replaced with a design of your own creation. All it takes is a graphics program that works with images in the PICT format, such as MacPaint or Photoshop. (PostScript applications such as FreeHand or Illustrator won't work.)

To create a custom icon, follow these steps:

1. Design the icon in the PICT-format drawing program of your choice.

2. Select the image and save to the Clipboard by using the Copy command under the Edit menu, or pressing ⌘-C.

3. From the Finder, highlight the icon you want to change and open its Get Info window.

4. Double-click on the icon in the upper left corner; a box will appear around it to indicate that it has been selected.

5. Select the Paste command from the Edit menu, or press ⌘-V: your new design will be resized to fit into the same general area as the old icon (Figure 9.14).

Working with Custom Icons

Custom icons aren't just another means of personalizing your Macintosh—you can use them to keep track of work on your hard disk, or to make information more accessible. Here are a few suggestions:

• If you work with several clients, and you distribute disk versions of files to them, you might want to create a custom icon for each client. That way, you can visually check the contents of each floppy to make sure that one client doesn't inadvertently receive files belonging to another. As an extra precaution, you could assign a unique label to the files as well (but under System 7, you're limited to a total of seven labels).

FIGURE 9.14

To create a custom icon, paste the new design into the file or folder's Get Info box

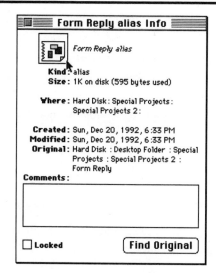

- If you want someone to read files in a certain order, or under certain conditions, you can assign custom icons to make the sequence or circumstance clear. A series of tutorials could have numerical icons, or a set of emergency instructions could have a stylized person shouting "Help!"

- Specially-formatted files, such as a spreadsheet or page layout, are often used as templates for multiple documents. If you'd like to keep track of which template was used to create which document, assign custom icons to the templates; the documents, if saved using the Save As command, will retain the icons. This way you'll be able to tell at a glance which Word files are new client proposals, or which PageMaker documents pertain to the staff newsletter.

- Custom icons can be especially effective when used in combination with aliases. You can create an alias for a project file, give the alias a name like "Do Today!", and assign it a particularly noticable icon. (If you want to make sure it doesn't get ignored, you could place the alias on the desktop.) Once the project has been completed, you could throw away the alias, create another link to the next project, and then give that alias the same name, icon, and location as its predecessor (you could design a macro to do this). That way, you can get in the habit of simply sitting down at the Macintosh and clicking on the "Do Today!" icon.

GIGABYTES AND BEYOND: HARD DISKS AND OTHER STORAGE MEDIA

FEATURING:

→ Multiple SCSI Devices

→ Tape and DAT Drives

→ Removable Media Drives

→ Optical and WORM Drives

→ Output Devices

→ A Look at the Future

For some people, a Macintosh and a hard disk may provide all the computing power they'll ever need. But others develop new needs and standards over time, and equipment that once seemed advanced can soon seem antiquated. Some users are tempted by the latest generation of faster, cheaper, and better products even though their hardware doesn't really hinder their work.

Our subject in this chapter is expansion: how to improve capability and performance while continuing to get the most out of your current equipment. I'll detail the process of adding devices to the SCSI bus, and describe some of the new hardware that's available—not just bigger and faster hard disks, but a new range of storage technology.

Working with Multiple SCSI Devices

The versatility of the SCSI standard is as impressive as its speed. Unlike data port bottlenecks on other systems, the Mac's single SCSI port can accommodate seven peripherals as easily as one. That's because the bus works as a sort of device-only network, administrating transfer priority along as well as actually transferring data. The single port can handle all SCSI devices because SCSI intercepts, identifies, and evaluates each data transfer before conveying it further along the bus, sequentially placing and removing each according to a changing set of priorities.

Because of this smooth and seamless coordinative ability, building and using a multiple-unit SCSI setup isn't much harder than getting your first drive up and running. Each new device requires only a single cable and power cord, and configuration matters are rarely more complex then they've been so far. You need to take some precautions and avoid some pitfalls, but don't worry: any mistakes you make won't endanger your hardware or software, unless you force connections or willfully ignore signs of trouble.

Setting Up the Daisychain

As noted in Chapter 2, daisychaining, the technique used to add external devices to the SCSI bus, avoids potential confusion by assigning each device a SCSI address, and prefixes all data placed on the bus with that address. If a device doesn't recognize the address as its own, it simply passes on the data.

To establish a functional daisychain, follow the steps detailed below. These will help you build a SCSI setup that not only meets your current expansion needs, but will accommodate future additions.

Connection and Termination

Begin by making the necessary physical connections, plugging in the power cord, and linking the new unit to one currently attached to the Macintosh. You can change the order of the devices if you want; the physical position of a device on a daisychain doesn't establish its address on the SCSI bus. Every SCSI device should have two ports; these ports may be one of two types: the 25-pin port identical to the one on the Macintosh, or the 50-point interlocking coupler. If your devices don't have the same port types, you'll need an adaptor cable or coupling, available in computer stores or from drive manufacturers.

But before you make the connections, remove the terminator from the currently attached device. As noted in Chapter 2, a SCSI bus must have a terminator at its physical end—otherwise, signals sent up the bus might "bounce" back down the bus, confusing the Macintosh and its devices, leading to malfunctions. Terminators absorb bus signals, which means that any devices connected to a terminated device will not be able to access the SCSI bus. Since any SCSI setup can have only one terminator, it should be placed on the last physically linked device; remove any others. Some terminators are hardware units placed between connector and port; these need only to be removed. Others are incorporated into the unit's design, and can be deactivated by flipping a switch or using a software utility; check your user's manual to determine which method to use. Still others are permanently installed; you'll have to place such a device at the end of the physical chain, or have the termination removed by a service technician or the unit's manufacturer.

Setting Multiple SCSI Addresses

Remember, each device connected to the daisychain must have its own unique SCSI addresses; otherwise, the system will soon come crashing down. You can determine a device's SCSI address by one of a number of means: some have numerical displays in the back of the case, and you can change the number by pushing a button. Others need to be set via software utility. Once again, consult the product's documentation.

When you have the option of setting the SCSI address, remember that the Macintosh searches for startup software and mounts in order of SCSI number. If you want one volume to be mounted before another, assign it a lower number. However, don't forget that number "0" is reserved for the Macintosh's internal hard disk.

Mirrored Hard Disks

For most people, daily or even weekly backup sessions provide all the insurance they need against data loss. But in some situations, the need for protection is even more critical. For example, say you were a scientist using your Macintosh for automated data acquisition; even the loss of five minutes worth of data could ruin an entire experiment. If constant backup is crucial, you should consider a mirrored hard disk setup.

Mirroring is the process of setting up a second hard drive, dedicated to real-time backup, on the same SCSI bus. When a file is created, modified, or deleted on the primary drive, the changes are made to the backup almost simultaneously, so fast that the user rarely notices a slowdown.

Mirroring is an expensive solution, considering that it requires a second hard disk (which can't be used for any other purpose) and specialized software, such as DiskTwin. It's also possible to buy complete "fault tolerant" systems with two drives already linked in a mirroring setup. If one drive fails, the other takes over immediately.

Although disk mirroring is the most comprehensive form of backing up available, it won't keep your data completely safe. Fire, system theft, and other physical mishaps can still occur.

Other Mass Storage Hardware

Most Macintoshes rely on floppies and hard disks for storage needs, but they're not the only game in town. There's a wide and growing field of alternatives to disks, offering different advantages. Some devices are hybrids of floppy disks and hard disks, combining high capacity with the convenience of a removable medium. Others represent a new generation of storage technology, which raise performance and potential to new heights.

Tape Drives

Tape drives save files on half- or quarter-inch tape cassettes, similar to those used for audio recording. Like floppy disks, these cassettes encode data magnetically; however, their capacity is much greater than floppies—up to 250 megabytes each. While that capacity may seem impressive compared to the average hard disk, it is only a fraction of the capacity of DAT drives, whose similar configuration can hold up to 1.3 gigabytes of data (see below).

Tape drives have their limitations: the tape can break or tangle, and data on cassette can't be accessed fast enough for regular work. However, these drives can make backups relatively painless, eliminating the need to stockpile and shuffle multiple floppies. Software capable of timed backups can make the process even easier, starting backups automatically at specified intervals.

Some tape drives are combined with a hard disk in a single unit, while others are stand-alone devices. Either type should be capable of backing up any volume on the SCSI bus; some can even work with several Macs connected to a network. You may want to determine if backups can be combined on one cassette or spread across several. If a backup can be distributed over multiple cassettes, you'll want to make sure that file restoration isn't too complicated a process.

Tape drives are slowly being supplanted by DAT drives. If you're in the market for a backup medium, you might be tempted by the low initial price of a tape drive (under $1,000), but on a per-megabyte basis, a DAT drive is more cost-effective.

Digital Audio Tape (DAT) Drives

Don't be put off by the "audio tape" in the name: DATs can digitize and store data as well as sound. In fact, since Macintosh data is already in digital form, you could argue that DAT is the ideal medium for backups. A typical DAT drive sells for $2,000- $3,000, which is more than a comparable removable media or tape cartridge drive—but DAT cassettes, at less than $20 apiece, are significantly cheaper than removable media cartridges. A DAT cartridge weighs under two ounces, looks like a cross between a cassette and a miniature VCR tape, and although it's roughly the size of a quarter-inch stack of business cards, it holds 1.3 gigabytes of data. If compression is used as part of the backup process, that amount can be even greater.

DAT drives have most of the same disadvantages as cartridge drives: they're not viable as primary drives, and the tape can jam or break. But if you need to backup an entire network, or if you routinely work with extremely large files, DATs are fast and reliable. If you want to transport large files through the mail or shipping services, DAT cartridges are a cheap and stable medium.

IP

When shopping for a DAT drive, look for one that is either self-cleaning or equipped with a light to indicate when cleaning is necessary. Tape manufacturers now offer both conventional DAT cartridges and "data-grade" ones; whenever possible, buy the latter. Although conventional DAT cartridges will work, data-grade cartridges are worth the extra price, for a number of reasons. Data-grade cartridges are encased in a special high-stress case designed to withstand the wear and tear of data backup (the process involves lots of fast-forwarding, reversing, and multiple writes). Secondly, data-grade cartridges have special binders added to the tape coating, to keep it from flaking off. And finally, all data-grades are tested far more rigorously than audio-grade cassettes and are certified defect-free. You'll also want to stick with the 60-meter length cartridges (which are also packaged as "120-minute" tapes). Longer tapes do exist, but they're thinner and more susceptible to breakage.

Videotape Cartridge Drives

An alternative to DATs and conventional tape cartridges is beginning to appear in the marketplace. The drive, marketed under different names but commonly known as the Exabyte drive (after the primary vendor), uses 8-millimeter videotapes much like those used by some video camcorders. Like DAT, Exabyte drives use a process known as helical scanning (which writes data in a series of angled stripes rather than as continuous tracks) to pack as much data as possible on the tape surface. Since the tape used is twice as large as DAT's 4-millimeter tape, it can store even more data: 2.2 gigabytes on a standard cartridge, and up to 25 gigabytes when compression is used. However, the cost of Exabyte cartridges and hardware is higher than DAT, and the drives are larger. In addition, DAT drives are being marketed more aggressively, which is likely to bring their costs down still further.

Removable Media Drives

The removable media drive is a version of the hard disk: it uses metallic, high-capacity platters contained in removable casings, often called cartridges or disk packs. While not as fast as conventional hard disks, they can be used both as a primary storage volume and as a backup. They're also more durable than tape cartridges or floppies, and rugged enough to be sent through the mail. While they're cheaper than DAT drives, they have a significantly smaller capacity: standard cartridge sizes are 44 megabytes and 88 megabytes.

There are two main types of removable media currently on the market. While they are similar in size and capacity, they are not compatible with one another.

SyQuest-compatible cartridge drives are the most common; the drives are produced by a number of manufacturers, but the disk packs themselves are manufacured by SyQuest. These are available in both 44 MB and 88 MB densities, but most of the older hardware can read and write to only the smaller variety. In addition, some of the newer drives can read and write to the 88 MB packs, but can only read the 44 MB variety. A SyQuest-compatible drive generally retails for $500-$1,000, and individual disk packs cost about $80 (44 MB) and $110 (88 MB) apiece.

Bernoulli removable disks, manufactured exclusively by Iomega, have a reputation for durability and reliability, but are somewhat noisier than SyQuest drives. Bernoulli drives use aerodynamics to protect against read/write head contact: air flowing beneath the rotating platter creates lift, which the drive uses to bring the disk close to the head. If a power surge, jolt, or other problem interrupts the air flow, the disk floats down and away from the head before contact can be made. A Bernoulli drive retails for approximately $800, and disk packs are available in 20 MB for about $60, 44 MB for $100, and 90 MB for $150.

Optical Disk Drives

Like hard disks, optical disks employ rotating platters organized in a track and sector system. But instead of a magnetically sensitive coating, these platters have a shimmering, mirror-like surface. The surface contains billions of microscopic indentations, or pits; when a laser beam is focused on these pits, the varying patterns of reflection are interpreted as bits and bytes.

In many respects, optical disks are a superior storage medium. They can contain copious quantities of data: a 5¼-inch platter holds as much as 550 MB while an 11-inch disk holds up to 4 gigabytes. Unlike hard disk platters they're not affected by dust and magnetic field problems, and can be removed and transported freely.

CD-ROM Drives

The first adaptation of optical storage for the Macintosh was compact disk read-only memory (CD-ROM), also known as optical read-only memory (OROM), These employ 5¼-inch platters that are identical to audio compact disks—in fact, some drives can also function as high-fidelity CD players. And like its musical counterpart, the information on a CD-ROM disk cannot be modified.

While the inability to add or change data keeps them from being a complete storage solution, CD-ROMs can provide huge directories and databases in a convenient online form. One disk can contain 700 megabtyes—enough for a complete set of encyclopedias, an unabridged dictionary, and a half-dozen or so phone books for major metropolitan areas.

Yet, for all its storage ability, CD-ROM is relatively slow: it takes about a half-second to open a file, whereas a hard disk can do the same task in a matter of milliseconds. Because of its inherent permanence, CD-ROM's greatest potential is as a "publishing" format, a medium for preserving and presenting not just documents, but high-resolution sounds and images as well.

IP

> Like most Macintosh hardware, CD-ROM drives are
> increasing in performance and decreasing in price. In you're
> in the market for one, look for a drive with an access speed of
> 500-milliseconds or less (older models have access speeds
> three times as slow!), and a price range of $500-$1,000.
> Since the majority of CD-ROM disks have been published for
> the MS-DOS compatible market, you may also want a model
> that comes supplied with software that lets you read data from
> DOS-formatted disks.

WORM Drives

More flexibility is offered by the write once, read many (WORM) drives. These drives write information to an optical disk, but they can't erase or change the data once written. The information is inscribed on the disk with a high-intensity laser, and then read with another, weaker beam.

WORMs generally run faster than CD-ROMs, and even though their contents can't be deleted, they're useful for maintaining permanent records. Multiple versions of a document on disk might be used to retrace mistakes or restore deletions, and records on a WORM disk are more compact and longer-lasting than their paper equivalents; current WORM disks have a shelf life of 100 years. Presently, WORM drives are limited by a lack of standardization and flexibility. Different models use different platter sizes (from 5¼" to 19") and different organization systems, which means that disks written on one drive type can't be used on the others. And even though the technologies are similar, WORM drives are unable to rcad CD-ROM platters. However, some erasable optical drives (see below) can read WORM disks. A 600 MB WORM drive sells for about $3,000.

Erasable Optical Drives

The latest generation of storage devices is the most promising of all, combining the functionality of magnetic media with the capacity of compact disks. Erasable optical drives, also known as magneto-optical drives, employ both magnets and lasers to read and modify high-capacity platters. The technology has been available for several years, but only recently have prices dropped enough to bring it into direct competition with other storage media.

In a nutshell, here's how erasable optical technology works. Each platter has one side with a magnetic coating. When data is written to a block on the platter, a laser heats up the nonmagnetic side of the data block to a temperature of about 150 degrees centigrade. Unlike with WORM drives, this doesn't carve a pit in the platter, but it does cause the block to reflect the polarity of the magnetic coating on the other side. A platter using this technology will wear out eventually, but not for a while—it takes about 10,000,000 erase/write operations, or about 15 years of useful life, before the drive is ready for the scrap heap.

The main drawback to these drives is speed: the coordination of laser and magnetic read/write head effectively doubles the time it takes for the drive to seek a file. Speeds are increasing, but at present, erasable optical performance lags behind SyQuest and Bernoulli drives.

Erasable optical media for the Macintosh are currently available in two main types: the 3½-inch format, which has a limit of 128 MB per disk, and 5¼-inch format, which offer capacities of up to a gigabyte. The larger format offers even greater capacity when packaged in a "jukebox" format, as an array of platters that remain in the drive, much like a multiple disk CD player. These drives have yet to establish significant inroads into the Macintosh market, primarily because of their prohibitive cost: a 6 gigabyte, 10 disk drive can cost over $13,000, while each individual disk costs approximately $500.

In contrast, the small-format erasable optical drive looks like a prime contender to snag a large segment of the storage marketplace. The 3½-inch disk cartridges are approximately the same size as floppy disks, and the drives themselves are small enough to fit into most desktop Macintoshes. The mechanisms are lighter than hard drives, and the disks are impervious to magnetic fields, so eraseable optical technology may soon find its way into portable Macintoshes as well.

External 3½-inch drives currently sell for approximately $2,000, with individual disk cartridges going for $150. However, these figures reflect the novelty of the technology more than any inherent cost of production, and in the future magneto-optical drives may become as cheap as today's hard disks.

Other SCSI Hardware

Not all SCSI peripherals are intended for storage and backup tasks. Although the majority of SCSI devices are used for storage, a growing number of other peripherals are being engineered to take their place along the SCSI bus: printers, scanners, and even cameras that produce full-color slides.

If SCSI is the fastest connectivity standard, why isn't it used by all devices? Some devices don't need the speed; modems, floppy disks, and dot-matrix printers handle data less quickly and in less quantity than the SCSI standard is designed to handle, and their own ports adequately meet their needs. Others (laser printers, file servers, other networkable products) are supposed to serve multiple Macs interchangeably (if not simultaneously), and a SCSI setup can work with only one computer at a time.

When properly designed, these products are as easy to integrate into a SCSI setup as hard disks, and like hard disks, they're usually capable of taking any address or daisychain position.

Input Devices

The SCSI bus is ideally suited for peripherals that need to identify and process large amounts of data at one time. Scanners are camera-like devices that read and interpret optical images into digital representations, which can be stored and modified like any other graphics file. Some can support optical character recognition software, which convert printed text to Macintosh documents with varying degrees of success. Video and audio digitizers also translate information into various Macintosh formats.

Output Devices

Every Macintosh has a printer port, but some printers can benefit from the greater transfer speeds of the SCSI port. Apple's Personal LaserWriter SC provides a good example. Unlike other LaserWriter models which connect to the Mac via LocalTalk, the LaserWriter SC connects to the Mac's SCSI port. Instead of generating images in PostScript, as other LaserWriters do, it generates printouts based on QuickDraw, the same graphic interpretation standard used to create and update the Macintosh's screen.

Other SCSI output devices include film printers, which produce photographic exposures of screen displays for slide generation and presentation graphics, and liquid crystal displays, which can be used in conjunction with overhead projectors to project the Macintosh display.

Other Expansion Options

For members of Macintosh II and Quadra families, daisychaining SCSI devices isn't the only way to expand your system. These models include expansion slots, which let you easily install additional circuit boards or other hardware, collectively known as expansion cards. The Macintosh IIsi has one expansion slot, the Macintosh IIci has three, and the Mac IIfx has six. Unlike internal floppy and hard disk drives, expansion cards are more than peripherals that share a case with the Macintosh itself; they're integrated with the computer, not just connected to it, and are as much a part of the computer as any soldered component. The expansion slots themselves are wired to the motherboard, the master circuit board that contains the CPU, the RAM, and the ROM. The multislot Macintosh II expansion system does function like a SCSI daisychain in that any or all slots can be occupied in any order, and cards can be removed and replaced at will.

Expansion slots on the Macintosh II and Quadra families are administered by another data bus: NuBus, a standard developed by Texas Instruments and adapted by Apple. The Macintosh LC's SCSI port can transfer data at a maximum of 1.25 megabytes per second, and the SCSI standard itself has been designed to accommodate speeds four times greater than that. But NuBus works at speeds of another magnitude altogether, transferring data at up to 37.5 megabytes per second. NuBus can also be accessed by more than one computer, and control of the bus can even be handed over to an expansion card, thereby turning the CPU itself into a peripheral. NuBus is primarily used to give the motherboard additional resources (extra RAM, special coprocessors), for high-speed communications (networks, bus linking), and for replacing standard functions with advanced alternatives (color video cards). However, just about any type of peripheral, including hard disks, can be designed to be connected to the Mac via an expansion port. Such products are beginning to materialize, and some ultra-high capacity drives overcome the limitations of SCSI by employing NuBus connectors.

Video cards coordinate all visual display functions. Compact Macs are designed to use only the 9-inch black-and-white screen integrated into the unit, so all video instructions are built into the ROM. Some commercially available adapter kits, however, enable you to connect a larger monitor to the compact Mac. The Macintosh II and Quadra families, on the other hand, are designed to work with a variety of monitors. These Macs do have built-in video support for some Apple monitors, but many monitor manufacturers have chosen to bypass that support in favor of a video expansion card provided with the monitors. There are three main reasons for doing so: (1) the screen sizes of some monitors are too large to be handled by the built-in video drivers, (2) some monitors are designed to operate at a higher resolution than the built-in support provides, and (3) some monitors display significantly more color information than the Apple monitors. For example, the Macintosh IIci's built-in video will operate Apple's 13-inch RGB monitor, with a resolution of 72 dots per inch and 8-bit color (i.e., 256 individual colors can be displayed at any one time). Video expansion cards, however, enable companies to market monitors with 25-inch screens, 94 dots-per-inch resolution, and 24-bit color (16,777,216 colors displayed at once). These high-resolution, multiple-color video cards are often more expensive then the monitor itself.

Memory cards supplement the factory-installed RAM provided with the Macintosh. Each SIMM can be installed with up to 8 megabytes which in eight-slot systems like the Macintosh II and Quadra means a total of 64 megabytes that can be directly installed on the motherboard. If that's not enough, NuBus can access up to four gigabytes of RAM, although that much RAM has yet to be packed onto an expansion card.

Bus linkages give two or more computers full access to the other's bus. Not only does this give the computers the ability to communicate, but such products can bridge Macintoshes together, or with even more powerful mini- and mainframe computers. Unlike a swiftest network, bus-linked computers don't just send and receive data amongst themselves: they handle it simultaneously, as multiple parts of a whole computing system. The collaborating CPUs can distribute data and then process different tasks or work in parallel on the same task as needed. A bus-linked Macintosh could access the files of, say, a Digital VAX as swiftly as those on its own hard disk, and the VAX could control the Mac's screen display with equal ease.

Looking Towards the Future

It's impossible to predict the future, but it's not too hard to spot potential trends in the fast-moving world of Macintosh computing. There are a number of developments on the horizon that may have an impact on the way you'll be working a few years from now. In the short term, look for the following:

- *Higher-capacity internal drives*. At present, the highest-capacity drive that can fit into the smaller modular Macintoshes (such as the IIci or Quadra 700) is about 210 MB. New drives will be able to hold a half a gigabyte or more of data while retaining the same size.

- *SCSI devices with "intelligent termination."* These devices will be able to determine exactly where they're placed in the SCSI bus, and configure their termination accordingly.

- *Macintoshes integrating new storage technology.* New Macintosh models will likely offer more media choices than floppy drives and hard disks. In addition, 3½-inch erasable optical drives will probably also become a configuration option, at least on the Quadra line.

- *"On-the-fly" file compression* will become a more prevalent feature, with special compression circuitry built into storage drives.

- *A new, faster SCSI standard will emerge.* Already, engineers are developing SCSI-2, which will allow faster transfer times, the ability to pack even larger quantities of data on individual volumes, and the ability to mount a greater number of SCSI devices at once. It's likely that future Macintoshes will be able to manage both SCSI and SCSI-2 devices.

THE WELL-CONNECTED MACINTOSH— NETWORKS AND HARD DISKS

FEATURING:

→ Local Area Network Types

→ Distributed and Dedicated Networks

→ Disk Sharing, File Sharing, and Groupware

→ AppleShare File Servers

→ System 7 and Networking

No Macintosh is an island…at least, it isn't designed to be one. Connectivity, or the ability to communicate with other computers, has been an intrinsic part of the Macintosh computer since the very first model. In the days before hard disks became common, this ability was often left untapped: if you wanted to share data, you would just pass it along on a floppy disk.

Now that file sizes have grown, direct network communications between computers is becoming more and more of a necessity. The successful configuration and maintenance of a network is both an art and a science, and a full treatment of the subject is beyond the scope of this book. But in this concluding chapter, we'll look at the various networking possibilities, and the technology and principles behind them. We'll start by looking at AppleShare, the most popular networking software. Next we'll explore some of the networking features of System 7. Then we'll move on to TOPS, AppleShare's largest competitor, and finally we'll touch upon remote-access software like Timbuktu.

Networks: An Overview

What is a network? By strict definition, a network is any configuration in which two or more computers are in direct communication. Of course, this definition can cover many different configurations. For example, some mini- and mainframe computer networks are highly sophisticated and wide-ranging, with users and machines connected around the globe via telephone lines, direct cabling, and microwave and satellite hookups. The costs of establishing and maintaining networks of this magnitude currently restricts their use to governments, academia, and very large corporations.

Fortunately, there is a microcomputer alternative: the local area network, or LAN. Although much smaller in scope, LANs give you many of the benefits of a full-scale network, including:

- *Information access.* With a network, you can swiftly transmit a file from one computer to another, or place it in a location accessible by all users. Some LANs also enable you to share data among computers of different standards: Macintoshes, IBM PCs, and others.

- *Interoffice communication.* LANs provide an electronic alternative to telephones, intercoms, memos, and other conventional means of workplace communication. An electronic message system delivers messages immediately and provides confirmation that a message was received.

- *Resource sharing.* Networked peripherals are more productive and cost-effective than units attached to individual machines. Most laser printers, some dot-matrix printers, FAX machines, CD-ROM players, and even modems can be shared among the various computers on a network.

Unlike full-scale networks, LANs can't accommodate thousands of users at once. Furthermore, the need for directable connections between computers usually confines the LAN to a single building. But networks, especially those designed for the Macintosh, are relatively easy to establish and expand.

AppleShare and TOPS are the two most popular network software packages. Both systems use the LocalTalk connectors located on the back of every Macintosh to communicate between the various machines. In fact, you can perform some network functions, such as sharing LocalTalk laser printers and network-savvy modems, with your Macintosh alone, without any additional software. To network a LocalTalk laser printer, all you need to do is install the proper printer driver in the System Folders of all networked Macintoshes, then connect it to with the nearest Macintosh with a standard LocalTalk cable. After that, all the Macintoshes on the network can share the printer.

One cautionary note: simple networking, such as the connection of three or four Macs and a couple of printers, can be done by the average computer-literate user, but more complicated networks really require the expertise of network specialists. A poorly configured network can end up hindering an office's productivity, so it's prudent to plan and build a network under the guidance of experts. Many Macintosh consulting firms specialize in networks, and if you envision connecting more than a half-dozen computers to the network, I'd recommend that you contact one of them.

N O T E

> You can network all Macintoshes, but you can't network all Macintosh peripherals. If you plan to place a printer, modem or other device on the network, make sure that it is networkable. In general, network-savvy devices cost more than their non-networkable equivalents.

LAN Types

Each computer connected to a LAN is classified as a file server, a client, or both. A file server accesses, locates, and opens files on the hard disks or other storage volumes to which it is attached. It does this when requested by the client computer. The client is the computer that initiates the access and receives the data.

Distributed Networks

Distributed network software allows each Macintosh in the network to act as both a file server and client, either alternately or simultaneously. In a distributed network, files either belong to one user exclusively or are designated for access by all users. Files, folders, and even entire volumes can be made accessible to other users in the network, and which users have access to which files is determined by the system administrator.

Each Macintosh can be connected to up to six SCSI storage devices (and have an additional internal hard disk), so distributed LANs can make a massive amount of files accessible on a network. However, the network software must shuttle between CPUs for the processor time it needs, so hooking up a lot of hard disks to a network slows down processing time considerably.

Dedicated Networks

One way to prevent slow network processing time is to establish a dedicated network. These networks require that one Macintosh be "dedicated" for the sole purpose of serving the other computers on the network. The networking software runs exclusively on this dedicated file server, and only those volumes attached directly to the file server can be accessed by the entire network.

Which Is Better?

Of the two main types of networks, neither is clearly superior: each has its own benefits and disadvantages, and you'll have to weigh them in light of your own resources and needs. In general, dedicated networks work significantly faster than distributed ones. But if your network is relatively small, you might not want to purchase another a Macintosh solely for use as a file server. Grouping your network files on a file server can also create a point of vulnerability: if the server goes down, the network fails, whereas the failure of a single Macintosh on a distributed network presents a much less significant loss of access.

Your solution depends in large part on the volume of your communication traffic. If you have several people working on complex projects at the same time, you'll probably find the speed of a dedicated network worth the investment. If you don't really need to do much more than send an occasional electronic message, a distributed network will probably do just fine. But no matter what your network choice, keep in mind that working with files on a remote volume isn't as fast or convenient as working with files on your own hard disk. Even the fastest network is noticeably slower than a SCSI bus, and transfer speed is reduced when the network's resources are taxed by several users.

Connection Hardware

Software is just part of the networking picture. The other part is hardware—the cables and connectors that convey information between machines. LocalTalk (formerly AppleTalk) is the built-in standard, requiring only the same kind of cables you use to connect your Mac to a LaserWriter; in fact, a Macintosh-LaserWriter setup is essentially a LocalTalk network consisting of one computer and one peripheral. While this type of network presents the least investment, it's also the slowest of all the commercially available network connection types.

Two significantly speedier solutions are EtherTalk and TokenTalk, which work in conjunction with EtherNet and Token Ring networks, respectively. These systems use expansion cards to accelerate network traffic up to ten times faster than LocalTalk. Since these cards must be installed in the individual Macintoshes before the LAN can be configured, the network cannot include Macintoshes without expansion slots (such as the Mac Plus). In addition, the cards are not cheap; their current prices range from $350 to $500 each.

Another way to maximize network speed is to add routers to the LAN. A router is a hardware or software device oversees network activity in its *zone*, or section the network. Zones come in handy when you need continuous access to some networked devices, and only occasional access to others. For instance, you might have three departments on three different floors, with a laser printer on each floor. The workers in one department will probably send the bulk of their print jobs to the printer on their floor, and the majority of their electronic mail will be to others in the same department. When a zone is created for each department, the router hardware will handle all traffic limited to it, which keeps network speed from slowing down. Of course, users can access other zones when necessary.

Some routers are stand-alone boxes, while others are software that runs concurrently with AppleShare on the file server. If speed is of the essence, a hardware router is the way to go. You see, normally transmitted data must pass through all networked devices between the source computer and the target device: if there are three Macintoshes on the LocalTalk cable between you and your laser printer, your print commands must be passed along by each of these Macs to the next one in line, resulting the in slowing of processing time for all units. In contrast, a hardware router will intercept the print command, bypass the other computers, and deliver the data directly to the printer, speeding both your print jobs and the other Macintoshes' work. A hardware router like Cayman System's GatorBox retails for around $2,000; Apple's AppleTalk Internet Router costs about $350.

What Is Shared?

How a network actually works isn't nearly as important as how it can help people work together. At present, there are three ways to share information on a network—disk sharing, file sharing, and groupware.

Disk Sharing

Disk sharing was the earliest form of networking for the Macintosh. It isn't true networking, however; it's simply partitioning, multiuser style. As explained in Chapter 8, partitioning is the process of breaking up a hard disk's storage capacity into separate, or logical, volumes. With disk sharing, each partitioned volume is assigned to a particular machine or user. In a typical disk-sharing setup, volumes may be opened and read by more than one user, but only the assigned user has the power to modify his or her "personal" volume.

Disk sharing has a few limitations. For example, transferring files between user partitions is awkward. To make changes to a document stored in someone else's partition, you must copy the file to your own partition, modify the duplicate version, and then request the "owner" of the other partition to replace the original file with your version. In addition, you can't eliminate or increase the size of a partition without reformatting the hard disk entirely. Also, since each partition is only a fraction of the size of the hard disk on which it resides, file fragmentation will occur more frequently.

The only real advantage of disk sharing is that it allows two or more Macintoshes to use a single hard disk. This was a big plus when hard disks were rare and costly items, but it's not as important today. If you're running System 7, a better solution is to keep hard drives unpartitioned and instead limit access with File Sharing commands.

File Sharing

Unlike disk sharing, which merely divides up storage space, file sharing allows you to freely exchange data from one computer to another. You can manipulate files on a remote volume as easily as files on your personal hard disk. File sharing's only limitations are those imposed by the network administration.

A file-sharing arrangement works best when access options are exercised—indiscriminate file access can lead to unwanted file changes and deletions. Most file-sharing LANs allow you to "publish" a file, so everyone on the network can read it, or archive a file, which stores a copy from which other copies can be made. It is up to the individual users and the network administrator to establish rules and privileges concerning file access.

Groupware

The ultimate goal of a network is not just connectivity, but interactivity. In other words, the network should not only enable users to easily transfer information, but also allow them to work together on collaborative projects. Thanks to groupware, programs designed specifically for use by more than one person, sharing work has become possible. Groupware is a rapidly growing part of the Macintosh software market.

There's no hard-and-fast definition of groupware. In general, the term refers to any application that can accommodate simultaneous and separate commands. In the past, networked Macintoshes could run the same application at the same time only when each was running an application copy of its own. Now, with groupware, you can collaborate on projects: each user can work on a document simultaneously, with the changes made by one user reflected immediately on the screen of the second user. They don't launch the same copy of the application, but each accesses the same document file.

It's easy to see the potential of groupware. For example, a large sales staff could use a groupware database to compile client and order information, with each salesperson consulting or updating the database. Similarly, with a groupware word processor, a committee drafting a report could incorporate suggestions from individual members without waiting for draft copies to be distributed, commented on, and collected.

Working with AppleShare File Server

The AppleShare File Server (called simply AppleShare in Systems software prior to System 7) is the most popular network standard for the Macintosh, in large part because it was created by Apple Computer. It is quite easy to use, and offers file sharing, groupware compatibility, and a wide range of access options. It is accessed via the Chooser control panel, which is also used for selecting printers (Figure 11.1). AppleShare File Server, however, is a dedicated system. To use it, you need at least a Macintosh Plus with an attached hard disk. In fact, for maximum performance, I recommend a more powerful model. If you buy a Macintosh IIci for file serving, you'll only need the computer itself; it won't need its own monitor and keyboard.

FIGURE 11.1

AppleShare File Server is accessed through the Chooser control panel

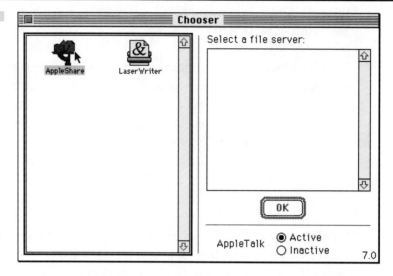

AppleShare File Server requires at least a Macintosh Plus with an attached hard disk, but will operate more effectively with a more powerful model.

A modular Macintosh that is used as a dedicated file server does not require a monitor and keyboard.

System 7 includes a non-dedicated version of AppleShare as part of its built-in networking software. The dedicated version of the AppleShare File Server software is available as a separate product. For a discussion of System 7's built-in networking capabilities, see "System 7 and Networking" below.

Macintoshes on an AppleShare network are linked by way of the LocalTalk port located on the back of each Macintosh. LocalTalk allows you to connect Macintoshes and other LocalTalk-compatible devices in a daisychain. Although LocalTalk is much slower than SCSI, it can daisychain more Macintoshes than the eight permitted by the SCSI standard.

Alternatives to the cable-connector method are available. Instead of cables, PhoneNET uses telephone wires to link computers, enabling you to extend your network beyond one room without knocking holes through walls and floors. PhoneNET will work with most phone wiring, so it is worth checking out if you plan to extend a network over a wide area or several floors. Ethernet, probably the most popular networking standard in the MS-DOS world, can also be adapted to accommodate LocalTalk, as can IBM's Token Ring network.

The AppleShare File Server automatically logs you onto the network when you boot up your Macintosh; you can, of course, configure it to request a password first before logging onto the network. Once you're on the network you can mount any of the file server's volumes by selecting them from the Chooser. A volume mounted this way functions like any other; it has its own icon on the desktop and file directory. To unmount a volume, you drag its icon to the trash.

AppleShare is one of the most "transparent" LANs available: file server volumes don't require a special format and the user interface lets you treat networked files like standard files. However, this harmonious design is also the network's Achilles' heel: the entire security system of passwords and privileges can be overcome by booting from a floppy instead of the startup hard disk. When you boot from a floppy, the file server functions like a typical Macintosh, which causes the network to stop functioning, and enables one to access (or erase) the file server volumes just as easily as any normal hard disk volume. To protect the data on the file server, keep it in a secure location where only authorized people have access to it.

System 7 and Networking

System 7 is the first System software to explicitly integrate networking into its functions. Bundled with the basic software is enough networking power to maintain all but the largest LANs, without the need for dedicated servers! However, if you want to set up a dedicated server system, System 7's AppleShare will work in conjunction with AppleShare File Server software. You can also use it with LocalTalk, EtherTalk, Token Talk, or some combination of the three to connect the various networked computers. Here's a look at some of the main features available with System 7.

File and Folder Sharing

Although Apple's documentation calls it "file sharing," that's actually a misnomer. Under System 7, you don't designate access level to individual files, but rather to individual folders, hard drives, or other volumes. Depending on the access level, other users on the network will be able to open, inspect, or modify whatever files happen to be residing in a particular folder. While this may sound awkward, it's actually quite handy: to change the access level of a particular file, you can simply move it from a folder with one setting to one with a different setting.

OTE

You can specify only ten items at a time for file sharing. While this might not sound like much, remember that each item (whether it's a folder, hard disk, or other volume) can contain as many files and nested folders as necessary. You designate an item for file sharing by selecting it, and then opening the Sharing command from the Finder's File menu (Figure 11.2).

FIGURE 11.2

*Designating the
share privileges
of a folder
under System 7*

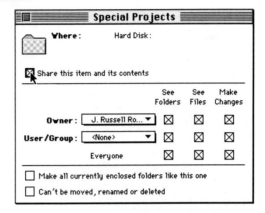

Once you've designated a folder or volume as shareable, you can then dictate exactly who can do what to the files contained within it. The Users & Groups control panel lets you assign names, access levels, and even passwords to other networked users (Figure 11.3). These users will need to register before accessing the files in the shareable folder or volume. You can even create a "drop folder" which would allow other people to add to the folder but not open or use its contents. This kind of folder is a good depository for confidential information.

Program Linking

By using "hot links" or "live links," many current Macintosh applications can pass information between themselves without the active effort of the user. For example, a chart graphic in Adobe Illustrator may be automatically generated from the data in an Excel spreadsheet; when the information in the spreadsheet changes, the graphic automatically changes to reflect the new information.

System 7's program linkage supports this sort of application-to-application communication within the parameters you set. You can select program linking as one of the privileges you assign to users via the Users & Groups control panel.

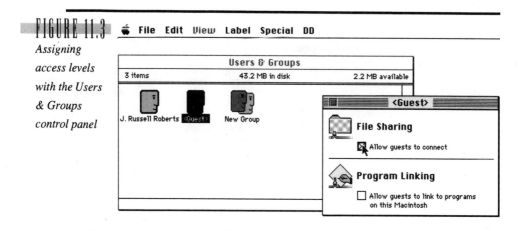

FIGURE 11.3

Assigning access levels with the Users & Groups control panel

Publish and Subscribe

Publish and subscribe is another form of program linking, but it's linkage that's done at your command. For instance, if you're producing a publication, you could begin the design process using the published files of stories. If the text of the stories changes at a later date, your layout will change as well. If your application has publish and subscribe capability, you can select all, or just a portion, of a file and designate it as a publisher. The specific command varies from application to application, but it's usually called either Publishing or Create Publisher under the Edit menu. The selected material will be saved as an edition file, which can then be accessed in other applications by way of the Subscribe command, which is also under the Edit menu. Unlike the connections established under program linking, the link is one-way; changes made to the subscriber file will be limited to that file, whereas changes made to the publisher file will be reflected in all files that subscribe to that file.

Say that you have a document with various bits of boilerplate text. You can select one bit of text and choose Publish. This bit of text will be saved to an "edition" file. You then create several documents in which this text should appear. At the proper location in each, you selected Subscribe. That boilerplate text will appear in each of the documents. If you edit the text in the subscription document, the changes will not be reflected in the edition file. If you change the text in the original publisher file, the text in the edition file will change, and therefore the text in all the subscription documents will also change.

For more information about the networking features unique to System 7, see *Introduction to Macintosh System 7* by Marvin Bryan (SYBEX).

Working with TOPS

TOPS originally stood for Transcendental Operating System, a good description of this pioneering distributed network. In the TOPS network, each Macintosh acts as both client and server, and files can be shared with non-Macintoshes almost as easily as they can among Macintoshes. There are versions of TOPS for MS-DOS, OS/2, and UNIX computers; various software and peripherals can be mixed and matched in a single network. However, you need an individual copy of TOPS for each computer.

TOPS is unobtrusive. Users aren't logged on automatically during startup; instead they're connected to the network but isolated until they choose the TOPS desk accessory (Figure 11.4). Once they have done that, they can place a file, folder, or complete volume on the network simply by clicking on the icon and selecting the Publish command from the desk accessory.

FIGURE 11.4

Using the TOPS desk accessory

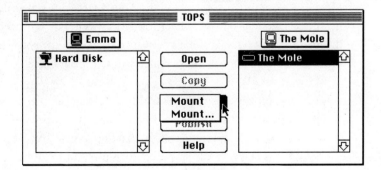

Text Translation: Sharing Files Between PCs and Macintoshes

The main difficulty of communicating between different machines is the fact that they have individual (and usually incompatible) file formats. Nevertheless, it's often possible to reconcile different formats with the use of a translation utility. Text can usually be transferred easily from Macintosh to PC, or vice-versa; graphics files, however, are a more complicated matter, and their translation methods are far from standardized. Here's a look at a few of the more popular options.

TOPS Translators

TOPS includes a utility called Translators with its Macintosh version. This program must be resident on the disk on which the TOPS network software is installed. When you run Translators, it presents two choice boxes for changing file formats, one listing Macintosh formats and the other listing "Foreign" formats. Select the format of the original file, and then the foreign format into which you want to translate it. TOPS Translators will only translate files between similar formats. For example, it can translate WordStar files into MacWrite files or Excel spreadsheet files into Lotus 1-2-3 files, but it cannot translate an Excel file into a dBASE III file.

Apple File Exchange

Apple provides a translation utility, Apple File Exchange (Figure 11.5), as part of the System software package. It easily converts text files from many MS-DOS word processors, including WordPerfect 5. Apple File Exchange can handle conversions between other formats as well, but you need a script file that describes the changes that you want to make. Some software manufacturers provide scripts to convert files created by their programs.

Apple File Exchange also has the ability to format floppies in MS-DOS format, which is a great time saver if you need to share files with a PC or compatible. And if your Macintosh is equipped with a SuperDrive, Apple's high-capacity 3½" 1.44 MB floppy disk drive, you can use Apple File Exchange to read and translate files directly from a DOS-formatted floppy.

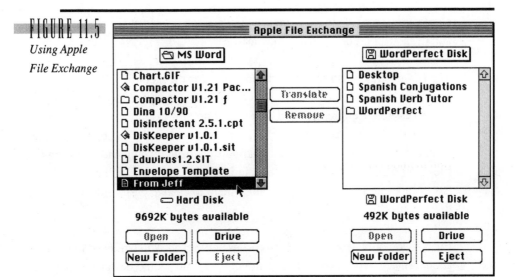

FIGURE 11.5

Using Apple File Exchange

Direct Translation

Increasingly, there's less and less need to use an intermediate utility to do the translating. More and more applications are being built to run on both the Macintosh and the IBM PC, so software manufacturers are adding file conversion utilities to their programs. WordPerfect on the Macintosh, for example, can save and read files in the format used by WordPerfect on the IBM PC. Microsoft Word on the Macintosh can also save files for Word in DOS format. Likewise, PageMaker files can be used on both the Macintosh and the PC—you don't need to translate them, but you do need to copy them to a disk that's readable by the other format.

Network Administration

Besides being installed and operated, a network needs to be administered by a person or group specifically responsible for the job. Network administration can be a full-time job in the case of a large LAN; for a small Macintosh network, the time demand is much less. An administrator keeps all the hardware elements properly connected, makes regular backups of networked hard disks, and deals with problems when they arise.

The administrator also establishes and maintains the hierarchy of user privileges, or who gets access to which files. It's not a good idea to give everyone access to the entire network; you would not, for example, want everyone to have access your payroll records. Therefore, it's usually best to set up a multi-level access system, in which you restrict users from reading and modifying files in certain directories. Only the administrator and a select few users should have "super-user" status, which enables them to change passwords or delete entire volumes.

Even if you only have a few Macintoshes networked, you still need to think about security. When you set up your network, you should design and apply a system for keeping confidential information secure. Here are a few suggestions:

- Delete the passwords of ex-workers, or other people who no longer need access to the system.

- Use the Users & Groups command to limit access to individual folders.

- Install password protection utilities on individual Macintoshes, so workers can "lock" them when they step away from their workspace. That way, they can leave networked volumes mounted on their desktop, but passers-by won't be tempted to tamper with them.

- Run periodic searches of files by "date last modified," to help you detect if an important file has been changed when it shouldn't have. If your Payroll file was changed last night but your accountant is on vacation, you'll want to find out why.

Network Administration Issues

Networks bring along their own set of topics and concerns, and you should address them carefully. While conditions and circumstances change, the general principles will always prove useful. Let's look at a few of them.

Structuring the Organization

Throughout this book I've stressed the importance of logical and systematic organization in hard disk management. The problems faced by an individual user are even more complex when it comes to networked hard disks. It's bad enough when you can't find a file in your own directory; imagine what can happen when a dozen people start moving files across as many hard disks.

From the beginning, your network should have a clearly defined storage strategy and each user should be made thoroughly aware of it. Moreover, the administrator should be willing to enforce the rules and regulations about accessing data on the network.

Eliminating Ambiguity

In effect, a network puts all your eggs in one basket. The potential for productivity is much greater but so is the potential for mishaps and mischief. To avoid confusion, keep things as clear-cut and aboveboard as possible.

Be scrupulous in the use of passwords—they're not only security devices, but also records of who was working at what time. Whenever possible, assign a unique password to each individual, not just to a department or work group. Make sure all passwords are confidential and purge the ones that aren't valid any longer. If you give users the option of choosing their own passwords, educate them to avoid obvious choices.

Making Backups

Making regular backups is very important when you're working with a LAN, since more people rely on a networked hard disk, and because the higher volume of use means that backups are outdated faster. You'll want to make backups as frequently as possible, and you'll probably need to do it after regular working hours, since networked volumes are unavailable while the backup is in progress. If the network consists of more than a handful of Macintoshes, you'll want to invest in an ultra-high capacity backup device, such as a

DAT drive, which can place the contents of an entire network on a single cartridge (see Chapter 10). For a smaller LAN, removable media such as SyQuest or Bernoulli drives would provide a cheaper solution.

Is It Working?

One of the hardest parts of operating a LAN is evaluating its usefulness. Nonetheless, you should periodically take a hard look at the realities of your workplace. Find out if the workers are ignoring the electronic message system in favor of scribbled notes; it might indicate that the software is inadequate or too difficult for them to use. If the network is so busy that performance has slowed to a crawl, it's time to consider adding another file server, or creating another AppleTalk "zone" with the addition of a router. On the other hand, if your department has been trimmed to a fraction of its former size, you might want to remove some Macintoshes and hard disks from the network. Finally, be sure that laser printers and other shared resources are in a convenient location; a trip to the printer to pick up your output shouldn't be a trek.

Remote Macintosh Access

A LAN can allow you access to the files of another Macintosh, but sometimes you might want an even greater degree of access. What if a co-worker on another floor is having problems operating a program and seeks your advice? You'll need to see just what she's doing before you can say what she's doing wrong. Or perhaps you'd like to look over the shoulder of a graphic designer while he develops that important company logo—but his studio is across town. In such cases, electronic mail simply won't do the trick. That's why remote access programs have been developed, which allow you not only to witness operations on another Macintosh while they're underway, but temporarily assume control of the other computer as well.

Remote access programs such as Timbuktu work across a network or via a simple modem connection. With them, you can monitor the actions of a distant Macintosh in a window on your screen. The user at the other end is notified that you're watching. These programs do have limitations—if the other computer has a larger monitor than yours, your view might be limited—but for the most part, what you see is what they're getting. And if the software is so configured, you can interact with the program launched on the remote computer, even if you don't have the same software loaded on your hard drive. You can even cut and paste between machines.

These programs also let you call up your office work environment while at home or on the road; instead of carrying an assortment of files with you (either on floppies or a portable hard disk), you can just dial in to your office computer and operate it remotely. Since you'll be working on the originals, this also saves you the trouble of updating files when you return.

GLOSSARY

access time: The measurement of how quickly the read/write heads of a hard disk can retrieve data.

address: The number that identifies a device on the SCSI bus or a location in the computer's memory.

AppleTalk: see *LocalTalk*.

application: A user-initiated program, such as a word processor or spreadsheet, that saves work in document form and that assists in performing a task. Applications are launched by double-clicking on an icon.

archival data: Information that the user has preserved, but does not need to have readily available.

archive: A stored collection of data, consisting either of copies of the originals, or of files for which immediate access is not necessary.

backup: A duplicate copy of data, automatically compiled and updated with a utility program and stored for use in case the original becomes damaged or inaccessable. Backups may utilize floppy disks, hard disks, or other mass storage devices.

bit: The smallest unit of information recognized by a computer; a single digit, either 0 or 1, that combines with others to represent numbers, characters, or instructions. Also known as a *binary digit.*

bit map: A set of dots or bits arranged by the computer to represent a graphic image.

block: The smallest discrete unit that a drive's controllers can read or write to in a single operation. The size of a block is dependent on the overall capacity of the drive.

bomb box: The dialog box displayed when a software problem has caused the operating system to lose control of the Macintosh. It is distinguished by the round bomb icon in the upper-left corner.

bombing: The sudden cessation of all software functions, signaled by the appearance of the bomb box.

boot: To start or restart the computer by switching on the hardware and loading the system software. Also called a *cold boot.* A *warm boot* refers to loading the system on an already- switched-on computer.

boot blocks: The tracks on a startup disk read by the Macintosh as part of the startup process. These identify the disk and help the computer display the disk's contents; missing or damaged boot blocks usually render a disk unreadable.

buffer: An area of RAM memory used as interim storage for data being transferred from the computer to a peripheral. Since the Macintosh can export data faster than most printers and other devices can import it, holding data in a buffer allows the CPU to return to other tasks.

bus: The connection between the Mac and expansion cards. The Mac SE uses the SE Bus and the Mac II uses NuBus. A third bus standard, called "030 Direct Slot," is used in the Mac SE/30, LC, and IIsi.

byte: A group of eight bits that the computer identifies as a number.

cartridge drive: A magnetic tape disk or optical disk that you can place on a disk drive without having to remove its container.

catalog tree: A group of sectors on each volume used to store the physical location of all files on that volume. When you launch a file, the Macintosh consults the catalog tree in order to move the read/write heads to the correct position. See also *extents tree.*

CDEV (Control Device): A resource file in the System Folder that contains device information and is used by the Control Panel desk accessory (found under the Apple menu).

CD-ROM (compact disk read-only memory): An optical device or medium capable of storing large amounts of permanent, unalterable data.

central processing unit (CPU): The core of the computer, built around the CPU chip, that processes information and coordinates all functions. See also *68000, 68020, 68030,* and *68040.*

client: A computer, connected to a network, that can access information from other computers or from file servers.

Command key: The ⌘ key, located in the lower left-hand corner of most Macintosh keyboards, used in conjunction with other keys for special functions.

commercial data: Any data that is purchased, such as applications, formatting files and extensions. Compare with *personal data.*

compact disk (CD): A storage technology, employing an optical rather than a magnetic media platter, on which data is created and accessed by a laser. CD drives for the Macintosh can store considerably more data than most hard disks. CD-ROM, WORM, and erasable optical disks are examples.

compact disk read-only memory: See *CD-ROM*.

Compact Macintosh: Any Macintosh of the "original" configuration, with a built-in monitor and a detatchable keyboard. These include the Plus, SE, SE/30, Classic, and Classic, II.

Control Device: See *CDEV.*

controller: The circuitry that manages a hard disk's physical data access operations, such as moving read/write heads and erasing tracks and sectors. The term is sometimes used to mean the software that runs this circuitry (more correctly called the driver).

copy protection: Hardware and software methods of limiting data duplication in order to discourage illegal use and piracy of software. Some copy-protected software can be copied only a few times, some not at all; others require a password or special floppy in order to work.

CPU: See *central processing unit.*

crash: When the Mac stops functioning or functions incorrectly.

creator ID: The distinctive four-character code in each document's resource fork—MacWrite's is MACA, HyperCard's is WILD—that identifies the parent application. If a creator ID is changed or deleted, the Macintosh may be unable to open an otherwise intact document. Appendix C has a list of creator IDs.

cursor: The symbol used to indicate position on the screen, usually manipulated with the mouse or keyboard. On the Mac, the cursor is a pointer arrow when items can be selected by pointing and clicking, an I-beam when text can be inserted, or a wait cursor when the computer is busy carrying out a command and can't acknowledge any new ones.

DA: See *desk accessory.*

daisychain: A configuration used by SCSI to connect multiple peripherals to a single Macintosh. Units are linked in a row, and each serves as an input/output relay for the others.

data encryption: A data protection method that makes use of codes. Data-encrypted files cannot be read except by users who have special decoder software.

data fork: The part of a Macintosh file in which numbers, text, and graphics are stored.

dead key: A keystroke or keystroke combination that modifies the subsequent character rather than producing a character of its own. Option-U, for instance, will place an umlaut (ü) over the following letter.

desk accessory (DA): A small program incorporated into the System file, such as Control Panel or Alarm Clock, that is run concurrently with applications. DAs are installed and removed with Font/DA Mover.

desktop: The icons and windows that the Finder displays. Also the area not occupied by any windows.

desktop file: The file in which the Finder stores the information it needs to accurately display and manage the contents of a volume. It records names, icons, directory structure, display formats, and instructions on loading and launching each file.

device: Any unit that can be controlled by the Macintosh to access, store, or display information. Hard disks and floppy drives are devices, and so is the internal speaker that emits warning beeps. In the Mac II, screen monitors also perform as devices.

dialog box: A box the Macintosh displays to request information or to issue warnings.

digitizer: A device that converts an image into a bit-mapped file that can be manipulated.

DIP switch: A small physical switch that can be in one of two positions, on or off. Often used to configure hardware.

directory: The organization of files on a disk or folder. In the Mac, files can be arranged by icon, small icon, name, date, size, kind, and color.

display font: Also known as the screen font, it is used to accurately display and manipulate a specific type style on the screen. The printer font is used to create type on a Postscript printer.

document: Any file that stores the results of work done while using an application.

downloadable fonts: Fonts for a PostScript printer that reside on the Mac and can be downloaded to a printer for temporary use.

driver: Software used by the Macintosh to access and control devices. Hard disks, floppy drives, and printers have their own unique drivers.

Encapsulated PostScript (EPS) format: A graphic image format that combines two versions of an image, one in PostScript and one bit-mapped for the Mac screen. They can be printed in detail only on a PostScript printer.

erasable optical disk: A mass storage device that records and writes files to a photo-optical medium.

expansion card: A physical circuit card that plugs into a slot on the computer to add more functions.

expansion slot: The physical location where additional circuitry such as expansion cards, is added to a computer. The Macintosh SE has one; the Macintosh IIci has three.

extents tree: An augmentation of the catalog tree. The group of sectors on each volume that lists where the segments of fragmented files have been store. See also *fragmentation.*

external hard disk: A hard disk drive with its own enclosure and power supply, designed to be connected to a computer rather than installed inside one.

FKey: See *function key.*

file: A group of bytes in which data is stored. On the Macintosh, applications, documents, and specialized software (such as fonts and DAs) are considered files as long as they have a specific name, icon, and directory location.

file compressing utility: A program that compresses files, making them both easier to store and less expensive to send over a modem.

file dialog box: The screen display used to open or save a document. Often it is modified for other purposes as well. The contents and configuration of the box vary depending on the application being used and the task being performed.

file server: A hard disk or other storage device connected to other computers in a network. Usually used to designate a drive with files that can be accessed by several users.

file type: A four-character code that identifies the category to which a file belongs. For example, all Mac-compatible applications have the file type APPL. Appendix C contains a list of file types.

Finder: The application launched automatically during startup, it displays and updates the desktop and directories of mounted volumes. It also performs basic functions such as opening, duplicating, relocating, and deleting files.

firmware: System software stored in read-only memory (ROM) and intended for continuous access by a computer. The Toolbox is an example.

floppy disk: A removable storage unit comprising a thin magnetic-medium platter in a protective enclosure. The Macintosh uses $3\frac{1}{2}''$ floppies, which can be single- or double-sided.

floppy disk drive: The internal or external mechanism that reads and writes data to and from a floppy disk.

folder: A subdirectory of a volume in which files and folders are grouped and stored.

font: An identifiable set of letters, numbers, and punctuation marks with a consistent design.

Font/DA Mover: The utility program provided with the System software (System 6 and earlier), used for installing and removing fonts and desk accessories to and from the System file.

formatting: The process by which the driver of a storage device organizes and addresses tracks and sectors. Hard disk formatting varies according to model and manufacturer.

fragmentation: When a file can't be placed on contiguous sectors on a hard disk, it is broken into parts and read to available sectors scattered around the platter surface. Because of these multiple sector locations, a fragmented file takes longer to open than one stored on contiguous sectors.

freeze: A condition when everything on the screen, including the mouse cursor, cannot be altered. Can be caused by faulty mouse and keyboard connections.

function key: A keystroke combination that activates a small program incorporated in the system file. For example, Shift-⌘ 3 saves the current screen as a MacPaint file and Shift-⌘ 4 prints the screen on an ImageWriter. Not to be confused with the keys labeled F1 to F15 on the extended keyboard.

gigabyte: A unit for data technically totaling 1,073,741,824 bytes. Usually defined as either a million kilobytes or a thousand megabytes.

hang: A condition when the Mac stalls and ignores commands from the mouse and keyboard.

hard disk: A storage device employing one or more permanently encased magnetic media-coated platters. Capable of storing and quickly accessing a large quantity of data, it can be attached externally or installed internally.

hardware: The physical elements of a computer and its peripherals.

head crash: The condition that occurs when the read/write heads of a hard disk collide with the surface of a platter and damage the magnetic coating and the data contained in the area of contact.

head parking: Moving a hard disk's read/write heads from their operational position (hovering above a platter) to a safe "landing zone" when the drive is shut down. Unparked heads may touch the platter surface when the drive is moved, possibly causing a head crash.

HFS (Hierarchical File System): A method of organizing applications, documents, and folders, with folders nested inside other folders. HFS is the second and current volume directory standard used by the Macintosh; MFS (Macintosh File System) was the first.

Hierarchical File System: See *HFS.*

I-Beam: The I-shaped cursor that indicates when text can be inserted.

incremental backup: A backup technique whereby only files altered since the previous backup are copied.

INIT: A program designed to be automatically launched whenever the Macintosh is booted up. To be activated, an INIT must first be placed in the System Folder of the startup volume. (Some INITs must be placed in the extensions folder or Control Panels folder.)

initialization: The process of configuring a hard disk, floppy, or other storage volume for use by the Macintosh.

initiator: The SCSI device that initiates communication with another device on the daisychain.

installer: A utility included with the Macintosh's System software, it allows the user to replace a System file while retaining any custom features (fonts, DAs) that may have been installed.

interleave ratio: The ratio of hard disk platter rotations to the number of sectors to which the read/write heads read or write. For example, a drive with an interleave ratio of 1:1 will read or write to each sector as soon as it passes underneath. One with a 2:1 ratio will skip alternate sectors, waiting for them to rotate one more time before proceeding.

internal hard disk: A hard disk drive installed in the same casing as the computer it serves. The Mac SE and II have internal chassis and connectors for this purpose; earlier models do not.

invisible file: A file whose icon doesn't appear in the Finder or standard File boxes.

kilobyte: A unit of memory totaling 1,024 bytes. Often abbreviated as *KB* or *K*.

launching: The act of starting an application, it is done in a number of ways: automatically during startup, by double-clicking on an icon, or when a document created with a particular application is opened.

loading: The process in which the Macintosh conveys data from a storage volume to a location where it can be used or rapidly accessed (usually the RAM).

LocalTalk: Apple's connection standard, which allows multiple Macs to share laser printers and other Localtalk devices. Formerly known as *AppleTalk*. LocalTalk sometimes refers to the connection hardware (connector boxes, cabling, etc.) while AppleTalk refers to the connection software.

logical volume: See *partition*.

Macintosh File System: See *MFS*.

macro: A sequence of commands distilled into a single, shorter command. Macro utilities save time by automating often-used functions. A complex series of commands can be activated with a single keystroke.

magnetic media devices: The types of media to which a computer can write magnetic patterns. These patterns are interpreted as data by the computer during the reading process. Magnetic tape, hard disks, floppy disks, and removable media are examples.

malfunction: Any or all of the conditions under which the Macintosh becomes entirely unusable. Bombs, crashes, freezes, and hangs are all malfunctions.

megabyte: A quantity of data equal to 1,024 kilobytes (or 1,048,576 characters).

MFS (Macintosh File System): The obsolete single-level directory standard incorporated into early editions of System software. It has since been replaced by HFS (Hierarchical File System), which offers true nesting of folders.

Modular Macintosh: Any Macintosh model without a built-in monitor, and with expansion slots for add-on cards and periperhals; also known as "open" Macs. Modular models include the Macintosh II and Quadra line.

motherboard: The circuit board which contains the most important parts of the computer system—the CPU, memory, keyboard controller, etc.

mounted volume: A volume already on the disk drive.

mounting: The act of rendering a storage volume usable during the current work session. A hard disk, floppy, or other volume is mounted when its icon appears on the desktop.

non-copy-protected: Software that can be transferred and duplicated.

NuBus: The data bus used by the expansion ports of most Macintoshes.

offline: A device not currently accessible by the Macintosh. It may be nonoperational, turned off, or improperly connected, or it may be that the computer does not have the software necessary to control it. Volumes are considered offline when not mounted on the desktop.

online: A device currently accessible by the Macintosh, properly powered and connected, with the necessary controlling software provided. Synonymous with "mounted" in respect to storage volumes.

optical disk: A mass media storage device, it uses the platter- track-sector system. A laser beam is shot at the platter and the resulting reflections are interpreted as bits.

parameter RAM: See *PRAM*.

parent application: The application used to create a document, as opposed to any others that may be able to open, convert or modify it. In order to know which application to launch when a document is opened, the Macintosh labels each document with the parent application's distinctive creator ID.

partition: A volume created by dividing the storage space on a hard disk into two or more separate entities. Also known as a *logical volume.*

path: The sequence of steps that must be taken in order to navigate from one directory point to another. Depending on the starting point and the target location, the path to a desired file may require opening a single folder, or leaping to another volume and descending far down the hierarchy.

peripheral: A hardware device directly controlled by the Macintosh, but not an integral part of it. Hard disks, printers, and modems are peripherals.

personal data: Any data that is not purchased, but created by the user in the course of working with the Macintosh, such as documents and preference settings. In contrast with commercial data.

platter: The flat, circular, rotating parts of a disk on which data is stored. Most hard drives have multiple platters.

pointer arrow: The cursor in the shape of a left-slanting arrowhead used to select items and initiate commands.

portable hard drive: A drive designed for durability, light weight and small size, which can be easily transported and attached to Macintoshes at various locations.

Portable Macintosh: Any Macintosh designed for mobile use, with battery as well as direct current power. Examples are the PowerBook series, the original Macintosh Portable, and third-party models such as the Outbound Laptop.

PostScript: The page description language developed by Adobe Systems and used by many laser printers to produce high-resolution output of text and graphics.

PRAM (parameter RAM): A semi-permanent part of RAM, used to store Control Panel settings. It retains its contents when the Macintosh is turned off, drawing power from a battery installed in the computer.

print spooler: A utility program that allows the user to operate the Mac and print at the same time. Print files are held by the spooler until the printer is ready to use them.

printer font: A file used by a printer or other output device to render text at a high degree of resolution.

progressive backup: A backup of only those files that have been modified or added since the last backup.

protection tab: The small shutter in the upper left-hand corner of Macintosh floppy disks. When the tab is pushed up to reveal a square opening, the disk's contents can be read but not deleted or added to. Pushing the tab down will restore the floppy to normal writing functions.

RAM (random access memory): The area in which the Mac places data it is currently working with. The storage is temporary; the data disappears when the electrical current is discontinued.

read/write heads: The component of a hard disk that records and retrieves data to and from the sectors.

removable-media storage: Mass storage technology which is similar to hard disks, but with platters encased in removable cartridge-style containers.

resource file: A file containing resources used by an application.

resource fork: The part of a Macintosh file in which specifications concerning the display and control of file contents are stored.

resource ID: A number that helps identify a resource in a resource file. Each resource must have an ID number.

resource type: A four-character code indicating the type of resource in a resource file.

ROM (read-only memory): The Mac's read-only memory for storing the Toolbox, the Operating System, and programs that will never be modified, such as QuickDraw.

router: a hardware of sortware device that maintains a *zone,* or subsystem, of a network.

scanner: A device for converting printed images into a format that can be stored or reproduced by a computer.

SCSI (Small Computer Standard Interface): An industry standard for electrical, functional, and mechanical interfaces for transferring data among hard disks, printers, and other peripherals.

SCSI bus: The bus which connects SCSI devices.

SCSI device: Any device that can be linked on the SCSI bus. Hard disks, printers, and optical disks are examples.

SCSI port: The communications port in the rear of the Macintosh or peripheral by which it is linked to the SCSI bus.

SE Bus: The bus used in the Macintosh SE.

sectors: The portion of the track on a disk that stores a specific amount of data. It is the smallest amount of data that can be overwritten on a disk.

serial hard disk: A hard disk designed to connect to the Macintosh via the serial port. Usually significantly slower than SCSI hard disks.

serial port: The outlet used for connecting the Mac to serial peripherals.

shareware: Software that is not distributed commercially, but through user groups and bulletin boards. Owners of shareware are requested to pay a user fee to the software's manufacturer or author.

shock rating: A durability measurement for hard drive mechanisms, expressing the amount of sudden movement a drive can undergo without damage.

signature: A four-character code with which the Finder identifies an application.

SIMMs (Single Inline Memory Modules): A package of memory that plugs into a Mac or other computer to increase memory size.

68000: The Motorola microprocessor chip that serves as the core for many Macintosh CPUs, in models including the Macintosh Plus, SE, and PowerBook 100.

68020: The Motorola microprocessor chip that succeeded the 68000, used in models such as the Macintosh II (original) and LC.

68030: The successor to the 68020, used in the IIci, PowerBook 140, IIsi, and other Macintoshes.

68040: The latest-generation Motorola microprocessor, used in the Quadra series.

slack: The extra unused space at the end of file, created when a file can't be evenly divided into sectors.

spliced applications: An application spread across several floppy disks that are installed one at a time. Usually one of the disks contains an installation program.

startup device: The device containing the active System file and the System Folder.

storage device: Any device that can store data. Examples are hard disks, floppies, and optical disks.

SuperDrive: Apple's product name for high-density (1.44 megabyte) floppy disk drives.

surge suppressor: A device that connects between the wall socket and the Macintosh and prevents surges of electricity from damaging the computer.

system extension: System 7 terminology for all programs that augment general operations, such as desk accessories, INITs, CDEVs and printer drivers.

System file: The program the Mac uses to start itself. It launches automatically when the Mac is powered up.

System Folder: It contains the System file, the Finder, and other System software for basic Mac functions.

System 6: The version of the Macintosh System software that immediately preceeded System 7, in versions from 6.0 to 6.0.7. Most features of System 6 were also available under Systems 4 and 5.

System 7: The most recent version of Macintosh System software, which introduced several significant changes to Macintosh operations. Font/DA management, networking and multitasking are some of the areas in which System 7 behaves differently from it predecessors.

target device: The device on the SCSI daisychain that receives requests from the initiator to carry out an operation.

terminator: A device that prevents commands in a daisychain from echoing, or bouncing back, on the SCSI bus. The first and last devices in a daisychain must have terminators.

Toolbox: The software in the ROM whose purpose is to present the user interface of an application.

track: Composed of eight to twelve sectors, it comprises one ring around the hard disk.

transfer speed: The rate at which data can be carried between devices.

Trojan horse: A type of rogue software that pretends to be a useful application but actually carries a virus.

user interface: The way a computer communicates, with dialog boxes, icons, etc.

utility: A program that does not generate a document but instead performs service-oriented tasks, like spell-checking or screen color customization.

view format: The various ways of seeing files and folders on the desktop. The Mac offers seven view formats: by icon, small icon, name, date, size, kind, and color.

virtual memory: A process by which free hard disk space is used to emulate RAM. A feature available only under System 7, and only on Macintoshes with a 68030 or later microprocessor.

virus: A destructive program designed to be passed unknowingly from computer to computer.

volume: Any distinct entity on which files can be stored, and with its own icon which can be mounted and dismounted on the desktop. A volume can be a floppy disk, a hard disk, a partition on a hard disk, a DAT cartridge or other medium.

volume bit map: The group of sectors on a volume that the Macintosh reads for directory information about that volume. It lists which groups of sectors are free and which are occupied.

volume info block: The group of sectors on a volume that establishes the identity of the volume itself. It includes such information as the name of the volume, how much free space is available, and where the System folder and other important files can be found.

wait cursor: Usually a wristwatch but sometimes a spinning beachball, hourglass or counting hand, it tells the user to wait while the Macintosh completes a task.

window: An enclosed area on the desktop which can be repositioned and resized. Disks and folder icons open into windows.

WORM (write-once read-many) drive: An optical mass storage device, it is used only for storing large amounts of data. Files are inscribed with a high-intensity laser and read with another, weaker laser beam.

zone: a subset of a network. Usually, a grouping of Macintoshes and peripherals that need to regularly communicate with one another. A department, floor, or workgroup may be placed in a zone.

PRODUCTS AND MANUFACTURERS

Adobe Illustrator
Adobe Systems Incorporated
1585 Charleston Road
P.O. Box 7900
Mountain View, CA 94039
(415) 961-4400

Adobe Photoshop
Adobe Systems Incorporated
1585 Charleston Road
P.O. Box 7900
Mountain View, CA 94039
(415) 961- 4400

AppleShare
Apple Computer, Inc.
20525 Mariani Avenue
Cupertino, CA 95014
(408) 996-1010

Bernoulli Box
Iomega Corp.
1821 W. 4000 South Street
Roy, UT 84067
(801) 778-1000

Disk First Aid
Apple Computer, Inc.
20525 Mariani Avenue
Cupertino, CA 95014
(408) 996-1010

DiskMaker
Golden Triangle Computers, Inc.
4849 Ronson Court
San Diego, CA 92111
(619) 279-2100

DiskQuick
Ideaform, Inc.
P.O. Box 1540
612 West Kirkwood Street
Fairfield, IA 52556

Disinfectant
c/o Berkeley Macintosh User's
Group (BMUG)
1442A Walnut St. #62
Berkeley, CA 94709
(510) 549-2684

DiskTopCE Software
P.O. Box 65580
West Des Moines, IA 50265
(515) 224-1995

Excel
Microsoft Corporation
16011 NE 36th Way
Redmond, WA 98052
(800) 828-6293

Font/DA Mover
Apple Computer, Inc.
20525 Mariani Avenue
Cupertino, CA 95014
(408) 996-1010

DiskDoubler
Salient
124 University Avenue, Suite 300
Palo Alto, CA 94301
(415) 321-5375

RGOfer
Microlytics
One Tobey Village Office Park
Pittsford, NY 14534
(716) 248-9150

HD Backup
Apple Computer, Inc.
20525 Mariani Avenue
Cupertino, CA 95014
(408) 996-1010

Hypercard Apple Computer, Inc.
20525 Mariani Avenue
Cupertino, CA 95014
(408) 996-1010

ImageWriter
Apple Computer, Inc.
20525 Mariani Avenue
Cupertino, CA 95014
(408) 996-1010

Interferon
c/o Sir-tech Software, Inc.
Charlestown Ogdensburg Mall
Ogdensburg, NY 13669

LaserWriter
Apple Computer, Inc.
20525 Mariani Avenue
Cupertino, CA 95014
(408) 996-1010

Last Resort for the Macintosh
Working Software, Inc.
P.O. Box 1844
Santa Cruz, CA 95061
(408) 423-5696

LocalTalk
Apple Computer, Inc.
20525 Mariani Avenue
Cupertino, CA 95014
(408) 996-1010

MacDraw
Claris, Inc.
440 Clyde Avenue
Mountain View, CA 94043
(408) 987-7000

MacPaint
Claris, Inc.
440 Clyde Avenue
Mountain View, CA 94043
(408) 987-7000

MacroMaker
Apple Computer, Inc.
20525 Mariani Avenue
Cupertino, CA 95014
(408) 996-1010

MacWrite
Claris, Inc.
440 Clyde Avenue
Mountain View, CA 94043
(408) 987-7000

The Norton Utilities
for the Macintosh
Symantec
10201 Torre Avenue
Cupertino, CA 95014
(408) 253-9600

Now Utilities
Now Software
520 S.W. Harrison St., Suite 435
Portland, OR 97201
(503) 274-2800

NuBus
Texas Instruments, Inc.
P.O. Box 655012
Mail Stop 57
Dallas, TX 75265
(800) 527-3500

PageMaker
Aldus Corporation
411 First Avenue South #200
Seattle, WA 98104
(206) 622-5500

PhoneNET
Farallon Computing, Inc.
200 Powell St., Suite 600
Emeryville, CA 94608
(510) 596-9000

PrintMonitor
Apple Computer, Inc.
20525 Mariani Avenue Cupertino,
CA 95014
(408) 996-1010

QuicKeys
CE Software
P.O. Box 65580
West Des Moines, IA 50265
(515) 224-1995

Redux
Microseeds Publishing, Inc.
5801 Benjamin Center Drive,
Suite 103
Tampa, FL 33634
(813) 882-8635

ResEdit
c/o Berkeley Macintosh User's
Group (BMUG)
1442A Walnut St. #62
Berkeley, CA 94709
(510) 549-2684

Sentinel
SuperMac Technologies
295 N. Bernardo Avenue
Mountain View, CA 94043
(415) 964-8884

StuffIt
Alladin Systems, Inc.
Deer Park Center, Suite 23A
Aptos, CA 95003
(408) 685-9175

Suitcase
Fifth Generation Systems, Inc.
10049 Reiger Road
Baton Rouge, LA 70809
(504) 291-7221

SuperPaint
Silicon Beach Software, Inc.
P.O. Box 261430
San Diego, CA 92126
(619) 695-6956

Symantec Antivirus for the
Macintosh (SAM)
Symantec
10201 Torre Avenue
Cupertino, CA 95014
(408) 253-9600

Symantec Utilities for the
Macintosh II (SUM II)
Symantec
10201 Torre Avenue
Cupertino, CA 95014
(408) 996-1010

TeachText
Apple Computer, Inc.
20525 Mariani Avenue
Cupertino, CA 95014
(408) 996-1010

TOPS
Sitka
950 Marina Village Parkway
Alameda, CA 94501
(800) 445-8677

TwinIt
Golden Triangle Computers, Inc.
4849 Ronson Court
San Diego, CA 92111
(619) 279-2100

Word
Microsoft Corporation
16011 NE 36th Way
Redmond, WA 98052
(800) 828-6293

CODE REFERENCE FOR TROUBLESHOOTING

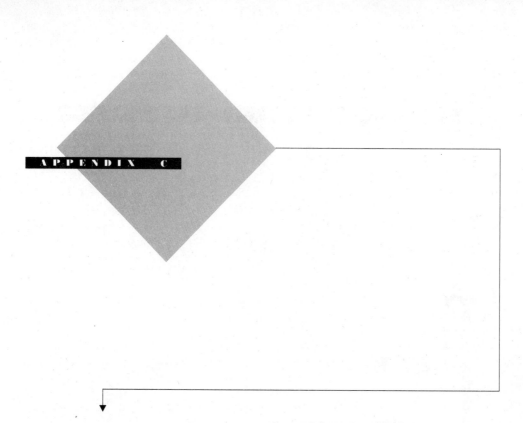

System Error IDs

In some bomb boxes, system error ID codes are displayed in the lower right corner of the box. Table C.1 lists the definitions and explanations of some of these codes.

 TABLE C.1

ID Number	Definition	
01	Bus error	The computer incorrectly accessed a portion of the RAM. This rare problem is limited to the Mac II and the obsolete XL (Lisa).
02	Address error	The computer incorrectly accessed a portion of the RAM. One of the most common problems, especially on the Mac Plus, it is usually caused by a programmer's oversight.

TABLE C.1

ID Number	Definition	
03	Illegal instruction	The currently running program used a command that the Mac didn't recognize.
04	Zero divide	The Mac was told to divide a number by zero, an illogical instruction that can't be carried out.
05	Check exception	The Mac has checked if a given value in some equation of the code is within a certain range of numbers, and isn't.
06	TrapV exception	A number that the program needs to continuously update, which is stored in a segment of RAM, has become too large for that segment before RAM can be reallocated.
07	Privilege violation	An instruction for the user mode was given, but the Mac always runs in supervisor mode.
08	Trace exception	A programming mistake—the trace bit in the status register is set.
09	Line 1010 exception	A programming mistake—the 1010 trap dispatcher failed.
10	Line 1111 exception	A programming mistake—there is an unimplemented instruction.
11	Miscellaneous exception	An exception other than the ID 05, 06, 08, 09, or 010, often of hardware origin, has caused a crash.
12	Unimplemented core routine	The programmer forgot to remove one of the temporary lines of code used to write an application.
13	Uninstalled error	Because it is running an application, the Macintosh's CPU can't access the routines it needs to carry out or give processing time to a problem initiated by a device.
14	I/O system error	A function failure of the ROM Toolbox has occurred.

TABLE C.1

ID Number	Definition	
15	Segment Loader error	A segment can't be found in memory or successfully loaded into memory.
16	Floating point error	The halt bit of an important number-crunching function has mistakenly been set, disabling the function. Most likely the System software has been damaged.
17 to 24	Can't load package	A PACK resource can't be loaded. PACKS, bits of code included in each System software release, update and augment the firmware resources in the ROM Toolbox. If one of these messages pops up, you may try reinstalling the System software.
25	Can't allocate requested memory block	The Macintosh has run out of RAM. The memory size of the application is set too low (check its Get Info window) or the application was not intended to be run on the Macintosh model you are using.
26	Segment Loader error	Either the application or the System file has been damaged severely and the launch process can't get underway.
27	File map destroyed	There is a bad sector in the MFS volume's directory. A good first step to correcting this problem is to rebuild the desktop.
28	Stack overflow error	Data assigned to one section of RAM has overflowed its boundaries and crashed into other segments.
30	Reinsertion request	The Macintosh needs to have an offline volume brought online. Usually, this means a floppy disk needs to be reinserted.
31	Wrong disk inserted	Disk inserted was not the disk needed by the Macintosh.

TABLE C.1

ID Number	Definition	
40	Macintosh Greeting	This ID number referrs to the resource that displays the "Welcome to Macintosh" greeting. If present in a bomb box, it indicates that the system error occurred while trying to display the greeting.
41	Can't load Finder	The Macintosh is either unable to locate or to load the Finder.
43	Can't find System file	The Macintosh is either unable to locate or to load the Finder.
51	Bad slot	One of the Macintosh's NuBus slots is damaged or unaccessible.
84	Menu purge	A menu has been mistakenly purged from RAM. Usually triggered when that menu is selected.
85	No MBDF resource	The Macintosh cannot locate an MBDF resource.
87	No WDEF resource	The Macintosh cannot locate an WDEF resource.
88	No CDEF resource	The Macintosh cannot locate an CDEF resource.
89	No MDEF resource	The Macintosh cannot locate an MDEF resource.
98	No patch	The System software cannot load a ROM patch (a software augmentation of ROM) for this particular model of Macintosh.
99	No patch resource	The System software cannot locate or load a resource belonging to a ROM patch.
102	Old System	This version of System software is too old for this Macintosh's ROM.
103	False 32-bit mode	An attempt was made to boot in 32-bit mode on a 24-bit system.

Negative System Errors

The system errors in Table C.2 can be distinguished by the fact that their number is preceeded by a minus (−) sign. Although the nature of many of these problems is too technical for the non-expert user to correct, I have tried to at least identify the general area of the System software that causes these errors as an aid to trial-and-error troubleshooting.

ID Number	Definition	
-9 to -21	Color Manager errors	Errors caused by Color Manager, the portion of the System dedicated to displaying and documenting color information.
-17 to -30	I/O System errors	These error messages are triggered by failures in basic Input/Output operations. The input port, connective cabling and the System software itself are possible suspects.
-33 to -61	File System errors	These are file-related problems, usually triggered by the inability to carry out a user command.
-33	Directory full	The directory file of a volume cannot accomodate another entry, either an update of a current file or the addition of another file.
-34	Disk full	The disk itself is full.
-35	Volume not found	The specified volume cannot be located.
-37	Bad file name	Through corruption or other malfunction, a file appears to have an incorrect name. This may mean that it contains "prohibited" characters, such as a colon (:).
-38	File not open	The Macintosh has treated a closed file as if it were open. For example, it may have attempted to update the window of a closed application.

TABLE C.2

ID Number	Definition	
-39	End of file	The Macintosh has abruptly reached the end of a file. Usually, this indicates that the file has been damaged, to the extent that it appears to end prematurely.
-41	Memory full	The available RAM won't allow the file in question to be opened.
-42	Too many files open	The Macintosh has reached its limit of opened files.
-43	Not found	A destination entity—a file, a folder, or a target volume—could not be located. If this occurs regularly when trying to copy to a mounted SCSI volume, the SCSI bus itself may be suspect.
-44	Volume locked (hardware)	In the case of a floppy disk, this means the floppy's write-protect tab is enabled. In the case of other storage media, it means the volume is locked by means of hardware.
-45	File locked	A command cannot be carried out, because the file in question is locked.
-46	Volume locked (software)	A volume is locked by software means.
-47	File busy	File could not be deleted, because it was active.
-48	Duplicate filename	Computer has discovered two files with the same name, or has confused a file with a folder by the same name.
-49	File already open	File is opened, with write permission enabled.
-53	Volume off line	Computer has attempted to access a volume that is not online.

TABLE C.2

ID Number	Definition	
-54	Read permissions error	Publish-and-subscribe operation failed, because subscriber was not valid.
-55	Volume online error	Computer has attempted to mount a volume that is already online.
-56	No such drive	Attempt to mount a volume failed, because incorrect or invalid drive number was given.
-57	Not a Macintosh disk	Recognition that a floppy disk does not appear to be formatted for the Macintosh. If the floppy is Mac-formatted, and if it is recognized by other Macintoshes, this can be an indication of damage to the floppy drive.
-60	Bad master directory block	At least one of the blocks containing the master directory is unreadable by the Macintosh.
-61	Write permissions error	Publish-and-subscribe operation failed, because publisher was not valid.
-64 to -66	Font Manager errors	
-78	Incorrect floppy read	The Macintosh mistakenly tried to read the second side of a single-sided floppy disk.
-79	Disk Speed error	The Macintosh was unable to correctly adjust the speed of a floppy disk.
-91 to -99	AppleTalk errors	
-108	Memory Full error	Macintosh ran out of memory in heap zone of RAM.
-120	Directory not found	An HFS directory could not be located.

TABLE C.2

ID Number	Definition	
-123	Wrong Volume Type error	Either an online volume is not an HFS volume, or an operation has been attempted that is not supported for MFS volumes.
-124	Volume Gone error	A server volume has been disconnected.
-147 to -158	Color Quickdraw & Color Manager errors	
-200	No Sound Hardware	The required hardware for a sound operation is not available. Usually, this means there is no hardware support for a specified synthesizer.
-201	Not Enough Sound Hardware	Insufficient hardware available for a specified synthesizer.
-203	Queue Full (sound)	No room in the Sound Manager queue.
-204	Resource Problem	Problem loading sound resource.
-205	Bad Channel (sound)	Sound channel is corrupt or unusable.
-206	Bad Format (sound)	Sound resource is corrupt or unusable.
-207	Not Enough Buffer Space	Insufficient memory available for the Sound Manager to operate properly.
-212	No More Real Time	Not enough CPU time available for the Sound Manager to operate properly.
-220	No Sound Input Hardware	Sound input hardware is not online.
-221	Bad Sound Input Device	An invalid sound input device has been specified.

TABLE C.2

ID Number	Definition	
--224	Hard Disk Too Slow	The selected hard drive operates at too slow a speed to adequately record sound information.
-225	Invalid Sample Rate	An incorrect sample rate has been chosen for sound sampling.
-226	Invalid Sample Size	An incorrect sample size has been chosen for sound sampling.
-227	Device Busy error	The chosen sound input device is busy.
-228	Bad Device Name	An invalid sound input device name has been given.
-230	Input Device error	The sound input device hardware has failed.
-250 to -261	MIDI Manager errors	
-470 to -489	SCSI Manager errors	
-602	Application Mode error	The Macintosh's memory mode is 32-bit, but the active application is not "32-bit clean," i.e., able to manage 32-bit memory.
-606	Demon Application	The application is of the "demon" type, designed to run in the background only ("demons" are not to be confused with viruses).
-620	Not Enough Memory	There is insufficient physical memory to carry out operation.
-850	Help Disabled (System 7 only)	Help balloon features are not enabled.

TABLE C.2

ID Number	Definition	
-853	Balloon Aborted (System 7 only)	Due to continuous cursor movement, a help balloon was not displayed.
-857	Skipped Balloon (System 7 only)	No text was found to display in a balloon.
-900 to -1272	AppleTalk (LocalTalk) errors	
-1300	File ID Not Found	File "thread" identifying file is damaged or lost.
-1305	Desktop Damaged	The desktop file has become corrupted. You can attempt to fix it by rebuilding the desktop.
-1700 to -1719	AppleEvent errors	
-3101 to -3109	Additional AppleTalk [LocalTalk] errors	
-4101	Printer Not Found	The LaserWriter printer specified in the Chooser is shut down, disconnected or otherwise unavailable.
-8132	Manual Feed timeout	A printing job failed whilie trying to process a manual feed command.
-8133	General PostScript error	An error was generated by the PostScript page description language.
-8150	No LaserWriter chosen	An attempt to print out a PostScript file could not be carried out, because a PostScript-compatible printer driver has not been chosen.

File Types and Creator IDs

Table C.3 below lists the file types and creator IDs of some popular applications. The creator ID identifies which application created a file; the file type specifies which application the file can be read by. The Finder uses the file type to display the proper document icon and to launch applications. If an application is corrupted or sometimes unusable, you can often open documents created by that application by changing their file type and creator ID to those of a similar program. A MacWrite file, for instance, can be modified to become a Microsoft Word document.

TABLE C.3

Application	File Type	Creator ID
DiskDoubler	DDO1	DDAP
FileMaker Plus	FMKL	FMKR
FreeHand 3.0	FHD3	FHA3
HyperCard	STAK	WILD
Illustrator 3.0	TEXT	ART3
ImageStudio	RIFF	FSPE
MacDraw	DRWG	MDRW
MacPaint	PNTG	MPNT
MacProject	MPRD	MPRJ
MacWrite	WORD	MACA
Microsoft Word	WDBN	MSWD
PageMaker 2.0	ALDD	ALD2
PageMaker 3.0	ALT3	ALD3
PageMaker 4.0	ALB4	ALD4
Photoshop	8BIM	8BIM
PixelPaint	SCRN	PIXR

TABLE C.4

Application	File Type	Creator ID
ReadySetGo!3	RSGJ	MRSN
SuperPaint	SPTG	SPNT
TeachText	TEXT	ttxt
TypeStyler	TSDC	TSLR
WriteNow	nX^d	nX^n
Xpress	XDOC	XPRS

In order to make such modifications, you'll need a utility such as DiskTop or the Norton Disk Editor. Whenever possible, try to make modifications only to copies of the original files. Note also that many programs are capable of saving documents in a variety of formats, each of which has a unique file type; here, only the primary file type is listed.

MACINTOSH ASCII TABLE

T

he following table shows the ASCII character equivalents of all characters belonging to the Chicago font. Other fonts may have additional characters, but in nearly all cases the basic alphanumeric setup is the same. You can use this information to interpret the contents of a file or to enter text with a file-editor program.

The box character (□) indicates that no symbol has been assigned to the specific character code. Equivalent symbols in fonts other than Chicago can be produced with the keystroke combinations below. The codes Control-P through Control-S may not work with all applications, but you can insert the symbols they produce by cutting them from the Key Caps DA and pasting them into your document.

TABLE D.1 — Macintosh ASCII Table

Dec	Hex	Keystroke	Character
000	00	Control-@	
001	01	Control-A	□
002	02	Control-B	□
003	03	Control-C	□
004	04	Control-D	□
005	05	Control-E	□
006	06	Control-F	□
007	07	Control-G	□
008	08	Control-H	□
009	09	Control-I	
010	0A	Control-J	□
011	0B	Control-K	□
012	0C	Control-L	□
013	0D	Control-M	
014	0E	Control-N	□
015	0F	Control-O	□
016	10	Control-P	⌘
017	11	Control-Q	⌘
018	12	Control-R	✓
019	13	Control-S	◆
020	14	Control-T	
021	15	Control-U	□
022	16	Control-V	□
023	17	Control-W	□
024	18	Control-X	□
025	19	Control-Y	□
026	1A	Control-Z	□
027	1B	Control-[	□
028	1C		□
029	1D		□

TABLE D.1   *Macintosh ASCII Table*

Dec	Hex	Keystroke	Character
030	1E		□
031	1F		□
032	20	space	□
033	21		!
034	22		"
035	23		#
036	24		$
037	25		%
038	26		&
039	27		'
040	28		(
041	29		)
042	2A		*
043	2B		+
044	2C		,
045	2D		–
046	2E		.
047	2F		/
048	30		0
049	31		1
050	32		2
051	33		3
052	34		4
053	35		5
054	36		6
055	37		7
056	38		8
057	39		9
058	3A		:
059	3B		;

TABLE D.1 *Macintosh ASCII Table*

Dec	Hex	Keystroke	Character
060	3C		‹
061	3D		=
062	3E		›
063	3F		?
064	40		@
065	41		A
066	42		B
067	43		C
068	44		D
069	45		E
070	46		F
071	47		G
072	48		H
073	49		I
074	4A		J
075	4B		K
076	4C		L
077	4D		M
078	4E		N
079	4F		O
080	50		P
081	51		Q
082	52		R
083	53		S
084	54		T
085	55		U
086	56		V
087	57		W
088	58		X
089	59		Y

TABLE D.1 *Macintosh ASCII Table*

Dec	Hex	Keystroke	Character
090	5A		Z
091	5B		[
092	5C		\
093	5D		]
094	5E		—
095	5F		
096	60		`
097	61		a
098	62		b
099	63		c
100	64		d
101	65		e
102	66		f
103	67		g
104	68		h
105	69		i
106	6A		j
107	6B		k
108	6C		l
109	6D		m
110	6E		n
111	6F		o
112	70		p
113	71		q
114	72		r
115	73		s
116	74		t
117	75		u
118	76		v
119	77		w

TABLE D.1   *Macintosh ASCII Table*

Dec	Hex	Keystroke	Character
120	78		x
121	79		y
122	7A		z
123	7B		{
124	7C		|
125	7D		}
126	7E		~
127	7F	space	
128	80	Option-u A	Ä
129	81	Shift-Option A	Å
130	82	Shift-Option C	Ç
131	83	Option-e E	É
132	84	Option-n N	Ñ
133	85	Option-u O	Ö
134	86	Option-u U	Ü
135	87	Option-e a	á
136	88	Option-‘ a	à
137	89	Option-i a	â
138	8A	Option-u a	ä
139	8B	Option-n a	ã
140	8C	Option-a	å
141	8D	Option-c	ç
142	8E	Option-e e	é
142	8F	Option-‘ e	è
143	90	Option-i e	ê
144	91	Option-u e	ë
145	92	Option-e i	í
146	93	Option-‘ i	ì
147	94	Option-i i	î
148	95	Option-u i	ï

384

TABLE D.1   *Macintosh ASCII Table*

Dec	Hex	Keystroke	Character
149	96	Option-n n	ñ
150	97	Option-e o	ó
151	98	Option-` o	ò
152	99	Option-i o	ô
153	9A	Option-u o	ö
154	9B	Option-n o	õ
155	9C	Option-e u	ú
156	9D	Option-` u	ù
157	9E	Option-i u	û
158	9F	Option-u u	ü
159	A0	Option-t	†
160	A1	Shift Option-8	°
161	A2	Option-4	¢
162	A3	Option-3	£
164	A4	Option-6	§
165	A5	Option-8	•
166	A6	Option-7	¶
167	A7	Option-s	ß
168	A8	Option-r	®
169	A9	Option-g	©
170	AA	Option-2	™
171	AB	Option-e	´
172	AC	Option-u space	¨
173	AD	Option-=	≠
174	AE	Shift Option-'	Æ
175	AF	Shift Option-o	Ø
176	B0	Option-5	∞
177	B1	Shift Option-=	±
178	B2	Option-<	≤
179	B3	Option->	≥

TABLE D.1   *Macintosh ASCII Table*

Dec	Hex	Keystroke	Character
180	B4	Option-y	¥
181	B5	Option-m	µ
182	B6	Option-d	∂
183	B7	Option-w	Σ
184	B8	Shift Option-p	∏
185	B9	Option-p	π
186	BA	Option-b	∫
187	BB	Option-9	ª
188	BC	Option-0	º
189	BD	Option-z	Ω
190	BE	Option-'	æ
191	BF	Option-o	ø
192	C0	Shift Option-/	¿
193	C1	Option-1	¡
194	C2	Option-l	¬
195	C3	Option-v	√
196	C4	Option-f	ƒ
197	C5	Option-x	≈
198	C6	Option-j	∆
199	C7	Option-\	«
200	C8	Shift Option-\	»
201	C9	Option-;	…
202	CA	space	
203	CB	Option-` A	À
204	CC	Option-n A	Ã
205	CD	Option-n O	Õ
206	CE	Shift Option-q	Œ
207	CF	Option-q	œ
208	D0	Option-–	–
209	D1	Shift Option-–	—

TABLE D.1   *Macintosh ASCII Table*

Dec	Hex	Keystroke	Character
210	D2	Option-[	"
211	D3	Shift Option-[	"
212	D4	Option-]	'
213	D5	Shift Option-]	'
214	D6	Option-/	÷
215	D7	Shift Option-v	◊
216	D8	Option-u y	ÿ
217	D9		□
218	DA		□
219	DB		□
220	DC		□
221	DD		□
222	DE		□
223	DF		□
224	E0		□
225	E1		□
226	E2		□
227	E3		□
228	E4		□
229	E5		□
230	E6		□
231	E7		□
232	E8		□
233	E9		□
234	EA		□
235	EB		□
236	EC		□
237	ED		□
238	EE		□
239	EF		·□

TABLE D.1 *Macintosh ASCII Table*

Dec	Hex	Keystroke	Character
240	F0	Option-k	
241	F1		□
242	F2		□
243	F3		□
245	F4		□
246	F5		□
247	F6		□
248	F7		□
249	F8		□
250	F9		□

Most of the Control-key hex characters marked 00–1B can be generated on Apple Desktop Bus (ADB) keyboards by holding down the Control key and typing the indicated character. For example, the hex character 07 is generated by typing Control-G. Hex characters generated with the Control key are used to make special symbols on the Macintosh and to control devices such as dot matrix printers. They are also used to access remote bulletin board systems. Some of the common Control-key hex characters used on both bulletin boards and the Macintosh are:

- Control-H (Backspace) moves the cursor move back one character space.

- Control-I (Tab) moves the next character to the next tab stop to the right. Tab stops are typically set at every eight characters. Some applications let you set tab stops at any location.

- Control-M (Return) moves the cursor to the beginning of the next line.

These functions are not usually used by the Macintosh, but are used by some bulletin board and telecommunication applications:

- Control-G sounds the speaker, beeper, or bell.

- Control-J (Line Feed) moves the cursor down one line.

- Control-L (Form Feed) moves the output to the top of the next page.

- Control-Q (XON) resumes output suspended by the Control-S command.

- Control-S (XOFF) suspends output until Control-Q is typed.

INDEX